CONSTRUCTING
MODERN
IDENTITIES

CONSTRUCTING
MODERN
IDENTITIES

Jewish University Students
in Germany

1815 · 1914

KEITH H. PICKUS

Wayne State University Press   Detroit

Library of Congress Cataloging-in-Publication Data

Pickus, Keith H., 1959–
    Constructing modern identities : Jewish university students in
Germany, 1815–1914 / Keith H. Pickus.
        p.   cm.
    Includes bibliographical references (p.   ) and index.
    ISBN 0-8143-2787-7
    1. Jewish college students—Germany—History—19th century.
2. Jews—Germany—History—1800–1933.   3. Jewish college students—
Germany—Societies, etc.—History—19th century.   4. Jews—Germany—
Identity.   5. Germany—Ethnic relations.   I. Title.
DS135.G33   1999
378.1'982'9924043—DC21   99-11845

Designer: S. R. Tenenbaum

Grateful acknowledgment is made to the Koret Foundation
for financial support in the publication of this volume.

For my parents
Art and Jean Pickus
with love and devotion

Contents

Preface

Few people today would challenge the claim that the intersection of German and Jewish history conjures up powerfully evocative images. The contorted face of Adolf Hitler delivering an emotionally charged speech, the minions of black-booted soldiers goose-stepping through the streets of Berlin and the smoke-belching crematorium of Auschwitz are but a few of the historical portraits that emerge when reflecting upon the subject of German Jewry. Not only does our historical memory of Jewish life in Germany focus on forces of destruction, but the tragic reality of the Holocaust casts a long and foreboding shadow over the historical scholarship that portrays Jewish life in Germany before the advent of Nazism. Given this situation, therefore, it is not surprising that much of the literature on nineteenth-century German Jewry is concerned with the rise of antisemitism and Jewish responses to it. Seldom does the historiography of German Jewry reflect the fact that anti-semitism was not the determinant influence on the lives of many German Jews.

The question, then, is how does one strip away the layers of historical memory that may distort the image of nineteenth-century German Jewry? Is it possible to sketch portraits of German Jewish existence that are not dominated by discrimination and defeat? If so, what investigative strategies can be employed to create them? These questions provide the impetus for the analysis presented in this book.

Constructing Modern Identities examines the identities of nineteenth-century Jewish university students in Germany, a small but important segment of German Jewry.[1] Educated as Germans and raised to expect that their lives would offer social and professional opportunities seldom experienced by previous generations, Jews studying at German universities between 1815 and 1914 redefined what it meant to be a Jew. Unlike the premodern era, when "religion, politics and personal life were so interfused that Judaism was perceived as a seamless garment," once German Jews discarded the protective veil of *Halakha* and transcended the boundaries of their autonomous communities, the formerly unambiguous distinctions between Christians and Jews were no longer valid.[2]

The process of emancipation and concomitant emergence of a civil society made it possible to separate one's religious and public identities. Before Germany was unified and the emancipation of the Jews was complete, most Jewish university students relegated their religious identity to the private sphere and avoided outward proclamations of their Jewishness. Although the privatization of Judaism enabled Germany's Jewish population to function as German citizens without converting to Christianity, the perpetuation of Christian influences in German society created a dialectical situation wherein the maintenance of Jewish identity was at odds with the Christian character of German society. As it became increasingly clear that Jewishness, even when expressed privately, prevented German Jews from enjoying the full benefits of citizenship, small groups of Jewish university students began to rearrange their self-images and publicly display what Jews had been reluctant to express in the past.

Members of Jewish student associations, all of which emerged after 1881, put forward public expressions of Jewishness that would have shocked previous generations. While the ideologies and foci of these organizations ranged from an integrationist agenda to Jewish nationalism and religious orthodoxy, membership in a Jewish student association provided one with an opportunity to openly proclaim one's Jewish heritage. At the same time, however, Jewish student groups were also imbued with sufficient German cultural characteristics to enable their members to function within the university environment.

Unlike their more organized brethren, students who did not join a traditional organization could not rely on a prepackaged identity to balance the demands of *Deutschtum* (Germanness) and *Judentum* (Jewishness). While some participated in nondenominational academic associations and others formed their own social coteries, most noncorporate Jewish students sublimated their Jewishness in favor of other concerns. Consequently, their public identity profiles were virtually indistinguishable from those of unincorporated Gentile students.

Contrary to the scholarship on German Jewry that depicts Jewish identity as a static ideological phenomenon,[3] this study emphasizes both the mutability and the social function of identity formation. Whom we socialize with, the organizations that we join, and how we position ourselves in society are integral to the process of self-definition. Individual German Jews were neither "assimilationists" nor Zionists operating on the margins of the continuum we call Jewish identity. Rather, their identities fluctuated throughout their lives, oftentimes within the course of a given day. Moving between Gentile and Jewish worlds and adjusting one's social relationships accordingly became the norm, not the exception, for Jews living in Germany during the nineteenth century. By personalizing the narrative and integrating analyses of Jewish student organizations with descriptions of individual Jews, this study reveals the paradoxical condition of German Jewry.

The primary materials for this study are culled from a variety of sources. The analyses of the corporate subculture at German universities and Jewish involvement within traditional student associations are based on the published manuscripts, student journals, and associational pamphlets located in the *Institut für Hochschulkunde* (Institute for Studies of Secondary Education) in Würzburg, Germany. The discussion of Jewish student organizations is derived from the monthly reports, newspapers, journals, and organizational histories that are housed in the Central Zionist Archive and the Jewish National and University Library in Jerusalem, and the Leo Baeck Institute in New York. The narrative accounts of individual Jews are drawn from the memoirs, autobiographies, and biographies contained within the Leo Baeck Institute.

The monograph's six chapters are organized both chronologically and thematically. Chapter one presents the process of self-definition as a series of historically contingent social relationships and depicts German Jewish identity formation as a synthetic act. By examining the nexus between education and identity, the opening chapter also demonstrates that as Jews abandoned traditional modes of education and entered German institutions of higher learning, they profoundly altered their identities. The second chapter investigates how Jewish students functioned within the university environment before German unification. Moving from the *Verein für Cultur und Wissenschaft der Juden's* efforts to align Jewish identity with the demands of an emerging civil society to the question of Jewish participation in traditional fraternal organizations, this section reveals the tensions inherent within the phenomenon of Jewish participation in German bourgeois society.

The third and fourth chapters discuss the emergence of Jewish student associations in the 1880s and 1890s. The *Freie Wissenschaftliche Vereinigung* was created in response to the student antisemitic movement of 1880 and remained the standard bearer of liberalism at German universities throughout its existence. In spite of a constituency that was almost exclusively Jewish, the *Freie Wissenschaftliche Vereinigung* neither presented itself as a Jewish association nor advanced a Jewish intellectual agenda. The *Akademische Verein für jüdische Geschichte und Literatur*, the *Kartell Convent Deutscher Studenten Jüdischen Glaubens*, and the *Bund Jüdischer Corporationen*, on the other hand, constructed public profiles that were self-consciously Jewish. While the three student societies pursued different social and academic agendas, students who belonged to these groups made two distinct statements about their identities: they rejected an identity that relegated Jewishness to the private sphere and they favored participation in an exclusively Jewish social coterie.

Based entirely on memoirs and biographical information, chapter five illuminates how students who did not belong to a Jewish association functioned within the university environment. Divided into four thematic sections that focus on the transition from the family home to the university, the importance of time and place, the formation of social coteries, and the relentless pursuit of *Bildung*, this chapter reveals the multifarious character of German Jewish identity. The paradigms of self-definition crafted by unaffiliated students were highly flexible, intimately linked to the location in which the students operated, and surprisingly unaffected by the antisemitic discourse of late nineteenth-century German society.

The sixth and final chapter evaluates Jewish life in Germany from the turn of the century until the onset of World War I. During this period women matriculated at German universities, challenged its exclusively male environment, and altered the dynamics of student identity formation. At the same time, religious Jews established their own organizations and students committed to Jewish nationalism aligned their associations with the Zionist movement. The combined effect of these developments was to accentuate the increasingly differentiated character of German Jewish identity.

The process of identity construction employed by German Jewish university students between 1815 and 1914 produced a variety of ways to express one's Jewishness. In developing modern paradigms of Jewish self-definition, German Jews created viable social relationships. Until the 1880s, most balanced the demands of *Deutschtum* and *Judentum* by relegating their Jewishness to the private sphere while publicly expressing their Germanness. The increasingly segregated social structure of the Kaiserreich, however, necessitated new identities. As a result, Germany's Jewish student population produced a colorful array of modern identities, some of which provided for the public expression of Jewishness while others perpetuated and accentuated the bifurcated pattern of identity formation. Whether they defined Jewishness as a nationality, a religious confession, or a common heritage, individual students and student organizations wove together the cultural threads of *Deutschtum* and *Judentum* into a beautiful, vibrant, and multifarious tapestry of German Jewish identity. Their efforts, although laden with tension and often controversial, have left an indelible imprint on contemporary Jewish culture.

Acknowledgments

Like most historical monographs, this book has experienced a lengthy gestation. From its inception in 1988 during a fellowship year at the Hebrew University in Jerusalem through its completion ten years later, I have benefited greatly from the support of colleagues, granting agencies, and family.

Special thanks go to Hillel Kieval, my mentor and friend, who nurtured my love for historical scholarship and guided my intellectual development with patience and skill. His role in this project and support for my career are the most precious gifts that a student can wish for. Alan Levenson, Michael Meyer, and David Sorkin provided critical insight and suggestions as I transformed the manuscript from a dissertation to a monograph. Their remarkable understanding of German Jewish history and interest in this work have been essential to the book's completion. Susannah Heschel's insightful assessment of the opening chapters and tireless efforts on my behalf have been invaluable assets, both for this project and for my professional development. Michael Berkowitz and Abraham J. Peck's valuable comments helped put the finishing touches on the manuscript. To all these individuals and the many others who assisted me over the years, I am deeply grateful.

Acknowledgments

The research for this book was made possible by many agencies. Grants from the Israeli Interuniversity Fellowship program and the Center for Middle Eastern Studies at the University of Washington financed a year's study in Israel. Funding from the German Academic Exchange (DAAD), the University of Washington Graduate School, and the Leo Baeck Institute supported initial research trips to Germany and the Leo Baeck Institute in New York. The Hazel D. Cole Fellowship in Jewish Studies from the University of Washington and a dissertation fellowship from the National Foundation for Jewish Culture provided the necessary funding to complete the dissertation. Return trips to New York and Germany were funded by awards from the American Historical Association and Wichita State University.

Above and beyond the intellectual succor of colleagues and the gracious financial assistance of institutions, I am fortunate for the support and guidance of a loving family. To Deirdre, who has witnessed the evolution of this book from its inception and has been my soul mate, editor, and best friend for many years, words simply cannot express what your companionship means. This book and life as I know it are unimaginable without you. To Maeve, Lila, and Claire, my beautiful daughters, thank you for being a part of my life and helping me remember that there is more to one's existence than work. To Art and Jean Pickus, my parents, I hope this book provides reassurance that your efforts were not in vain. No child could hope for better parents, no adult better friends. It is with tremendous respect and ceaseless appreciation that I dedicate this book to you.

Organizations

ORGANIZATION	FOUNDED	DESCRIPTION
Corps	18th C.	Nonpolitical, religiously neutral dueling organization
Burschenschaften	1816/17	Christo-Germanic dueling organization with a political agenda
Verein für Cultur und Wissenschaft der Juden	1819	Association for the promotion of Jewish intellectual discourse
Wingolfsbund	1850s	Christian dueling organization
Cartell-Verband	1860s	Catholic dueling organization
Landsmannschaften	1870s	Nonpolitical dueling association
Turnerschaften	1880s	Formerly gymnastic associations—dueling
Verein Deutscher Studenten (V.D.St.)	1880	Promoted anti-Jewish agenda
Freie Wissenschaftliche Vereinigung (F.W.V.)	1881	Nondenominational, although largely Jewish membership—standard-bearer of nineteenth-century liberalism

Akademische Verein für Jüdische Geschichte und Literatur	1883	Promoted the academic study of Judaism
Viadrina	1886	First Jewish dueling association—later followed by Badenia, Licaria, and Sprevia
Jung Israel-Jüdisch Nationaler Verein	1892	First Jewish nationalist student association
Vereinigung Jüdischer Studierender/Bund Jüdischer Corporationen (V.J.St./B.J.C.)	1895/1901	Coalition of Jewish nationalist associations
Kartell Convent Deutscher Studenten Jüdischen Glaubens (K.C.)	1896	Umbrella association for Viadrina, Badenia, Licaria, Sprevia, and other like-minded groups
Finkenschaften	1896	Association of unaffiliated students. Also known as "Free Students"
Bund Jüdischer Akademiker (B.J.A.)	1903	Association of religious/*halachic* Jews
Kartell Zionistischer Verbindungen (K.Z.V.)	1906	Umbrella association for Zionist groups
Kartell Jüdischer Verbindungen (K.J.V.)	1914	Fusion of B.J.C. and K.Z.V.

I

THE TRANSFORMATION
OF JEWISH
EDUCATION

1

Identity and Education
in the
Modern Era

For individuals concerned with the contours of Jewish life in the modern era, few topics are as emotionally laden and politically charged as the subject of Jewish identity. As rabbis in the United States work tirelessly to promote a Jewish consciousness among a constituency increasingly distanced from traditional Judaism and the Israeli rabbinate militantly lobbies to maintain its absolute authority over those who can lay claim to being Jewish, identity politics rage on campuses throughout the Western world. It is against this backdrop that academics wrestle with the question of who is a Jew.

With the onset of emancipation in the early nineteenth century, European Jews constructed paradigms of self-definition that were no longer completely harmonious with the dictates of the *halachic* tradition. As the traditional structures of authority and social cohesion broke down, Jews redefined their relation to the broader social and national frameworks. In the words of Michael Stanislawski, they lived "with one foot in their tradition and the other outside it . . . [trying] to reconcile the way of life of their parents with the attractions and challenges of modern existence."[1] Over the course of many generations, European Jews diminished the extent to which religious practice defined their Jewishness and fashioned identity profiles that would have been completely alien to their parents and grandparents.

In Germany, Jewish university students were on the forefront of the emancipationist movement. From the close of the Napoleonic era in Europe to the eve of World War I, Jews studying at German universities crafted patterns of Jewish identity that have influenced and inspired Jews for generations. Before investigating the content of these identities, however, we need to first consider the process of self-definition and examine the relationship between education and identity formation.

THE SOCIAL FUNCTION OF IDENTITY FORMATION

Since Sigmund Freud's pioneering studies of the human mind, academics across the disciplines have attempted to chart the path of psychological and social development. Erik Erikson's pathbreaking work in the 1950s set the standard for social scientists and humanists.[2] The explosion of minority studies programs at universities during the 1960s, followed by women's and ethnic studies programs in the 1970s and 1980s, has made the term *identity* commonplace in the scholarly literature and at conferences. While much has been written about German Jewish identity, historians of German Jewry seldom state explicitly what they mean by the term.[3] Hence, religious practice, organizational ideology, and political affiliation are mined for information regarding the content and character of German Jewish identity. Although Jewish student organizations occupy considerable space in this narrative, the study's primary goal is to illuminate the Jews' evolving position in nineteenth-century German society by analyzing the social function of identity formation.

Stuart Hall's observations on the topic of identity provide an appropriate point from which to assess the paradigms of self-definition employed by German Jews. Hall argues that an identity is best understood as a "process of identification . . . something that happens over time, that is never absolutely stable, that is subject to the play of history and the play of difference."[4] Because people reformulate their self-definitions in relationship to historical contingencies and, therefore, their identities are in a constant state of flux, Hall advises us to think of an identity as a "production

[that] is never complete, always in process, and always constituted within, not outside, representation."[5]

Identities can also be understood as a set of relationships that are continually contested and repositioned.[6] On the one hand, identity formation is a consciously creative process necessitating that individuals position themselves in relation to their families, communities, and social environments, and calling for them to make choices about their lifestyle, friends, organizational participation, and careers. Since, however, individuals are also positioned by the societies in which they live, identity formation is passive as well. In this regard, the determinant influences of one's parents, home environment, neighborhoods, and schools during the formative years of life constitute an unconscious component of identity construction.[7] In both cases, whether operating at the active/conscious or the passive/unconscious level, identities are historically contingent social constructions. As Sharon Macdonald argues, "Identities do not exist outside their making. Rather, they are *socially created in specific historical circumstances,* though they may be reified and perpetuated through all kinds of essentialist models."[8]

Not only are identities socially constructed, but they also are synthetic creations. In the words of A. L. Epstein, the act of identity formation "represents the process by which the person seeks to integrate his various statuses and roles, as well as his diverse experiences, into a coherent image of the self."[9] For German Jews, the act of synthesis integrated secular, religious, political, and social components that, when fused together, provided the building blocks of German Jewish culture.

The link between culture and identity is integral to understanding German Jewish identities. Anthony Cohen cogently argues that "culture is the means by which we make meaning, and with which we make the world meaningful to ourselves, and ourselves meaningful to the world." Rather than being a monolithic determinant of behavior, culture is a versatile metaphor that functions as an "eloquent representation of identity."[10] According to David Sorkin, German Jewish culture is best understood as a "subculture," one that is composed in large measure of "elements of the majority culture, [but] is nevertheless identifiably distinct and functions as a self-contained system of ideas and symbols."[11] Although I agree that German Jewish culture was distinct, I feel that cultural boundaries are considerably more porous than

Sorkin's definition allows for. Given that culture, by definition, is a versatile metaphor of meaning, it follows logically that German Jews did not create a single subculture, but a variety of them. The Reform, Conservative, and neo-Orthodox movements in Judaism, as well as the academic study of Judaism, *Wissenschaft des Judentums,* represent the diverse religious creations of the German Jewish subculture.[12] Similarly, the variety of Jewish organizations in existence at the close of the Kaiserreich demonstrate further diversity within German Jewish culture.

Although Jewish organizations and institutions were important vehicles for the creation and transmission of German Jewish culture and identity, they were not the only mechanisms at work in the process of identity formation. As Herbert Kelman reminds us,

> [G]roup identity is carried by the individual members of the group, but it is not coterminous with the sum of the conceptions of individual group members. For one thing, it has an independent existence in the form of accumulated historical products, including written documents, oral traditions, institutional arrangements, and symbolic artifacts. For another, different segments of the group differ widely in their degree of active involvement and emotional commitment to the group: various leadership elements and particularly active and committed subgroups are far more instrumental in defining the group identity than the rank-and-file members.[13]

Focusing exclusively on organizations when evaluating German Jewish identity is highly problematic. Not only is membership in an organization only one facet of a person's identity, but also not all German Jews participated in Jewish associational life. Consequently, studies of Jewish organizational structures cannot possibly comment on the paradigms of self-definition fashioned by individuals who were not affiliated with a Jewish organization. Moreover, given that the primary German Jewish organizations were created and run by German Jewish men, evaluations of these organizations offer no insight into the process of identity construction employed by German Jewish women.[14]

To appreciate the complex and often paradoxical existence for Jews living in Wilhelmine Germany and to uncover the lives buried beneath the archival legacy of Jewish organizational structures, one must distinguish between the act of self-definition that takes place among one's family and most intimate friends, a social sphere that I designate as one's "private" identity, and that developed while participating within the public sphere. This conceptual distinction is, in many ways, analogous to Milton Gordon's understanding of "primary" and "secondary" social groups.

> The primary group is a group in which contact is personal, informal, intimate, and usually face-to-face. . . . In direct contrast, the secondary group is a group in which contacts tend to be impersonal, formal or casual, non-intimate, and segmentalized. . . . The intimate friends we invite to our house regularly for dinner and to whose parties we are invited in return constitute a primary group. The civic committee for the preservation of the community's parks to which we belong and which meets twice a year is a secondary group.[15]

The key concept for both Gordon and myself is the question of social groupings. When in the company of intimates, we do not compartmentalize our lives, but rather we give free play to all facets of our identities. Conversely, when operating within the public sphere, only specific portions of our identities openly manifest themselves. Although one's public and private identities clearly overlap and are never completely separate, distinguishing between the two spheres of identity formation is a useful heuristic devise that enables us to evaluate how individuals position themselves as they maneuver in a range of societal settings.[16]

Such maneuvering, or the process of self-definition, can be understood as a person's attempt to determine a "fixed point of thought and being" from which to orient oneself in a confused and chaotic world.[17] Stuart Hall writes that "identities are a kind of guarantee that the world isn't falling apart quite as rapidly as it sometimes seems to be. It's a kind of fixed point of thought and being, a ground of action, a still point in a turning world."[18] In writing about twentieth-century American Jewish university students, Ilene Philipson claims that "identity politics furnishes a way to negotiate what seems to be an increasingly competitive and alienating experience within the university."[19] It strikes me that this statement is equally valid for nineteenth-century German Jewish students.

For German Jewish university students adapting to university life and the attendant departure from the nurturing and relatively secure environment of a family home, fashioning an identity helped counter feelings of alienation and isolation often associated with university studies. Jewish university students describe their attempts to counter the loneliness of a first semester of university studies by seeking out companionship at every opportunity, even if it meant calling upon individuals with whom they had no contact other than a "letter of introduction" from an acquaintance back home.[20] The process of self-definition for students making the transition from adolescence to young adulthood involved forming social coteries, joining student associations, and participating in the cultural, political, and intellectual opportunities available to university students. These are the activities that will occupy center stage in this study of Jewish university students, once we have examined the crucial nexus between education and identity.

EDUCATION AND IDENTITY

The appearance of Jewish students at German institutions of higher learning is a relatively recent phenomenon. Before the parallel movements of *Haskalah* (Jewish Enlightenment) and *Aufklärung* (German Enlightenment) opened the doors of Gentile society to Jews at the end of the eighteenth century, the majority of German Jews participated in an exclusively Jewish educational system. The most decisive factor preventing Jews from obtaining a non-Jewish education was the all-encompassing Jewish *Weltanschauung* (worldview) of traditional Jewish society. Before the rise of the absolutist state in the seventeenth century, European Jews lived out their lives in a world defined by Jewish law, or *Halakha*. Life's every contingency was accounted for in either the *halachic* code itself or the exegetical body of Jewish law known as the Talmud. All facets of Jewish life, from one's familial associations to one's education, were carried out in an exclusively Jewish environment. Non-Jewish society, according to Jacob Katz, "was neither a field of social aspiration nor a source of acute spiritual danger."[21] As long as Jewish law reigned supreme and retained its authority over the Jewish community, a non-Jewish education held no cultural or social value for Jews.

Apart from the few Jews who ventured abroad to study medicine at Italian and Dutch universities,[22] the vast majority of German

Jews were educated within the secure cultural walls of two traditional Jewish educational institutions: the *heder* and the *yeshivah*. At the age of five or six, Jewish boys were sent to a *heder*, an educational institution responsible for instructing Jewish males in the basics of Torah and the commentary of the medieval Jewish scholar, Rashi. The pedagogical goals of the *heder* were neither systematic nor comprehensive, but they facilitated the practice of normative Judaism by preparing Jewish males to participate in organized communal worship. The curriculum employed by the *heder* provided the basis of a "national-religious consciousness" for the Jewish community and was a vehicle for the transmission of Jewish religious and cultural traditions.[23]

The *yeshivah* was the Jewish equivalent of an institute of higher learning, one exclusively reserved for the academic elite. The educational goal of the *yeshivah* was to turn its pupils into scholars—masters of the Talmud and the work of its codifiers. The rearing of Jewish scholars, in fact, was the ultimate objective of the entire Jewish community. Unlike the *heder*, the *yeshivah* was not a communal organization, but a school that attracted students from a wide variety of towns and villages. *Yeshivah* studies truly anticipated those of latter-day universities in that their public lectures could only be understood by people who had devoted several years of intensive study to the nuances and minutiae of the Talmud.[24]

The essence of Jewish culture, its values, customs, and legal structure, was embodied in the Jewish educational system. Traditional Jewish society had perpetuated itself for centuries by adhering to a static and narrow educational system predicated on the study of Torah and Talmud. With the perpetuation of Jewish cultural values intimately intertwined with the educational curriculum of the *heder* and *yeshivah*, it is little wonder, therefore, that suggestions to supplement it with subjects outside the body of Jewish law were vehemently opposed.[25] By the last quarter of the eighteenth century, however, traditional Jewish society was under siege, facing challenges from a minority of its own constituents and a small segment of Gentile society. Proponents of the *Aufklärung* and the *Haskalah* lobbied to end the social and cultural isolation of German Jewry and formulated a program that, among other goals, advocated restructuring the Jewish educational system. Enlightened critics argued that educational reform was critical to the process of Jewish emancipation and the eventual Jewish participation in a newly emerging civil society.

An important voice among those calling for the reform of Jewish educational structures was Moses Mendelssohn (1729–86). Improvement of instruction and recommendation of the German mother tongue were favorite themes of Mendelssohn's. To promote the acquisition of the German language by traditional German Jews and to offer a path of return for the growing segment of Jewish society distanced from the basic tenets of Judaism by their inability to read Hebrew, Mendelssohn translated the Torah into high German. His translation of the Pentateuch, the first five books of the Old Testament, and his suggestions for educational reform were the first tangible steps in the transformation of the German Jewish educational system.

The move toward educational reform received additional impetus and legitimacy when Christian Wilhelm von Dohm (1751–1820), a Prussian bureaucrat and close friend of Mendelssohn's, published his classic emancipationist manifesto, *"Über die bürgerliche Verbesserung der Juden* (Concerning the amelioration of the civil status of the Jews).[26] Dohm's treatise argued that the debased condition of the Jews resulted from conditions imposed on them, and in order for Jews to become "better men and useful citizens . . . it [was] first necessary to give them equal rights with all other subjects."[27] In exchange for citizenship Jews would be encouraged to alter their educational system.

> The government should take care that, besides the holy teachings of his fathers, the Jew is taught to develop his reason by the clear light of knowledge, the science of nature and its great creator, and that his heart is warmed by the principles of order, honesty, love for all men and the great society in which he lives; . . . This would have to be done either in Jewish schools, or if teachers and funds are for the time being lacking, the Jews should be permitted to send their children to the Christian schools.[28]

According to Dohm, the reform of the Jewish educational system would not only initiate the moral improvement of the Jews, but it would also facilitate the restructuring of their economic profile. The restructuring of the Jewish educational system and the alteration of their economic profile were necessary prerequisites, Dohm felt, to Jews becoming more serviceable to the state.

The premise that education was key to the transformation of the Jewish character and the successful incorporation of Jews into civil society formed the cornerstone of the emancipationist movement. Shortly following the publication of Dohm's treatise, many of its ideas were incorporated into Joseph II's (1741–90) Edicts of Toleration.[29] As Holy Roman Emperor (1765–90), Joseph intended his pathbreaking decrees to alter the educational profile of his Jewish subjects. The legislation, issued in 1782, sought "to make the Jewish nation useful and serviceable to the State, mainly through better education and enlightenment of its youth as well as by directing them to the sciences, the arts and crafts." Toward this end, Joseph II decreed "that the tolerated Jews [could] send their children to Christian primary and secondary schools [where they would have] the opportunity to learn reading, writing and counting."[30] As the chorus of voices clamoring for a thorough restructuring of the Jewish educational system crescendoed, the pressure on Jewish communities intensified. Yet, until the call for educational reform resonated favorably within the walls of the Jewish community, the tone and tenor of traditional Jewish education never wavered.

To garner support among traditional Jews for Joseph's educational reforms, Naphtali Herz Wessely (1725–1805), a leading figure within the early *Haskalah*, attempted to reconcile the conflicting worldviews of German and Jewish societies. In his essay *Divrei Shalom ve'Emet* (Words of peace and truth), Wessely differentiated between human knowledge(*Torath ha' Adam*) and the teachings of God (*Torath ha' Elohim*), arguing that the former was an important and logical prerequisite for the study of God's laws.

> He who possesses "human knowledge" will gain much from the poetic expression of the divine Torah and from the ways of God that are written therein. . . . Similarly history, geography, astronomy and the like—which are inscribed in the mind as innate "primary ideas" whose foundation is reason— produced truths in every matter of wisdom. . . . Now, "human knowledge" is anterior to the exalted divine laws. Hence it is proper that in his youth man should crown himself with the fear of God, with the rule of etiquette and with the knowledge to which the appellation "human" is appropriate. With this knowledge he will prepare his heart to learn the laws and teachings of God. . . .[31]

Wessely's thoughts on education are, to a large extent, representative of Jews who supported the *Haskalah*. As a traditional Jew, Wessely did not envision that Jews would abandon the study of Jewish texts, but that "human knowledge," or nontraditional Jewish subjects, would complement a classical Jewish education. His specific educational proposals encouraged Jews to learn the language of the country in which they resided and to develop a proficiency in Hebrew sufficient to fully understand the Bible. A useful pedagogical tool in this regard, according to Wessely, was Moses Mendelssohn's German translation of the Bible.[32]

Wessely's opponents were quick to point out the threat his program posed to the integrity of traditional Judaism and the perpetuation of Jewish culture, especially as it promoted the benefits and validity of a body of learning outside the domain of traditional "Jewish" knowledge. In an essay entitled "A Sermon Contra Wessely," David Ben Nathan of Lissa (d. 1792) accused Wessely of being an impious and uneducated Jew, one who lacked all understanding of the "sublime wisdom of Torah."[33] Wessely's opponents, and opponents of Jewish educational reform in general, wanted to preserve the status quo of traditional Judaism by preventing changes to either the structure or content of Jewish education. Had they been successful, the existential question of Jewish identity would never have materialized. Their efforts, however, were insufficient to stem the tide of enlightened thought from penetrating the cultural walls of traditional Jewish society.

The spread of enlightenment principles throughout Jewish and non-Jewish German society provided the impetus for the creation of the first modern Jewish schools, the so-called *Freischule*. Founded by Jews in Berlin (1778), Breslau (1791), and Dessau (1799), the pedagogical objective of the *Freischule* was to teach poor Jews the subject matter necessary for commercial endeavors and thereby to enable them to improve their economic position. For the first time within the context of a Jewish educational environment, secular topics were given equal billing with traditional Jewish subjects. Fewer hours were spent on Hebrew, the Bible was taught in the vernacular, and the study of the Talmud was eliminated altogether. Moreover, the new curriculum employed by the *Freischule* included course work in "biblical history" and "religious instruction," two subjects predicated on Christian models. Biblical history stressed the moral and universal principles of the Bible and, in a thoroughly non-Jewish fashion, presented the Holy Book in a biographical and chronological format. Religious instruction prepared the individual for his confirmation, a celebration entirely foreign to traditional Judaism.[34] The curriculum employed by the *Freischule* not only altered the means by which Jewish children learned about their religious and cultural heritage, but it also transformed the process of Jewish identity formation employed by those who attended the *Freischule*.

Even though only nine hundred Jewish children enrolled in *Freischulen* in 1812, they pioneered the secularization of Jewish education in Germany. In the decades that followed, the number of German Jews attending nontraditional Jewish schools increased dramatically. By the middle of the nineteenth century, 50 percent of all German-Jewish male schoolchildren attended modern, secular educational institutions, and by 1867 the number had increased to 75 percent of the Jewish school-aged population.[35] Changes in the content and structure of Jewish education, especially the increased reliance on the German language for pedagogical purposes and synagogal ritual, bridged the cultural void that had separated Christian and Jewish society for centuries.

At the time that Jews first entered the German universities, following the Prussian defeat at Jena (1806), the entire pedagogical foundation of German educational institutions was in the midst of a complete renewal in accordance with the principles of *Bildung*, or self-formation. Religious instruction, once central to the curriculum of German and European schools, was gradually deemphasized in favor of a secular, humanistic education.[36] Germany's *Gymnasien*, the preparatory schools for study at German universities, drilled students in Greek and Latin and emphasized the development of reason over faith. At German universities, the educational system of the preceding century had utilized a rigid educational structure with little or no concern paid to the unique talents of individuals. As the leaders of the reform movement, Karl von Hardenberg and Karl Freiherr von Stein in the civilian government and Gerhard von Scharnhorst and Neithardt von Gneisenau in the military, attempted to rally the Prussian populace around the state's sagging fortunes, they recognized the benefits of fostering individual initiative as an indirect means of educating a productive and loyal elite. With this goal in mind, *Bildung* became the guiding principle for the reorganization of the German university system.[37]

The educational reforms that embodied the concept of *Bildung* and had the greatest impact on the future development of the

German university system were those instituted by Wilhelm von Humboldt, head of the Section for Religion and Education in the Ministry of the Interior from February 1809 through June 1810.[38] Humboldt's reforms were carried out in accordance with the neohumanist conception of *Bildung*, which sought to limit state power in favor of individual freedom. The modern state, according to Humboldt,

> must wholly refrain from every attempt to operate directly or indirectly on the morals and character of the nation. . . . Everything calculated to promote such a design, and particularly all special supervision of education, religion, sumptuary laws, etc., lies wholly outside the limits of its legitimate activity.[39]

Humboldt's proposed reforms for Germany's system of higher education contained three important provisions. The first called for the state to assume all financial responsibility for the schools and, in so doing, allow its citizens to educate themselves. Second, Humboldt suggested that educational barriers that perpetuated the segregation of the nation be removed and that universities be opened to all qualified individuals. German universities, according to Humboldt, should no longer be the exclusive purview of the privileged estates. In making a university education accessible to all qualified applicants, Humboldt envisioned that universities would become vehicles for social integration. It is little wonder, therefore, that Jews who entered the halls of academia in the first half of the nineteenth century considered a university education to be an effective method of integrating into German society.

Humboldt's third educational reform was predicated on the assumption that the needs of the state are best met when individuals are allowed to develop their unique character rather than being subjected to a rigid vocational training. In his opinion, "persons educated to be free individuals will ultimately be better citizens than men educated to be citizens." On the subject of the student's course work Humboldt argued that "one [should care] not that this or that be learned; but rather that in learning memory be exercised, understanding sharpened, judgment rectified, and moral feeling refined." Consistent with this view, Humboldt's final proposal called for universities to employ a general curriculum, based on mathematics, classical languages, and history—a system that he believed was best suited to encourage the unique development of each student and foster the acquisition of *Bildung*.[40]

Historian Fritz Ringer elaborates on Humboldt's thesis by contrasting the concepts of *Bildung* (cultivation) and *Unterricht* (instruction). While *Unterricht* is understood as the acquisition of specific knowledge necessary for the fulfillment of one's professional duties, *Bildung* is defined as

> forming the soul by means of the cultural environment. *Bildung* requires: (a) an individuality which, as the unique starting point, is to be developed into a formed or value-saturated personality; [and] (b) a certain universality, meaning richness of mind and person, which is attained through the empathetic understanding and experiencing of the objective cultural values. . . .[41]

The curriculum developed by Humboldt and employed by German universities throughout the nineteenth century emphasized formation of character over the mere acquisition of knowledge.

While not all of Humboldt's reform measures were implemented, the concept of *Bildung* central to his pedagogical philosophy was so thoroughly embraced by German academics that it carried over into the organizational structure of the universities. German universities were completely open to any student who had successfully completed his *Abitur* (the formal exam marking the completion of *Gymnasium*, or university preparation), with absolutely no restrictions placed on enrollments. The choice of institution was up to the student. Once registered at a university, the arrangement of one's academic program, its subjects, lectures, and exercises, was left entirely to the discretion of the student. Moreover, no course exams were given, nor were grades assigned. Students prepared themselves for the various state exams that followed their university studies in any way they saw fit.[42] The university required only that students register for at least one lecture course in each semester and did little, if anything, to ensure that they attended.

In spite of the fact that professional qualifying examinations were administered by the appropriate government ministries and no formal relationship existed between academic degrees and state exams, attending a German university was an important stepping stone on the path to a professional career. The right to sit for an examination was reserved for individuals who had acquired their *Abitur,* enrolled at a university for a minimum of three years, and registered and paid fees for specific courses within their subject area.[43] Although passing the examination was a prerequisite for acquiring a civil service position, whether or not one had performed well in a specific set of required courses was completely irrelevant. The assumption was that if one had lived up to the underlying principle of *Bildung* and made the most of the opportunities for self-cultivation during his years of university study, he would be well prepared to assume a professional post.

Obtaining a university education in Germany and, specifically, the acquisition of *Bildung,* was also recognized as a way to improve one's social position. The German sociologist Max Weber once wrote that a university education was crucial to overcoming firmly entrenched social barriers, "especially in Germany, where almost all privileged positions inside and outside the civil service are tied to qualifications involving not only specialized knowledge, but also general cultivation [*Bildung*] and where the whole school and university system has been put into this [idea of] general cultivation."[44] During the eighteenth century, non-nobles sought to improve their societal position by acquiring as much education as was within their financial means. Once employed by the state, they were designated as "servants of the state," a title that clearly distinguished them from those employed in the private sector. A university diploma, irrespective of one's social origins, entitled the holder to a prestigious and respected position in the hierarchy of German society. In many respects, graduates of German universities were considered a "substitute nobility."[45]

Once *Bildung* was institutionalized in the German university system, Jews living in Germany's urban centers who desired to break away from their traditional Jewish communities and participate in German society viewed a university education as the most expedient method of doing so. It is not surprising, therefore, that following the Wars of Liberation (1812–13), Jewish attendance at German universities started to rise. Although the emancipatory legislation of the preceding years contributed to this increase, it is also likely that the growing economic prosperity of German Jewry, a development that began at the turn of the century and continued for the next seventy years, also contributed to the rise in the number of Jewish university students.[46] As the material success of German

Jews increased, they attempted to translate their prosperity into the higher social standing bestowed upon those who had acquired *Bildung* by sending their sons to university, a move that emulated the social strategies of wealthy non-nobles.

By attending German institutions of higher learning, Jewish students participated in an educational system that imparted a cultural heritage alien to traditional Jewish society. Whereas a classical Jewish education predicated exclusively on the study of Jewish texts transmitted Jewish cultural and religious traditions and prepared Jews to participate in Jewish society, German universities provided the means for students to engage in the process of self-cultivation and to prepare for life within German society. Before the *Aufklärung*, German Jews exhibited little or no inclination to challenge the underpinnings of a Jewish education. Only in the nineteenth century did Jewish university students begin to question the validity of classical Jewish education and, as they did so, they were forced to reconcile the conflicting cultural, pedagogical, and philosophical orientations of two vastly different educational traditions. The efforts of Jewish university students to balance the demands of their German and Jewish heritages required the creation of new Jewish identities. It is to these students and their processes of identity formation that we now turn.

2

Jewish University Students in Preunification Germany

The political climate within the German lands during the first two decades of the nineteenth century simultaneously presented Jews with tremendous opportunities and serious challenges. The emancipatory legislation in Baden (1809), Prussia (1812), and other German states made it appear as though Jews would be granted citizenship and the door to Gentile society would be opened, albeit tentatively. At the same time, however, conservative legislation in Bavaria, Saxony, and Hanover perpetuated the inferior status of the Jews and spurred thousands to seek the more promising environs of Austria and Prussia. When the fall of Napoleon (1814–15) generated a reaction against Jewish advances and the Congress of Vienna (1815) failed to universalize Jewish emancipation throughout the German lands, Jews living in central Europe confronted the ambiguous legacy of the preceding decades of revolutionary ferment.

One consequence of the tentative move toward Jewish incorporation into an emerging civil society was an increase in the number of Jewish university students. Whereas Jewish attendance at German universities totaled approximately three hundred students during the eighteenth century, the number of Jews registered at the universities of Heidelberg, Breslau, Bonn, and Tübingen during the *Vormärz* era (1815–48) rose from 3 to 232. Nearly 40 percent of these students studied medicine; the remainder pursued studies within the faculties of philosophy and law.[1] Regardless of their chosen academic careers, the ambivalent and oftentimes hostile attitudes of Gentile students toward their Jewish colleagues exacerbated the process of identity formation. Jewish students who attended German universities in the aftermath of the Napoleonic era had to determine if the promises of emancipation were only a mirage in a barren desert, or if the ideals of enlightened society would eventually carry the day. Their assessments of the political and social landscape profoundly influenced the manner in which they positioned themselves in German society.

FIRST ENCOUNTERS

Some of the first German Jews to address this challenging dilemma were members of an organization known as the *Verein für Cultur und Wissenschaft der Juden* (The Society for the Culture and Science of the Jews). While not all of its members were university students, nor all of its concerns university related, members of the *Verein* were among the first German Jews to leave a written legacy of their efforts to construct a modern Jewish identity.[2]

The *Verein für Cultur und Wissenschaft der Juden* evolved out of an organization known as the *Wissenschaftliche Zirkel*, a group founded in 1816 by Jewish students looking to alleviate their sense of alienation and to interact socially with other students.[3] In the wake of the *Hep Hep!* riots of 1819, Joel Abraham List (1780–c.1848) invited six young Jewish intellectuals to his Berlin apartment to discuss the fate of German Jewry. Present at the meeting were List, Isaak Markus Jost, Leopold Zunz, Joseph Hillmar, Isaac Levin Auerbach, Eduard Gans, and Moses Moser, a veritable who's who of German Jewish intellectuals. Among those present only Moser, Hillmar, and possibly List had not studied at a university.[4]

In the opening presidential address to the association, List stated that "behind our decision to found a society for Jews seems to have been an apprehensiveness that in the future we, as individuals, will not be able to continue to live as Jews, or at least not in the way we would like to."[5] Unlike premodern Jewish society, which was held together by religious bonds, List argued that in the future "our venerable religion must cease to constitute the bond of our nation, not only because of its aforementioned mistaken goal [the perpetuation of Jewish isolation] . . . but also because of the severity of its [heteronomous] laws."[6]

List's inaugural comments reveal several concepts central to his image of modern Jewry. First, he was cognizant that if Jews were to participate in a rapidly changing German society, then their Jewishness needed to be redefined. Accordingly, religious Judaism could no longer constitute the distinguishing feature of one's Jewishness. In an attempt to delineate the essential characteristics of modern Jewry, List put forth the following propositions.

> We are aware of a substance within us, an essence of timeless existence. In that we are conscious of our existence as Jews, we wish to preserve our Jewishness, and since we *wish* to preserve our Jewishness, we *must* preserve it. We therefore have a clear conception of our being, of our common being, for otherwise we would no longer be ourselves and hence nothing at all. . . . For us, however, there must be no greater concern than the integrity of our nation, and we must not shy away from any sacrifice to preserve it. With respect to the Jewish nation, we should regard as meritorious only those deeds which further the realization of this goal.[7]

List's claim that modern Judaism centered on a national rather than a religious ideal marked a radical departure from the position of both traditional Jews and proponents of the *Haskalah*. Yet, in spite of his desire to end Jewish social isolation without abandoning a distinctive Jewish identity, List failed to formulate a viable road map for this unprecedented journey.

In addition to the presentation given by List, Moses Moser (b. 1796) also addressed the young Jewish intellectuals who had gathered to discuss the fate of German Jewry. Like List, Moser referred to the Jews as a "nation."

> Our goal is the advancement of the outer and inner culture of our nation which complement one another. . . . The opposition of Jewish culture against the general European (or, if you prefer, Christian) culture must be resolved . . . not in the manner of our compatriots through conversion . . . but rather, ideal Judaism must be completely reconciled with the state

insofar as it is determined through the culture of its citizens; but it must be in sharp opposition to the ruling church as such in regard to its dogma.[8]

Moser's formulation of the task confronting Jews is significant in that he equated European with Christian culture and expressed the need to "reconcile" Jewish culture with the prevailing Christian-Germanic culture of German society. Although opposed to the authority of church dogma, be it Jewish or Christian, Moser recognized that modern German society was in fact a Christian construction. To participate in German civil society, therefore, German Jews would have to negotiate a path between their Jewish culture and the dominant Christian society. Opposed to conversion as a solution to this dilemma, Moser was unable to postulate what constituted a Jewish identity once Judaism was no longer defined in religious terms.

The challenge of positioning one's self in German society without converting to Christianity was one faced by many members of the *Verein*. For Sigmund Wilhelm Zimmern, the task proved insurmountable. Born in Heidelberg in 1796 to a "merchant" family, Zimmern began his legal studies in Heidelberg in 1813 and later attended the universities in Berlin and Göttingen. While in Berlin, Zimmern participated in the *Wissenschaftliche Zirkel* and later in the *Verein* itself. After receiving his Ph.D. in 1817, Sigmund Zimmern became a *Privatdozent*, the first step on the academic ladder, and he looked to advance his university career. When his application to become an *Ordinarius* (full professor) was denied on account of his being Jewish, Zimmern confronted the reality that professional advancement in an academic setting was not possible if one chose to remain a Jew. Faced with the dilemma of choosing between his religious heritage and his desire to become a professor, Zimmern ultimately chose the latter.[9] His path was by no means unique.

Two years after its founding, the Society for the Culture and Science of the Jews continued its effort to construct a modern Jewish identity that would enable Jews to participate in German society without converting to Christianity. In a report delivered to the association in April 1822, Eduard Gans (1798–1839), the group's leading ideologue and current president, could do little more than speculate on the nature of modern Judaism. Utilizing Hegel's dialectical interpretation of history to explain how the essence of Judaism would be preserved, Gans offered the following consoling lesson of history:

> Everything [in history] passes without perishing, and yet persists, although it has long been consigned to the past. That is why neither the Jews will perish nor Judaism dissolve; in the larger movement of the whole they will seem to have disappeared, and yet they will live on as the river lives in the ocean.[10]

Reminding his fellow members of their role in the historical process, Gans explained that in order

> to hasten the coming of this day [when Jews would be indistinguishable from Christians], to bring it about with all of our power at our disposal, . . . we wish to help in pulling down the barrier which still exists between the Jew and the Christian, between the Jewish world and Europe; we want to reconcile that which, for thousands of years, has been moving along side by side without so much as touching each other.[11]

Clothed in the garments of a Hegelian worldview, Gans's speech failed to define the essence of modern Judaism or reconcile its continued existence in the historical development of humankind. When evaluated within the context of his tumultuous personal life and growing professional frustrations, Gans's speech both presages his own apostasy and offers a philosophical justification for it. Unsuccessful in his attempt to secure a position as a professor of law at a German university, Gans followed in Zimmern's footsteps and was baptized in Paris on December 12, 1825. Upon returning to Berlin as a Christian, he received the university position he coveted dearly and had previously been refused. Apparently Gans was unable to wait patiently for the day when "no one in Europe will ask any longer, who is a Jew and who is a Christian."

The *Verein für Cultur und Wissenschaft der Juden* represents the first attempt by German Jewish university students to establish the philosophical basis for Jewish participation in the cultural arena of secular society. The organization's inability to articulate a viable program for the cultural reorientation of German Jewry underscored the complexity of the existential problem of Jewish self-definition in the modern period. Living at a time when Jews were denied equal status with Gentiles and conversion was seen by both Christians and many Jews as the entry ticket into European society, the members of the *Verein* could do little more than outline the agenda for the redefinition of German Jewry. As Michael Meyer so eloquently suggests, "Again and again a mute Jewish consciousness reached out for self-explanation, but ever fell short of an adequate justification."[12] Its failures aside, the *Verein für Kultur und Wissenschaft der Juden* made two significant contributions to the creation of a modern Jewish identity: it redefined Judaism in national as opposed to religious terms, and it provided its members with a location within student society where they could share the burdens associated with negotiating a path between *Deutschtum* and *Judentum*.

THE THEORY OF JEWISH MEMBERSHIP IN THE *CORPS* AND *BURSCHENSCHAFTEN*

Although the dissolution of the *Verein* in the 1820s temporarily ended the efforts of Jewish university students to establish their own organizations, it did not preclude the possibility of their participating within the vibrant associational life of German universities. A hallmark of German society throughout the nineteenth century was the spread of a cross-regional network of special interest *Vereine*, or associations. Appearing first at local levels and developing later into an interterritorial phenomenon, the vast network of formal associations is recognized as an important feature of a *bürgerliche Gesellschaft* (civil society).[13] Formulated on the principle of a "free association of individuals" and opposed to membership based on coercion, the German *Vereine* transcended the limitations of class and profession established at birth and transformed enlightened notions of individuality into practice. Voluntary associations came into being as a "public sphere" was created outside of the family and the state. Both contemporary commentators and historians reporting on the associational movement claimed that the early organizations brought together "cultivated (*gebildeten*) men and women from both the educated and merchant classes."[14]

An important feature of the German associational movement was its incorporation of the ideals of *Bildung* (self-cultivation) into the organizations' raison d'être. Whether they were reading societies, singing clubs, or gymnastic associations, the modern *Vereine* subscribed to the theory that every individual possessed the potential for self-improvement. By upholding this basic principle of enlightened ideology, the *bürgerlich* organizations facilitated the acquisition of *Bildung* among a greater segment of the German population than had previously been possible.[15] Although Jewish participation in Germany's bourgeois associations was problematic and not always tolerated, the desire to do so and subsequent attempts to emulate the activities of the Gentile middle class are important for our understanding of Jewish integration into German society. At German universities, the two most important and influential student associations were the *Corps* and the *Burschenschaften*.

The ideological roots of the *Corps* can be traced to organizations at the University of Erlangen in 1796 and the University of Halle in 1799, with the first use of the name *Corps* occurring at Heidelberg in 1810.[16] The *Corps'* self-defined purpose was to "arrange for the lively interaction of like minded and honest young university men who desired the natural satisfaction of their social needs."[17] Like its predecessors, the *Corps* emphasized lifelong friendships. The areas in which the *Corps* distinguished itself from other nineteenth-century student associations were its understanding of *bürgerlich* honor and its position on religion. Members of the *Corps* viewed themselves as belonging to a *bürgerlich* society, a fact necessitating that they act as gentlemen and be treated as such. The organizational statutes of every association emphasized the importance of conducting one's self in an honorable way, and the following is but one example of these ubiquitous exhortations:

> Each [member] should consider his word of honor as holy. He who gives it, should carefully consider whether he is speaking to a friend or a foe, and if he can fulfill his pledge. Broken or false declarations of honor will be punished by the association without exception.[18]

Not only was it incumbent upon members of the *Corps* to conduct themselves in an honorable manner, they were also required to stand ready to defend all violations of their honor. Any slanderous comment, perceived or actual, demanded an apology or retribution. If an apology was not forthcoming, a *Corpsstudent* was obligated to demand *Satisfaktion* from the person who had violated his honor by challenging the perpetrator of the insult to a duel. The immediate and unimpeachable demand for the satisfaction of one's defamed honor became known among the *Corps* as the principle of *unbedingte Satisfaktion mit der Waffe* (unconditional satisfaction with weapons). The association's organizational statutes contain detailed regulations that not only stipulated the appropriate periods of time to wait before issuing a challenge, but also the types of weapons that could be used and how the duels were to be fought.[19]

In spite of their aristocratic constituency, however, the *Corps* were the first university student associations to open their membership to all honorable students, regardless of their religious beliefs. When considering a student's worthiness for admission, questions of religion, race, and nationality did not enter into discussion. The constitution of the *Corps Franconia* in Leipzig claimed that "every young man of spirit and heart whose upright nature and honesty are readily visible to all, can be accepted into our brotherly association."[20] According to Albin Angerer, a historian of the *Corps,* religious differences between members never entered into discussions of how to settle their disputes, and the religious views of the individual remained inviolable.[21]

The religiously neutral stance of the *Corps* was founded on its commitment to the concept of *Bildung* and belief in the perfectibility of humankind.[22] The underlying principle of *Bildung* maintained that all individuals, regardless of religious orientation, were capable of cultivating themselves and participating in civil society. The fact that the *Corps* drew largely from the upper classes of German society and were comprised of individuals who retained a strong affinity for a monarchical form of government does not discount the association's commitment to *Bildung,* religious toleration, and the willingness to accept Jewish members. While not all *Corps* had Jewish members or were comprised of both Protestant and Catholic students, the theory of religious toleration was central to the ideology of the *Corps* throughout the period from 1815 to 1871. Even though the number of Jews at German universities during the period before the revolutions of 1848 was not great, their Jewishness never prevented them from joining the *Corps.* There was no overt "Jewish Question" within the *Corps* and the organization remained open, in principle, to the idea of Jewish membership. As for the *Burschenschaften,* however, the *Corps'* counterpart and rival organization, the question of Jewish membership was extremely problematic.

The *Burschenschaft* movement was started in the years following the German Wars of Liberation by students who had interrupted their university studies to join the military campaigns against Napoleon. The war with France had infused these students with strong nationalist ideals and a desire to unify the German lands. After the conclusion of the war, the student volunteers resumed their studies and created *Burschenschaften*, student associations whose principles reflected their newly acquired worldviews. The theme of the organization was unity; unity of both the fatherland and all university students, and its rallying cry was "honor, freedom, and fatherland." The program of the various *Burschenschaften* resonated favorably among the entire student body and, by the time of the *Wartburgfest* in 1817 (the first interuniversity gathering of German university students held in commemoration of both the defeat of Napoleon and the tricentennial of the Reformation), its popularity had eclipsed that of the *Corps*.[23]

The immediate success of the *Burschenschaft* movement was due in large part to the ties it retained to previous student organizations. Even though the founders of the *Burschenschaften* portrayed themselves as reformers of student society and railed against the socially exclusive nature of the *Corps*, the vast majority of original members had previously belonged to this rival organization.[24] In developing the ideological and structural basis of their new student association, the founding brothers established important lines of continuity between themselves and the *Corps*. The concepts of honor and community were integral to the ideology of the *Burschenschaften*, and *Bildung* was a basic philosophical tenet. The organizational structure of the *Burschenschaften* was borrowed from the *Corps*, and the first *Burschenschaft* constitution was practically a replica of those written by the *Corps*.[25] The incorporation of these ideological and structural positions into the founding principles of the *Burschenschaft* movement made the new student association readily acceptable to most former members of the *Corps* and enabled it to cultivate an active and loyal membership from its inception.

The *Burschenschaften* parted ways with the *Corps* over politics and religion, however. Unlike the *Corps*, which was a politically and religiously neutral student association, the *Burschenschaft* movement had deep Christian roots and took an active political stance. The new organization's main political goal was to establish a unified German nation, an aim that stood in stark contrast to the existing situation in Germany, wherein regional differences were accentuated and the ruling political order demonstrated little inclination to relinquish its hold on power. The experience of foreign occupation under Napoleon and the military activities of the students during the Wars of Liberation were sufficient to motivate a small but active group of returning students to stake out this political platform.[26] Immediately following its creation in 1815, the *Burschenschaft* movement became the single most important social force at German universities. Out of a student population of approximately ten thousand men in 1815, roughly one to two thousand belonged to the *Burschenschaft* movement.[27]

The political agenda of the *Burschenschaften* extended beyond the question of German nationalism and the desire to establish a single student association representative of all German university students. The founding members of the organization understood that, upon completion of their studies, they would be expected to assume positions of importance within German society and to take part in the political process. To facilitate the transition from student to responsible citizen, the *Burschenschaften* believed that a university education attuned to the concept of *Bildung* necessitated that students be introduced to the issues and societal concerns on which they would one day pass judgment. Unlike the *Corps*, which defined *Bildung* solely in terms of *Wissenschaft* (academics), the *Burschenschaften* adopted an understanding of self-cultivation that claimed that a student's political as well as academic development was central to the ideology of *Bildung*. The differences between the *Corps* and the *Burschenschaften* were articulated within the pamphlet literature produced by the two organizations in the 1860s.[28]

The political education advanced by the *Burschenschaften* was influenced by the organization's definition of a civil society. The *Burschenschaften's* self-proclaimed love of the German fatherland was coupled with a "deep seated, Christian oriented moral and religious attitude." A united Germany, according to the statutes of the *Burschenschaften* organizations, required the "training of all physical and spiritual powers for the service of the fatherland."[29] In other words, *Burschenschaft* ideology defined civil society and citizenship in Christian terms. Although the core of the *Burschenschaften's* Christian ideology was of Protestant origin, efforts were made in the years following the *Wartburgfest* to reach out to Roman

Catholic university students and promote the organization's inter-confessional nature. Attempts, however, to establish a unified po-sition on the relationship between Christianity and the formation of a civil society eluded the *Burschenschaften*. Nowhere were the differences in philosophical and religious orientation within the *Burschenschaft* movement more pronounced than in the debates over Jewish membership.[30]

In spite of the fact that relatively few Jews attended German universities prior to 1848, the question of Jewish membership was discussed during the initial phases of the *Burschenschaften's* development (c.1815–1830). Proponents of Jewish membership articulated the same arguments as those employed by German liberals who, in support of Jewish emancipation, claimed that if society were based on the rational philosophical ideals of the *Aufklärung* (German Enlightenment), people of all religious per-suasions were entitled to participate in civil society. Students in favor of Jewish membership argued that as a *bürgerlich* association, it was incumbent upon the *Burschenschaft* movement to admit all worthy members, regardless of religious orientation.[31]

During the initial phase of the *Burschenschaften's* development, Jewish membership depended upon a given association's inter-pretation of the Christian character of the organization.[32] In the *Burschenschaften's* original charter of 1815, there was no mention of either Jewish membership or exclusion. The constitution stated only that "eternal enemies of the German people," specifically the *Welschen*—a nineteenth-century German term used to designate the peoples of southern Europe who speak a romance language—and the French were excluded from membership in the *Burschen-schaften*.[33] The students at Jena and other ideologically like-minded associations differentiated between foreign nationals and Jews at-tending German universities, identifying the former as clearly non-German and hence, ineligible for membership. Jewish students, on the other hand, were seen as an organic and indigenous segment of the German populace and therefore fully entitled to membership. The position of the Jena *Burschenschaften* on Jewish membership was commensurate with the enlightened ideal of civil society, which postulated that membership was not contingent upon one's religious orientation.

As was the case with German society at large and with its view of Jewish emancipation, members of the *Burschenschaften* could not agree on Germany's religious orientation. The *Burschenschaft* association at the university in Gießen, a group commonly known as the *Gießener Schwarzen*, was the first organization to insist on the Christianity of its membership.[34] Led by the ardent German nationalist and ideologue of Germanic culture Karl Follen (1796–1840), the *Gießener Schwarzen* argued that German society was an inherently Christian construction. When Follen began his university studies in 1814, he immediately established a reading association that concentrated on his ideological role models, Schiller, Fichte, and Arndt. In 1815, Follen, along with his brother and a group of like-minded Christian radical students, formed an association called *Germania* that became known as the *Schwarzen* (the Blacks) on account of the color of their academic coats and their stern moral outlook. The Blacks issued a set of resolutions that supported the establishment of a student court to settle all questions of honor and called for the creation of "an assembly of all Christian German students, united in a free student community, . . . [which should be authorized to] exercise all legislative and judicial functions in all student affairs." When this resolution failed to win over the students of Gießen, especially members of the *Corps*, the *Schwarzen* pushed ahead with their plans to establish a student court and unify the German student body under the banner of a "Christian-German *Burschenschaft*."[35]

Although the *Gießener Schwarzen* represented an extreme anti-Jewish position within the *Burschenschaft* movement, they were not alone in their opinion that the *Burschenschaften* should be Christian organizations. The Heidelberg *Teutonia*, the first student association at Heidelberg to associate itself with the *Burschenschaft* movement, adopted a similar anti-Jewish position. According to the memoirs of *Teutonia* member Ferdinand Walter, only individuals of German heritage and Christian orientation were eligible for membership.[36] In a similar vein, the *Burschenschaft* organization at the university in Erlangen also excluded Jewish students. Its 1818 constitution stated that "foreigners, meaning non-Germans and Jews, could not be members of the German *Burschenschaften*."[37] Unlike the students at Jena who distinguished between foreign and Jewish students, members of the Erlanger *Burschenschaften*, along with the *Burschenschaften* at Gießen and Heidelberg, saw no difference between the two groups and excluded both from their student associations. While these three branches of the early *Burschenschaft* movement were not representative of the entire organization, by 1818 even the associations that did not explicitly exclude Jews had incorporated "Christian articles" into their constitutions. Even the *Burschenschaft* organization at Jena called for the Christian education of its membership.[38]

Extensive discussion of the "Jewish Question" among the *Burschenschaften* came to an abrupt halt following the 1819 murder of the dramatist and purported czarist informer, August von Kotzebue. Prince Klemens von Metternich (1773–1859), foreign minister of Austria and chief advisor to the Habsburg emperor, utilized the assassination by the mentally unstable *Burschenschafter* Karl Sand as a pretext to dissolve the *Burschenschaften* and to clamp down on all nationalist activists within German universities. The imposition of the Karlsbad Decrees in 1819 forced the *Burschenschaften* underground until 1827 and temporarily quieted discussion of the "Jewish Question."[39]

When the organization emerged from its clandestine existence and met openly under its black, red, and gold banner in Bamberg in 1827, the influence of the *Gießener Schwarzen* had significantly diminished. Over the next four years references to Christianity were gradually removed from the statutes of the individual constitutions, and the *Burschenschaft* organizations moved toward a position on Jewish membership similar to that of the *Corps*. At an 1831 general meeting of the *Burschenschaften* in Frankfurt, the organization changed the wording of the general constitution to read that "all German students, without regard to their homeland or faith," were eligible for membership.[40] From this time until the reemergence of the "Jewish Question" at German universities in 1879, associations of the *Burschenschaften* and the *Corps* were theoretically open to all university students, regardless of religious orientation. Whether the theory of religiously neutral membership policies translated into practice when it came to admitting Jewish students as members, however, is yet to be determined.

Unfortunately, comprehensive enrollment figures that allow for a statistical analysis of Jewish participation in the corporate subculture of German universities are only available for the University of Heidelberg. Although limited to Heidelberg, such a study raises important questions about the rate of Jewish acculturation. Why, for example, did it take three decades for Jews to begin participating, to any significant degree, in traditional student associations? Was the decade following the revolutions of 1848 a high-water mark in Gentile acceptance of Jews in student corporate associations or did the trend continue until the completion of the emancipatory process in 1871? To answer these questions and examine the process of Jewish integration into German society, we now turn to the situation at the University of Heidelberg between 1815 and 1871.[41]

JEWISH MEMBERSHIP IN THE *CORPS* AND THE *BURSCHENSCHAFTEN* OF HEIDELBERG

Heidelberg University was sanctioned by Ruprecht I, the prince elector of the Rheinland, in 1386 and officially named the Ruperto Carola University in 1803 by Prince Karl Friedrich of Baden. Surrounded by forested green hills and nestled along the banks of the Neckar River, Heidelberg's idyllic setting has delighted residents, tourists, and students alike for centuries. The picturesque beauty of "Old Heidelberg" has captured the imagination of Goethe, Longfellow, Mark Twain, and scores of other luminaries, and it has inspired one historian of German student life to proclaim Heidelberg as "the most beautiful university city in the world."[42] Although devoid of a central campus along the lines of an American or British university, Heidelberg University spawned a vibrant and colorful student tradition. During the nineteenth century, the students of Heidelberg actively participated in both the *Corps* and *Burschenschaft* movements.[43]

One activity central to the existence of the Heidelberg *Corps* was the *Mensur*. The *Mensur* never derived from an actual insult, but rather, it was a competition between members of different student associations, arranged by senior members to allow the young initiates, or *Füchse* (foxes), to demonstrate their courage. Most *Mensuren* in Heidelberg took place at the renowned *Hirschgasse*. Although the rules of the *Mensur* varied from place to place, its form remained consistent.[44] Participants were clothed in protective garb, which consisted of a thickly padded vest covering the torso and the throat. The head was protected by a loosely worn cap and the arms were swathed in layers of protective padding, arranged in such a way as not to hinder the action of either the wrist or the elbow.[45] Displaying one's courage in a *Mensur* became a rite of passage for all students wishing to join the *Corps*. More importantly, the association believed that only upstanding and honorable individuals were worthy to fight with swords and, in so doing, to demonstrate their qualification for membership. Students unworthy of defending their honor in this manner were, in fact, excluded from membership.

The question of whether Jews were perceived as "honorable" students by members of the Heidelberg *Corps* is open to debate. Although theoretically a religiously neutral association and open to students of all religious views, membership figures for the five Heidelberg *Corps* associations reveal that very few Jews actually joined. Between 1815 and 1848 there were only four Jewish members, followed by seven more in the next decade and five additional Jewish *Corps* men in the ten-year period before the unification of Germany. (See table 2.1.) Even more telling of the underrepresentative nature of Jewish membership in the Heidelberg *Corps* is the low participation rate of Jewish students as compared to that of their Gentile colleagues. The Gentile rate of participation in the *Corps* ranged from 9.28 percent during the years 1815–48 to 16.66 percent between 1849 and 1859 and 9.27 percent for 1860–70. The corresponding participation rates for Jewish students were 0.99 percent, 3.65 percent, and 1.58 percent. (See tables 2.2 and 2.3.)

The low rate of Jewish participation in the *Corps* can be interpreted on many levels. One factor that may have affected the rate at which Jewish students joined the *Corps* was the inconsistent support of German liberals for Jewish emancipation. While liberals advocated the concept of a religiously neutral civil society, not all who held liberal views felt that Jews were worthy of citizenship. This was apparently the situation among the Heidelberg *Corps*. Before 1848, Jewish membership was concentrated in two organizations, *Suevia* and *Vandalia*. After 1848, five Jewish students joined *Suevia*, two became members of *Saxo-Borussia*, and one joined *Vandalia*. At no time during the period 1815–70 were Jews admitted to *Guestphalia*. What we see, therefore, is that the religiously neutral governing principles of the *Corps* did not automatically translate into Jewish membership in every organization. The fact that some groups had Jewish members while others did not suggests that Jewish participation in a particular chapter of the *Corps* depended on the attitudes of the specific members at a given point in time. Such a pattern suggests that the organizational ideologies of German bourgeois associations did not translate into the social reality of Jewish membership.

A second explanation for the lack of Jewish participation in the *Corps* pertains to the emancipatory process itself and what

Table 2.1 Jewish Membership in the Heidelberg *Corps*

	1815–48	1849–59	1860–70
Suevia	3/349	5/201	0/78
Guestphalia	0/476	0/140	0/106
Saxo-Borussia	0/377	2/180	0/163
Vandalia	1/101	0/194	0/109
Rhenania	0/0	0/100	5/101

Source
These figures were derived by cross-referencing the names of Jewish students enrolled at Heidelberg University and listed in *Die Matrikel der Universität Heidelberg*, Gustav Toepke, ed., Vols 5 and 6 (Heidelberg: Carl Winter's Universitätbuchhandlung, 1904) with membership lists found in the following documents: *Corps Rhenania zu Heidelberg: Mitglieder-Verzeichniss der Jahre 1849 bis 1879* (Heidelberg, 1879); *Corps Suevia zu Heidelberg, 1810–1935 Zum 125. Stiftungsfeste Juni 1935* (Heidelberg, 1935); *Mitglieder der Guestphalia zu Heidelberg, 1818–1928* (Heidelberg, 1928); *Die Mitglieder der Vandalia zu Heidelberg, Juni 1907* (Heidelberg, 1907); and *Rhenania, 1862–1869: Von der Wiedererrichtung 1862 bis zur Feier des zwanzigjährigen Stiftungsfestes 1869* (Heidelberg, 1869).
Note
The first number represents the total number of Jewish members for the period, with the second number representing the total number of members.

Table 2.2 Gentile Participation Rate in the *Corps*

Years	Gentile Students	Gentile Members	Participation Rate
1815–48	14103	1309	9.28%
1849–59	4891	815	16.66%
1860–70	6008	557	9.27%
Totals	25002	2681	10.72%

Source
These figures were derived by cross-referencing the names of Jewish students enrolled at Heidelberg University and listed in *Die Matrikel der Universität Heidelberg*, Gustav Toepke, ed., Vols 5 and 6 (Heidelberg: Carl Winter's Universitätbuchhandlung, 1904) with membership lists found in the following documents: *Corps Rhenania zu Heidelberg: Mitglieder-Verzeichniss der Jahre 1849 bis 1879* (Heidelberg, 1879); *Corps Suevia zu Heidelberg, 1810–1935 Zum 125. Stiftungsfeste Juni 1935* (Heidelberg, 1935); *Mitglieder der Guestphalia zu Heidelberg, 1818–1928* (Heidelberg, 1928); *Die Mitglieder der Vandalia zu Heidelberg, Juni 1907* (Heidelberg, 1907); and *Rhenania, 1862–1869: Von der Wiedererrichtung 1862 bis zur Feier des zwanzigjährigen Stiftungsfestes 1869* (Heidelberg, 1869).
Note
The Gentile participation rate is derived by dividing the number of Gentile members of the organization by the total number of Gentile students at the university.

Table 2.3   Jewish Participation Rate in the *Corps*

Years	Jewish Students	Jewish Members	Participation Rate
1815–48	404	4	0.99%
1849–59	192	7	3.65%
1860–70	316	5	1.58%
Totals	912	16	1.75%

Source
These figures were derived by cross-referencing the names of Jewish students enrolled at Heidelberg University and listed in *Die Matrikel der Universität Heidelberg*, Gustav Toepke, ed., Vols 5 and 6 (Heidelberg: Carl Winter's Universitätbuchhandlung, 1904) with membership lists found in the following documents: *Corps Rhenania zu Heidelberg: Mitglieder-Verzeichniss der Jahre 1849 bis 1879* (Heidelberg, 1879); *Corps Suevia zu Heidelberg, 1810–1935 Zum 125. Stiftungsfeste Juni 1935* (Heidelberg, 1935); *Mitglieder der Guestphalia zu Heidelberg, 1818–1928* (Heidelberg, 1928); *Die Mitglieder der Vandalia zu Heidelberg, Juni 1907* (Heidelberg, 1907); and *Rhenania, 1862–1869: Von der Wiedererrichtung 1862 bis zur Feier des zwanzigjährigen Stiftungsfestes 1869* (Heidelberg, 1869).
Note
The Jewish participation rate is derived by dividing the number of Jewish members of the organization by the total number of Jewish students at the university.

might be referred to as a "generational" rate of acculturation. In the years before the revolutions of 1848, Jews who attended German universities were on the forefront of the emancipatory movement. Many came from traditional Jewish homes and most had received instruction in both classical and secular subjects. The decision to attend a secular institution of higher learning was one of the first steps of acculturation for German Jews, rather than a final stage in the process of affiliation with the host culture.[46] It would be incongruous to think, therefore, that the first and second generations of Jewish university students plunged into the heart of traditional student culture immediately upon entering a German university. German Jews would have to be better acquainted with German student culture before membership in a traditional student association became a "field of social aspiration." Jacob Katz posits that bridges to the Gentile world had to be established before Jews would aspire to participate in it.[47] The gap between traditional Judaism and Gentile culture was simply too great to span in one movement. As successive generations of Jewish students acquired greater knowledge of German student culture, the desire and ability to immerse oneself in the social and cultural environment of the *Corps* gradually increased. Hence, the growing rate of Jewish participation between 1815 and 1859. To explain the precipitous drop in Jewish membership within the *Corps* after 1859, however, we need to examine the rate of Jewish membership in the *Burschenschaft* movement.

The Heidelberg *Burschenschaften*, like similar organizations at other German universities, experienced a stormy beginning. The first Heidelberg chapter of the *Burschenschaften* was established in 1815. Under the influence of the German philosopher Jacob Friederich Fries (1773–1843), it excluded Jews from joining. With the arrival of the reform-minded law student Friederich Wilhelm Carové in 1817, the organization adopted a more liberal attitude toward Jewish membership. After the *Wartburgfest*, at which Carové represented the Heidelberg *Burschenschaften*, an internecine struggle developed between students who supported Carové and others who favored the position advocated by Fries and the *Gießener Schwarzen*. The dissolution of the Heidelberg *Burschenschaften* following the proclamation of the Karlsbad decrees prevented the establishment of a united organizational front. Until 1856 the Heidelberg *Burschenschaften* led a fragmented and precarious existence.[48] Given the tenuous legal position of German Jews during this period, it is highly doubtful that Jewish students would have jeopardized their academic careers and subsequent prospects for economic advancement by joining a *Burschenschaft* organization that had yet to secure its position at the University of Heidelberg. It is no surprise, therefore, that the *Corps* remained the organization of choice for Jewish students who joined a traditional student society before 1856.

The situation within the student body changed abruptly in 1856, when the Heidelberg university senate temporarily dissolved the five *Corps* and simultaneously lifted many of the restrictive regulations that had hindered the development of a permanent *Burschenschaft* association. In November 1856, the *Burschenschaften* *Allemania* and *Frankonia* were founded.[49] Both organizations opposed the exclusion of prospective members based on either political or confessional beliefs and between 1856 and 1870, the Heidelberg *Burschenschaften* exhibited a greater degree of receptivity to Jewish students than their rivals, the *Corps*. During this period, *Allemania* initiated five Jewish members and *Frankonia* three. The comparative rates of participation in both organizations show that Gentile students at Heidelberg were six times more likely to join one of the *Corps* than were Jewish students, whereas among the *Burschenschaften* the ratio was only two to one. Between 1860 and 1870, 4.39 percent of all Gentile students joined either *Allemania* or *Frankonia* and 2.22 percent of Jewish students did likewise. These figures compare to a participation rate within the *Corps* of 9.27 percent for Gentiles and 1.58 percent for Jewish students during the same period of time. (See tables 2.4, 2.5, and 2.6.)

In the decade before German unification, Jewish university students at Heidelberg who wanted to join a traditional student society joined one of three organizations: the *Rhenania Corps*, the *Allemania Burschenschaften*, or the *Frankonia Burschenschaften*. By joining one of these associations, Jewish students immersed themselves in a society that was strictly regulated by the rules, regulations, and symbolism of a corporate society completely removed from Jewish society. Every waking hour was devoted to fulfilling the obligations and social expectations of membership, or attending to the demands of a university education. Upholding the laws of kashrut, attending prayer services, or even socializing with fellow Jews were beyond the realm of possibility for Jewish students who joined either the *Corps* or the *Burschenschaften*. It is self-evident that in order for these students to fully participate within a non-Jewish societal structure, they had completely distanced themselves from traditional Judaism.

Yet, as important as these facts are for our understanding of German Jewish identity in the decade before German unification, we cannot lose sight of the fact that key pieces to the puzzle are still lacking. While we know that the public identities of Jewish members of the *Burschenschaften* and the *Corps* were constructed largely in reference to the corporate structures in which they operated, we know absolutely nothing of their private identities. What connection to Jewish society did their families maintain, and how did the students position themselves when they returned home during periods of vacation or after they had completed their university studies? Did they continue to move almost exclusively within a Gentile social environment? Were Jewish members of traditional student societies so far along the path to the baptismal font that they ultimately broke entirely from their Jewish past? Unfortunately, a lacunae in source materials prevents us from answering these questions. We have little choice but to rely on a discussion of the *Verein für Cultur und Wissenschaft der Juden* and of Jewish members in the *Corps* and *Burschenschaften* for a

Table 2.4 Membership in the Heidelberg *Burschenschaften*

	1815–48	1849–59	1860–70
Allemania	0/0	1/73	4/170
Franconia	0/0	0/52	3/94

Source
These figures were derived by cross-referencing the names of Jewish students enrolled at Heidelberg University and listed in *Die Matrikel der Universität Heidelberg*, Gustav Toepke, ed., Vols. 5 and 6 (Heidelberg: Carl Winter's Universitätbuchhandlung, 1904) with the membership lists found in the following documents: *Die Burschenschaft Allemania zu Heidelberg: Ein Album herausgeben zum dreißigjährigen Stiftungsfeste und fünfhundertjährigen Universitätsjubiläum* (Heidelberg, 1886); *Die Burschenschaft Franconia zu Heidelberg, 1856–1886: Eine Festgabe zum dreissigjährigen Stiftungsfest* (Heidelberg, 1886).
Note
The first number represents the total number of Jewish members for the period and the second number represents the total number of members.

Table 2.5 Gentile Participation Rate in the *Burschenschaften*

Years	Gentile Students	Gentile Members	Participation Rate
1856–59	1869	125	6.69%
1860–70	6008	264	4.39%
Totals	7877	389	4.94%

Source
These figures were derived by cross-referencing the names of Jewish students enrolled at Heidelberg University and listed in *Die Matrikel der Universität Heidelberg*, Gustav Toepke, ed., Vols. 5 and 6 (Heidelberg: Carl Winter's Universitätbuchhandlung, 1904) with the membership lists found in the following documents: *Die Burschenschaft Allemania zu Heidelberg: Ein Album herausgeben zum dreißigjährigen Stiftungsfeste und fünfhundertjährigen Universitätsjubiläum* (Heidelberg, 1886); *Die Burschenschaft Franconia zu Heidelberg, 1856–1886: Eine Festgabe zum dreissigjährigen Stiftungsfest* (Heidelberg, 1886).
Note
The Gentile participation rate is derived by dividing the number of Gentile members of the organization by the total number of Gentile students at the university.

glimpse into the process of identity formation employed by Jewish university students in Germany before 1871.

For the period after 1871, however, the sources allow for a fuller portrayal of Jewish students than is possible for the earlier period. Not only have the Jewish student associations that emerged after

Table 2.6   Jewish Participation Rate in the *Burschenschaften*

Years	Jewish Students	Jewish Members	Participation Rate
1856–59	70	1	1.43%
1860–70	316	7	2.22%
Totals	912	8	2.13%

Source

These figures were derived by cross-referencing the names of Jewish students enrolled at Heidelberg University and listed in *Die Matrikel der Universität Heidelberg*, Gustav Toepke, ed., Vols. 5 and 6 (Heidelberg: Carl Winter's Universitätbuchhandlung, 1904) with the membership lists found in the following documents: *Die Burschenschaft Allemania zu Heidelberg: Ein Album herausgeben zum dreißigjährigen Stiftungsfeste und fünfhundertjährigen Universitätsjubiläum* (Heidelberg, 1886); *Die Burschenschaft Franconia zu Heidelberg, 1856–1886: Eine Festgabe zum dreissigjährigen Stiftungsfest* (Heidelberg, 1886).

Note

The Jewish participation rate is derived by dividing the number of Jewish members of the organization by the total number of Jewish students at the university.

1880 left a considerable written legacy, but there is also a substantial body of memoir literature that provides insight into the process of self-definition employed by Jewish students who did not participate in organizational life. Together, these materials provide the fabric for the narrative that follows.

II

THE ORGANIZATIONAL
IMPULSE

3

Emancipation and
The Reintroduction of the "Jewish Question"
at German Universities

STUDENT ENROLLMENT IN THE POSTEMANCIPATORY ERA

Following the unification of Germany in 1871, enrollment at German institutions of higher learning increased at an unprecedented rate. From 1830 to 1860, between 12,000 and 13,000 students enrolled annually. By 1871, the figure reached 14,000. With the onset of the depression in 1873, students flocked to German universities in record numbers. There were 28,820 students registered during the winter semester of 1889–90, and on the eve of World War I more than 60,000 students enrolled for the summer semester at German universities. The growth in student enrollment increased the number of students per 100,000 of the population from 32.4 in 1870–71 to 93.7 in 1914.[1] Simply put, a university education was available to more Germans during the Kaiserreich than at any previous time in German history.

German Jews took advantage of the widening opportunities for advanced education by registering at German universities in unprecedented numbers. The pattern of Jewish "over-representation"[2] that first emerged at the Universities of Heidelberg and Breslau during the *Vormärz* era was clearly entrenched at all Prussian universities during the Kaiserreich. Whereas Jews accounted for approximately 1.3 percent of the population in Prussia, they represented 8.98 percent of the Prussian university student population in 1886–87 and 8.11 percent in 1899–1900.[3] Although there are a variety of explanations for the growth of the student body as a whole, the tremendous increase in Jewish enrollment figures results from three factors: Jews' attendance at postelementary educational institutions, the entrance of women into German universities, and the increasing numbers of foreign students studying at German universities.

After 1834, the *Abitur* was recognized as the formal entrance certificate for German universities. Traditionally, German *Gymnasium* prepared students for the *Abitur*. In the decades before the unification of Germany, the numbers of German *Gymnasien* and *Gymnasium* students steadily increased. From approximately 50 institutions and thirteen thousand students in 1820, the numbers ballooned to 205 institutions and fifty-nine thousand students by 1874.[4] These figures suggest that growth at German universities derived, in part, from the expanding number of qualified individuals ready to begin their university careers. While not all *Gymnasium* graduates moved on to study at a German university, the fact remains that the number of students qualified to study at German universities increased throughout the nineteenth century.[5]

The *Gymnasium*, however, was not the only institution that awarded the *Abitur*. During the Kaiserreich, graduates of the *Realschulen* and *Oberrealschulen*, two alternate high school options, also earned the right to study at German universities. Consequently, increasing student enrollments were dependent on a huge expansion of postelementary education.[6]

A close evaluation of the students who continued their education beyond the primary years reveals that the percentage of Gentile students who went on to study at one of Germany's upper schools (i.e., *Gymnasien, Realschulen,* or *Oberrealschulen*) lagged behind that of students from the Jewish population. In 1886 only 6 percent of all Gentile schoolchildren in Prussia continued their education beyond the elementary level, compared to 47 percent of Jewish children. By 1911 the disparity was even greater: 64 percent of all Jewish schoolchildren continued their education beyond elementary school, as compared to 9 percent of Gentile schoolchildren.[7] Put another way, for every ten thousand citizens of each religious group in 1860, there were 36 Protestant, 21 Catholic, and 152 Jewish pupils attending one of Prussia's upper schools. In the decades that followed, the number of Jewish pupils per ten thousand Prussian Jews rose from 152 in 1860 to 260 in 1870 and then to 336 in 1880, thereafter decreasing slightly to 327 in 1890 and to 307 in 1900. The corresponding figures for Protestant students are 43 in 1870, 52 in 1880, 50 in 1890, and 51 in 1900. For Catholics, the figures are even lower: 24 in 1870, 23 in 1880, 29 in 1890, and 32 in 1900.[8] Clearly, the pool of potential university students was proportionately larger for Jews than for either Protestants or Catholics.

The second factor accounting for the expanding number of university students in general and Jewish students in particular was the entrance of women into German universities. During the last decade of the nineteenth century, women were allowed to audit courses, provided that they had obtained the approval of both the instructor and the Ministry of Education. In 1901 Baden was the first state to formally allow women to matriculate, while the Universities of Munich, Erlangen, and Würzburg officially admitted women in 1904. Prussia was the last holdout in this regard and did not allow women to matriculate at its universities until 1908.[9] By 1914, female students accounted for 6.9 percent of the Bonn student body and 7.44 percent of the student enrollment at Prussian universities.[10] In the same year, Jewish women comprised 12.9 percent of all women studying at German universities and an astonishing 21.7 percent of the women students at the University of Berlin.[11] Marion Kaplan believes that the reasons for the disproportionate number of Jewish women studying at German universities range from the "predominantly bourgeois socioeconomic profile of German Jewry which allowed for the luxury of supporting a daughter's education," to the increasing tendency for Jewish women to marry later in life and therefore to have "six to ten years of uselessness before they would be ready to marry." According to Kaplan, Jewish women's acute awareness of their parents' concern about status enabled them to prevail "upon their parents to let them pursue an education beyond dancing and tennis lessons."[12]

The third development that contributed to the rising enrollment of Jewish university students during the Kaiserreich was the growing number of foreign students attending German institutions of higher learning. In 1871 slightly more than 5 percent of the student body came from beyond the borders of Germany. In the decade before the First World War, this figure increased to 8 percent.[13] Jews were strongly represented among this particular subgroup of German university students. During the academic year 1886–87, Jewish students of foreign origin comprised 17.11 percent of the foreign student population in Prussia. This figure rose to 24.34 percent in 1899–1900 and 39.72 percent in 1911–12.[14] The remarkably high number of Jews among the foreign student population stems from developments outside of the German Reich and it highlights an important facet of German Jewish demography during the Kaiserreich. Beginning in 1887, the czarist regime implemented a *numerus clausus* on Jewish enrollment at Russian universities, limiting the number of Jewish students to 10 percent of the total student body within the Pale of Settlement, 5 percent outside of the Pale, and 3 percent in St. Petersburg. Even more deleterious for Russian Jewish students was the fact that after the turn of the century, enrollment quotas were applied to each faculty rather than to the university as a whole. Since most Jews were concentrated in the medical and philosophy faculties, the opportunities for Jewish students to enroll in these fields of study at Russian universities were significantly decreased.[15] While not all Russian Jews studying abroad went to Germany, on the eve of World War I, half of all foreigners enrolled at German universities were Russians, and more than 78 percent of the Russian students were Jewish.[16] As Russian Jewish students tended to concentrate at universities located in Germany's large cities—Berlin, Breslau, Königsberg, Leipzig, and Munich—they remained particularly visible. These factors, combined with the "social aloofness" of Russian Jewish students, perpetuated the image of German universities as being inundated with foreign or, in other words, Jewish students.[17]

The demographic development of Russian Jews constituting an expanding percentage of Jewish students studying at German universities parallels the situation of the entire German-Jewish population. In 1871 there were approximately 512,000 Jews living in the newly created German Reich, accounting for 1.2 percent of the total population. Even though the number of Jews living in Germany had increased to 615,000 by 1914, the Jewish percentage of the German populace had shrunk to 0.95 percent. Given that an estimated 200,000 German Jews emigrated overseas between 1830 and 1910 and that the natural growth rate of German Jews slowed after 1871, it is surprising that the percentage of German Jews did not decrease even further.[18] Yet, like the situation at the universities, Jewish numbers in the general population were bolstered by a steady flow of immigrants from eastern Europe. Whereas foreign-born Jews accounted for 3.9 percent of German Jews in 1890, or

22,000 individuals, by 1910 their numbers had risen to 78,746, or 12.8 percent of the German-Jewish population.[19]

The increasing number of foreign Jews both in the population at large and among the university student body in particular exacerbated the process of Jewish integration into German civil society and altered the dynamics of Jewish-Gentile relations. Native-born German Jews were sensitive to the fact that the arrival of eastern European Jews accentuated the image of "the Jew as foreigner" and jeopardized their efforts to participate fully in German society.[20] Among the student body, the growing ranks of foreign Jews contributed to an already tense situation between Jewish and Gentile students, especially among the medical faculties to which the majority of Russian Jews belonged. Although the increase in foreign Jews at German universities occurred too late for their arrival to be a cause of student antisemitism (the student antisemitic movement was already well underway before large numbers of Russian Jews were matriculated in Germany),[21] the presence of foreign Jews provided fuel to the rhetoric of student antisemites who sought to prevent all Jews, foreign or otherwise, from participating in German civil society. Before we can explore the impact of Russian Jewish students on the process of Jewish identity formation, therefore, we need to first examine the rise of the antisemitic movement at German universities.

THE STUDENT ANTISEMITIC MOVEMENT

The antisemitic movement of 1879 resonated deeply within the walls of German universities and, by the end of 1880, many students had joined the campaign to curb the rights of Germany's recently emancipated Jewish population. Adolph Stöcker's (1835–1909) call for the re-Christianization of German society and Heinrich von Treitschke's (1834–96) claim that the Jews' failure to remove all vestiges of their distinctive identity violated the underpinnings of the emancipationist bargain, struck particularly responsive chords among the student body.[22] Stöcker's close contact with the ruling elite made his brand of antisemitism palatable to university students, while Treitschke's position as a university professor legitimized antisemitic discourse in the eyes of many young academics.[23]

In Stöcker's harangues against Jews, he criticized orthodox Jewry for being "dead at its very core" and called reform Judaism a "pitiful remnant of the Age of Enlightenment." The court chaplain's most venomous attacks, however, were reserved for his diatribes against "modern Jewry," a somewhat nebulous code word symbolizing the segment of German Jewry responsible for undermining the Christian-Germanic state.[24] "The truth is," claimed Stöcker, "that modern Jewry is most certainly a power against religion; a power which bitterly fights Christianity everywhere, uproots Christian faith as well as national feeling in the people, in their stead offering them nothing but the idolatrous admiration of Jewry such as it is, with no other content but its self-admiration." To prevent the Judaization of the German spirit and the impoverishment of the German economy, Stöcker proposed that the number of Jewish judges appointed to the bench be commensurate with the percentage of Jews in the population at large. To reduce Jewish influence in German society, he also suggested that Jewish teachers be barred from teaching in German schools. These proposals, according to Stöcker, would promote a return to "Germanic rule in law and business . . . [as well as] a return to the Christian faith."[25]

Stöcker's vision of a Christian-Germanic state, and especially his desire to limit Jewish influence on German society, appealed to university students chagrined at the prospect of sharing their privileges with a recently emancipated and upwardly mobile Jewish population. But Stöcker's prescriptions for Germany's social ills were neither innovative nor unique. His discourse merely echoed the views of students who had been opposed to Jewish membership in the *Burschenschaften* during the debates of 1815–30. In the seven decades since the "Jewish Question" had first been taken up by German university students, the discussion had come full circle. The arguments employed in the early decades of the century to prevent Jews from joining Germany's traditional student societies were now resurrected to limit the impact of Jewish emancipation.

While Stöcker's anti-Jewish agitation was received favorably by university students anxious to stem the tide of social transformation, an aura of academic legitimacy and social respectability was bestowed upon antisemitism when the well-known historian and political theorist, Heinrich von Treitschke, published an article in the 1879 edition of the *Preussische Jahrbücher* entitled "A Word About Our Jewry."[26] In this essay Treitschke chastised the Jews for clinging to vestiges of their religious heritage and demanded that they "become Germans, regard themselves simply and justly as Germans, without prejudice to their faith and their old sacred past . . . [for he did] not want an era of German-Jewish mixed culture to follow after thousands of years of German civilization."[27] As a paradigmatic model for assimilation, Treitschke pointed to the Sephardic Jews living in western and southern Europe as Jews who had "always adjusted easily to the Western way of life." In fact, Treitschke went on to say, "the great majority of them [Sephardim] have become good Frenchmen, Englishmen, Italians, as far as can be expected from a people of *such pure blood and distinct peculiarity.*"[28] With this last sentence Treitschke distanced himself from the traditional, religious-based antisemitism of Stöcker to make the argument that the Jews of Germany, especially the *Ostjuden,* were alien to the "German national character," and hence, unassimilable.

As a former member of the Liberal Party, Treitschke did not oppose Jewish emancipation per se. Rather, his understanding of the German national spirit did not allow for non-Christian elements to be incorporated into German society. Treitschke's notion of religious toleration, delineated both in his essay about German Jewry and within his earlier works on German history, made allowances for Christian denominations only.[29] Yet, Treitschke's understanding of Christianity was not predicated on religious dogma, but rather, it was a vision imbued with racial conceptions that prevented Jews, even if they converted, from becoming Germans. For Treitschke and other racial antisemites, the terms "Christian" and "Jewish" functioned as dialectical code words, with the former used to demarcate the Jew as an "other," or alien component of German society, while the latter symbolized every negative aspect of German life.[30] Treitschke wrote that "there will never be a complete solution [to the "Jewish Question"]. There has always been an abyss between Europeans and Semites"[31] Accordingly, Jews would always remain a foreign and necessarily unequal component of German national life. Following the publication of this essay, an open debate ensued between Treitschke and other members of the academic community.

The subsequent exchange of ideas between Treitschke and his colleague and fellow historian, Theodor Mommsen (1817–1903), had a great impact on German university students. In an essay entitled, "Another Word About Our Jewry,"[32] Mommsen challenged Treitschke on a number of specific points. With regard to the nature of the Jewish character, Mommsen adopted the classic emancipationist position first formulated by Christian Wilhelm Dohm, which argued that Jews, through no fault of their own, did have a number of character "defects." Even though Mommsen was a dedicated liberal and strong proponent of emancipation, like Treitschke, he understood German society to be predicated on Christian principles and was opposed to the preservation of Jewish identity. In his opinion, the specifically Jewish societies of Berlin served no "positive purpose at all," and he argued that it was the duty of the Jews to "do away with their particularities wherever they [could] do so without offending their conscience."[33] Although willing to tolerate the continued existence of Jews within German society, Mommsen, like Stöcker and opposed to Treitschke, left no doubt that conversion offered the best solution to the "Jewish Question."[34]

The ongoing academic exchange between Treitschke and Mommsen, coupled with the rhetoric of Stöcker, effectively reintroduced the "Jewish Question" as a topic for debate among German university students.[35] As with the discussions of Jewish emancipation and the right of Jewish students to join traditional associations immediately following the Wars of Liberation (1813–14), the theoretical composition of civil society and corresponding relationship of Jews to it were once again highly contentious issues at German universities. What had been an unarticulated social norm at German universities for decades—that is, the desire to prevent Jews from integrating into traditional student society—regained a platform for public debate. Antisemitism in its modern, German parlance turned the issue of Jewish emancipation on its head by attempting to reverse its course. German antisemites of the 1870s and 1880s were heirs to the opponents of emancipation who fought to retain the Christian character of German society by preventing the Jews from obtaining citizenship.

While the ideological debates between Treitschke and Mommsen concerning the place of Jews in German society and the nature of a postemancipatory Jewish identity provided grist for heated student discussions, it was the signature campaign in support of the so-called antisemitic petition of 1879–80 that provided a rallying point for organized student action. Germany's antisemitic petition was drawn up by Bernhard Förster, Max Liebermann von Sonnenberg, and Ernst Henrici, three individuals whose anti-Jewish animus was equal to, if not greater than that of Stöcker and other German antisemites.[36] The title of their petition, "The Emancipation of the German People from the Yoke of Jewish Rule," was obviously inspired by Wilhelm Marr's best-selling antisemitic pamphlet *Der Sieg des Judenthums über das Germanenthum vom nicht confessionellen Standpunkt* (The victory of Judaism over Germandom) and by individuals who during the revolutions of 1848 announced that the time had come to "emancipate [Germany] *from* the Jews."[37] The petition, which ultimately was passed on to Bismarck, called for the restriction of Jewish immigration into Germany, the dismissal of Jews from all responsible government posts, and the reestablishment of an official census for Jews.[38] The introductory section of the document offers the following rationale for turning back the pages of emancipation:

> For a long time the minds of the patriots of all classes and parties have been apprehensive over the growing dominion of the Jewish part of the population. The former hopes that the Semitic elements would merge with the German proved to be deceptive, although Jews were granted equal rights. Now, it is no longer equalizing Jews with ourselves, but rather of the diminishing of our national privileges due to the predominance of the Jews. The ever growing influence of these peoples stems from racial peculiarities which the German nation does not wish to and cannot adopt without detrimental consequences to itself. The danger is imminent, and many are aware of it. . . . Judaism is an actual power which can be fought only through practical means of government authority.[39]

The crux of the argument is clear. Jews were not interested in equality; they wanted to dominate German society. Emancipation had only whetted the appetite of German Jews. Conversion did not solve the "Jewish Question" because one's Jewishness was an immutable consequence of race. Moreover, the threat of Jewish domination actually increased when Jews converted to Christianity. Unlike Jews who remained true to the faith and were readily recognizable as such, Jewish converts could undermine German society from within. The classic articulation of this viewpoint was given by Karl Eugen Dühring (1833–1921), who wrote that "a Jewish question would still exist, even if every Jew were to turn his back on his religion and join one of our churches. . . . It is precisely the baptized Jews who infiltrate furthest, unhindered in all sectors of society and political life."[40] Individuals in favor of the petition, therefore, sought to maintain the so-called purity of German national society by returning Jews to the status of second-class citizens and perpetuating their social segregation. It was this theme that provided the impetus for the development of antisemitism at German universities.[41]

Organized student involvement in the antisemitic movement was initiated by Paul Dulon (1858–1927), a law student at the university in Leipzig and the son of a royal Prussian government surveyor. In October 1880, Dulon received Treitschke's blessing to stir up anti-Jewish agitation among university students when the two met to discuss the matter of an organized campaign to limit Jewish involvement in university social life.[42] At Friedrich-Wilhelms University in Berlin a "Committee for the Promotion of the Petition Among the Student Body" (*Comitee zur Verbreitung der Petition unter der Studentenschaft*) was established under the leadership of the law student Erich von Schramm (1851–97), the son of a Prussian officer and himself a veteran of the Franco-Prussian War (1870–71). The *Comitee* exploited the political tension created by the debates between Mommsen and Treitschke to draw attention to its cause and win the support of students for the antisemitic petition.[43] In November 1880, the *Comitee* drafted a student version of the petition which contained the following rider:

> German students believe that they must not lose the opportunity of adding their support to the feelings expressed in what has been said above [referring to the petition itself], although their civic position and their point of view on social questions might not allow them to support every single demand. This is done in the full knowledge that the continuation of the struggle to maintain our nationality will to no small extent one day be put into their hands. . . .[44]

This addendum allowed a degree of latitude to students who were in basic agreement with the petition's objectives, but took issue over particular items. In this manner, individual students could reject specific aspects of the "Jewish Question" as they were articulated in the document and still support limiting Jewish integration into, and advancement within, German society. This strategy turned out to be particularly effective, as support for the petition among the student body exceeded all possible expectations of the *Comitee*. Of the approximately 265,000 adult male citizens who signed the petition, 4,000 of them were university students. The significance of this number is apparent when one compares the 0.6 percent of the entire population which supported the petition to the 19 percent of university students who affixed their names to the document.[45] Even more astounding is the fact that approximately 1,700 out of 4,107 students matriculated at the university in Berlin in the winter of 1880–81 signed the petition, representing 41 percent of the student population. Similar results were achieved at the university in Göttingen, where nearly 41 percent of the student body supported the student petition (400 out of 979 students), and at the university in Halle, which boasted the signatures of 350 out of 1,211 students (approx. 29 percent).[46]

Norbert Kampe addresses the issue of why so many students supported the antisemitic petition by exploring the relationship between the number of Jewish students at a given university and the number of students willing to sign their names to the petition. Interestingly enough, there is not a consistent correlation between a high percentage of Jewish students and a high number of signatories. In Berlin, where the Jewish student population approached 17 percent of the student body, the correlation holds. In Göttingen, Halle, and Kiel, however, where large numbers of students signed the petition, the proportion of Jewish students was only 1–2 percent. Moreover, in Breslau, where Jewish students comprised 17 percent of the enrollment, not one student supported the petition. It is also important to remember, as Kampe points out, that one's signature on the petition does not necessarily mean that one was an avowed antisemite. Apparently, many of the student signatures were obtained at the pub rather than at any formal, sober organizational meeting.[47]

Flush with the success of their efforts to support the antisemitic petition, members of the *Comitee* decided to create a permanent student association dedicated to the cause of German nationalism vis-à-vis the preservation of a racially defined Christian-Germanic society. After formally dissolving the *Comitee* in 1880, the members of the group established a new student organization known as the *Verein Deutscher Studenten* (V.D.St.), or Association of German Students. The first chapter of the organization was founded in December 1880 at the Friedrich-Wilhelms University in Berlin, and by March 1881, additional associations were established at the universities in Halle, Leipzig, Breslau, and Göttingen. Like all university student societies, the V.D.St. had to be sanctioned by the university's academic senate. To receive the blessing of university officials, the Association of German Students needed to denounce all political activities and convince the proper authorities that their association would make a positive contribution to the university environment. At the Friedrich-Wilhelms University in Berlin, the academic senate refused to sanction the *Verein Deutscher Studenten* for fear of increased agitation among the student population. The senate at this time was dominated by liberal-minded professors, among whom was the outspoken critic of organized antisemitism, Theodor Mommsen. The struggle for official approval lasted until the summer of 1882, at which time the members of the academic senate had changed and the new body was no longer opposed to a student organization dedicated to promoting antisemitism at German universities.[48]

Once sanctioned by the university senate, the V.D.St. no longer hid its antisemitic agenda. As one member of the Association for German Students put it, "Not only were Jews excluded from membership from the V.D.St., but the struggle against Jewry was the sole reason for its existence [*Daseinszweck*]."[49] Distancing himself somewhat from the religious-based antisemitism of Stöcker and relying heavily on themes articulated by Treitschke, the leader of the V.D.St. in Berlin, Diederich Hahn, challenged every Christian-German student to join the campaign to eradicate foreign influences from German society. In his opening speech at the *Kyffhäuserfest*, the first interuniversity gathering of members of the *Verein Deutscher Studenten*, Hahn identified Jewry and Frenchness (*Franzosentum*) as the mortal enemies of the German Reich. This juxtaposition of *Judentum* and *Franzosentum* offers clear evidence of the national-racial orientation of the V.D.St.'s conception of a Christian-Germanic society. Portraying the V.D.St. as the heir to the nationalist spirit of German students following the wars of 1813 and 1870, Hahn issued a poignant emotional appeal to his audience, saying that the V.D.St. would "strive once again for the ancient ideal of Christianity and Germanness [*des Christentums und des Deutschtums*]. For 1500 years our German forefathers have recognized Christian faith to be the fundamental principle of their national life [*Volksleben*] and held on to it with all of their strength."[50] The *Verein Deutscher Studenten* held true to its vision of a racially defined, Christian-Germanic society as it spearheaded the campaign to limit Jewish involvement in traditional university society and, in essence, to isolate Jewish students from their Gentile colleagues.

The institutionalization of antisemitism at German universities represented by the V.D.St. sparked a countermovement from members of the student body. Organized opposition to student antisemitism at the universities of Leipzig, Göttingen, and Berlin focused on producing a petition to challenge the claims of the V.D.St.[51] Interestingly enough, however, the initial steps taken by students in Berlin to counter the growing tide of student antisemitism were not carried out by Jews alone. In keeping with the liberal conception of society that still held sway among a diminishing segment of the student population, Gentile and Jewish students joined together to create the *Comitee zur Bekämpfung der antisemitischen Agitation unter den Studierenden* (The Committee for Combatting Antisemitic Agitation Among the Student Body). Established in January 1881 under the leadership of Oskar Schubert (d.1928), the committee immediately published a pamphlet to challenge the antisemitic petition and successfully garnered four hundred signatures in support of its cause. Pressured by the rector of the university to dissolve his committee, Schubert helped organize the *Freie Wissenschaftliche Vereinigung* (F.W.V.), a *paritätisch*, or nondenominational association that, for the next thirty years, carried the banner of liberalism among the student body.[52]

The efforts of the F.W.V. to stop the spread of antisemitism at German universities were challenged at every juncture by the *Verein Deutscher Studenten*. When the V.D.St. heard that a group of students had organized a liberal association to thwart its activities, the organization was quick to take up the challenge. On June 23, 1881, as a number of students gathered in front of the *Waßmann Kneipe* (a pub located on Leipziger Straße in Berlin) anxious to participate in the F.W.V.'s first organizational meeting, they were told by the owner of the establishment that they would have to go elsewhere for their gathering. It seems that the owner had been forewarned by members of the V.D.St. that a "political" meeting was going to be held in his restaurant. An alternate meeting location was spontaneously arranged and, before long, approximately one hundred students were present at *Lauters Bierstuben*, where Max Spangenberg (1860–91), the F.W.V.'s first president, spoke. Even the appearance of the Berlin police could not deter the group from its objective, for when the police entered the pub, the members implemented a prearranged plan and pretended as if they had gathered only to drink, chat, and play skat. In the meantime, however, they surreptitiously circulated a list containing the founding statutes of the *Freie Wissenschaftliche Vereinigung* and, in this manner, gave birth to their organization.[53]

In his first speech as president of the *Freie Wissenschaftliche Vereinigung*, Spangenberg bemoaned the fact that the efforts of the V.D.St. had divided the student body and rendered the spirit of German university students in a shameful and apathetic condition. To remedy this malady, Spangenberg proposed that the *Freie Wissenschaftliche Vereinigung* dedicate itself to the "general scholarly and social intercourse of Berlin students in all faculties, without distinction of faith."[54] Acknowledging that diversity was fundamental to the pursuit of science, the F.W.V. encouraged freedom of expression among its membership and refused to tolerate the system of compulsion common within traditional associations that regulated the dress and behavior of their members. The most extreme form of compulsion among the *Corps* and the *Burschenschaften* occurred during the ritualistic drinking bouts for which these student fraternities were renowned. In an effort to distance itself from the extremely detailed and structured regulations of traditional student associations, the organizational statutes of the F.W.V. functioned only as a general operating directive.[55]

The most salient feature of the *Freie Wissenschaftliche Vereinigung* was its desire to be a multifaceted organization and to avoid a one-dimensional social and academic agenda. The commitment to diversity is underscored by the association's loyalty to Wilhelm von Humboldt's philosophy of *Bildung*, the lifelong commitment to self-cultivation, as the cornerstone of its existence.[56] "The sign of a sound student," argued Spangenberg, "is a positive universal interest. The alma mater offers its sons not simply the opportunity to prepare for a specific profession . . . but also hopes that students will acquire a form of encyclopedic understanding for all of their professional life which only an abstract schematicism can render practical."[57] "He who pursues no more than the mere acquisition of knowledge while at the university," claimed F.W.V. member Franz von Liszt, "is no true student." The true student pursues his subject in connection to the spiritual life of his people. He should strengthen his character, build and sharpen his political views, and formulate his worldview through a rigorous exchange of ideas with his fellow students.[58] Members of the *Freie Wissenschaftliche Vereinigung* held firmly to the belief that the acquisition of *Bildung* was the core of a German university education. In so doing, the organization appealed to Jewish university students loyal to the emancipationist ideology, which viewed the acquisition of *Bildung* as their entry ticket into German society.[59]

The F.W.V.'s position on the "Jewish Question" outlined by Max Spangenberg in an address to the association on October 30, 1882, was also in keeping with the liberal view of emancipation. After a lengthy introductory prologue typical of Spangenberg's flowing rhetorical style, he formulated the following three questions: 1) Who and what is an antisemite? 2) Who and what are Jews? 3) Viewed from the limited terrain of academia, what is the F.W.V.'s position on antisemitism and the Jews?[60] In responding to the first question, Spangenberg stated that an antisemite was one who harbored ill feelings toward all Jews. Here he simply differentiated between a dislike of individuals, be they Jew or Gentile, and opposition to an entire group of people predicated solely on their religious affiliation. From the perspective of the F.W.V., the goal of an antisemite was to repeal all emancipatory legislation and return German Jews to the status of second-class citizens.[61] Spangenberg's comments on antisemitism reveal very little about the F.W.V.'s views on German Jewish identity. To illuminate the association's position on this issue, we must turn to Spangenberg's responses to his second and third questions.

"In spite of an uninterrupted history of 3,000 years," thundered Spangenberg from the podium, "the Jews of today are no longer what they once were in Palestine: a distinct nationality [*eine gesonderte Nationalität*]." Ignoring the fact that the mother tongue for millions of Jews was Yiddish, Spangenberg argued that there was no "Jewish language" and that Jews only spoke the language of the land in which they lived. Jews were not merely "German, French, English, or Italian Jews, but were [exactly the same as] Germans, Frenchmen, Englanders, Italians, and so forth." Jewish loyalty to the Fatherland was unassailable, a fact proven by the willingness of German Jews to sacrifice their lives for the cause of German nationalism. Moreover, the spiritual connection between German Jews and their German homeland was beyond reproach. For evidence, one need only evaluate the writings of Berthold Auerbach, who, according to Max Spangenberg, was a Jewish poet who produced "truly German works" (*echt deutscher Werke*).[62] Spangenberg believed that only Jewish students studying for the rabbinate were clearly recognizable as Jews and could be regarded as "un-German" (*undeutsch*). These students he blithely dismissed as a minority group, one not at all representative of the majority of Jewish university students.[63] As is clear from Spangenberg's rhetoric, the F.W.V.'s position on the "Jewish Question" was the same as that voiced by Christian and Jewish proponents of emancipation throughout the nineteenth century. Spangenberg and the F.W.V. contributed nothing new to the debate; they chose, instead, to rehash old arguments. For more than a century, Gentile proponents of Jewish emancipation had envisioned that once Jews became citizens of the lands in which they resided, Jewish distinctiveness would disappear. Members of the *Freie Wissenschaftliche Vereinigung*, Jew and Gentile alike, held firmly to the classical liberal theory of emancipation, even when faced with the increasing agitation of students claiming that Jews were unassimilable and incapable of shedding their cultural particularities.

Given its stand on Jewish integration into German society, it is not surprising that the F.W.V. was accused of being a Jewish organization. In response to this charge, Spangenberg defended his association in the following manner:

> Many classes of the urban population assume that the F.W.V. is nothing more than a bulwark of Judaism which reinforces the national, confessional and social isolation of the semitic race (*Abkömmlinge*) from the Memel to the Rhein. Against the villainous misrepresentation of our organization as being *prosemitisch* or *philosemitisch*, I enter, once again, a protest on your behalf which has previously been met with your lively approval. . . . We defend German Jews not because they are the chosen people and therefore claim special privileges, but because they are people of good soul, intellect, creativity and just as ourselves, they are fallible. . . .[64]

Sensitive to the charge that the *Freie Wissenschaftliche Vereinigung* was merely a Jewish organization operating under the guise of

nondenominationalism, Spangenberg cautioned his cons
not to overemphasize the F.W.V.'s opposition to studer
semitism for fear that it would jeopardize the association's cc
ment to a liberal social and political agenda. In so doing, he
in a manner consistent with the tradition of German liber____,
which, in spite of its support for Jewish emancipation, sought to
avoid being labeled a "Jewish" movement.[65]

The desire of the *Freie Wissenschaftliche Vereinigung* to play
down all external manifestations of Jewishness is evident in Spangenberg's comments on the public behavior of his Jewish colleagues and the merits of intermarriage. To prevent the opposition
from denouncing the *Freie Wissenschaftliche Vereinigung* as "un-
German," Spangenberg encouraged the members of the F.W.V.,
especially his Jewish colleagues, to eliminate all foreign characteristics. Toward this end, he condoned marriages between Christians
and Jews as the best method for the F.W.V.'s Jewish members to
shed their "foreignness" and to promote their complete amalgamation.[66] Spangenberg was so enamored with intermarriage as the
solution to the existential question of Jewish self-definition that he
reveled in relaying the news from a fellow member that "once
again a Christian and Jew had been married within his family."
Not only did Spangenberg recognize the utility of intermarriage,
he sincerely believed that such unions were "beautiful and praise-
worthy."[67]

Spangenberg's assessment of intermarriage as a solution to
the "Jewish Question" was consistent with that of Christian proponents of Jewish emancipation, as well as that of a small group
of German Jews who argued that intermarriage would lead to
the complete amalgamation of the Jews. Jews in favor of mixed
marriages "considered the assimilation of the Jews a far more
important goal than the preservation of Judaism." Such a stand
differed from both Liberal and Orthodox Jewish camps, which
refused to yield on the question of abandoning their Jewish identity
in exchange for civil and social equality. For them, the bargain of
emancipation did not necessitate such a trade-off. Even though
leading reformers like Abraham Geiger, Ludwig Philipson, and
Samuel Holdheim recognized the legal necessity of intermarriage,
they recoiled at the thought that it would lead to the disinte-
gration of a distinctive Jewish identity.[68] The F.W.V.'s position on
intermarriage not only differed from that of the vast majority of
German Jews, but it raises an important question: What does the

Freie Wissenschaftliche Vereiningung's stand on intermarriage and its views on the composition of German society tell us about the identities of Jewish students who joined the organization?

Due to the fact that the composition of the organization changed considerably during the decade following its establishment, the answer to this question fluctuates according to the period of time under consideration. Before 1890, the F.W.V. contained both Gentile and Jewish students. Jewish members at this time rejected a social milieu comprised exclusively of either Jews or Gentiles and they adopted a position in student society that maximized social interaction between students of all faiths. We can assume, therefore, that their Jewishness was not a determinant feature of their identities; but neither was it so diminished that they were willing to distance themselves entirely from their Jewish heritage. During the first eight years of its existence, the *Freie Wissenschaftliche Vereinigung* genuinely conformed to the image of a civic society envisioned by liberals throughout the nineteenth century. Given, however, that support for liberalism diminished precipitously both in German society at large and at German universities during the 1880s, the period of harmonious social interaction between Gentiles and Jews under the auspices of a single university organization was brief. Not only did the F.W.V.'s membership decline from 179 students in the summer of 1882 to approximately 50 students by the middle of the decade, the *Freie Wissenschaftliche Vereinigung* had become an almost exclusively Jewish association by the decade's end.[69]

Students who joined the F.W.V. after 1890 made a number of statements about their identity. First, they wanted to be part of a student organization that functioned as an important but not an all-encompassing component of their social coterie. Second, they chose to socialize primarily with other Jews. And third, they had no interest in accentuating their Jewishness in the manner that members of the Jewish fraternal organizations did. This process of self-definition is clearly evident in the memoirs of Eduard Isaac, a German Jewish university student who joined the *Freie Wissenschaftliche Vereinigung* in 1900 when he began his studies.[70]

Born in Cologne in 1882, Eduard Isaac was the oldest son of the owner of a firm that provided chemicals for shoe manufacturers. The success of his father's business provided a secure, middle-class existence for the Isaac family. The descriptions of the daily fare in the Isaac household—meats, cheeses, and sausages, coupled with the absolute lack of discussion about religious observance, suggest that Judaism was not the focus of Eduard's identity. It was not, however, entirely absent. We know, for example, that Eduard's religious studies in *Gymnasium* were supervised by a rabbi, an arrangement that was not uncommon for Jews during the Kaiserreich.[71] In addition, his religious heritage informed his decision to study chemistry as opposed to physics at the University of Berlin. Eduard Isaac was well aware that Jews were unlikely to secure an academic appointment at a university or as an instructor in a *Gymnasium,* the two primary careers for individuals who earned a university degree in physics. Last, but not least, Eduard Isaac's decision to join the *Freie Wissenschaftliche Vereinigung* tells us that he considered it a priority to establish a network of Jewish friends.[72]

Eduard was first introduced to the F.W.V. by the half-cousin of a good friend and fellow student at his *Gymnasium.* In describing the association, he explains that by the time he joined the *Freie Wissenschaftliche Vereinigung,* it had adopted a corporate character commensurate with that of the *Burschenschaften* and *Corps* and the number of non-Jewish members was minimal. The activities of the association included regular lectures, discussions, and occasional evenings at a local *Kneipe,* or pub. Eduard writes that he gave his heart and soul to the F.W.V. and that he "enjoyed himself most when he was in the company of friends and fellow F.W.V.ers." While members of the F.W.V. had absolutely no interest in maintaining Jewish traditions, what attracted Eduard Isaac and other Jewish university students to join the association was the opportunity to socialize and exchange ideas with fellow Jews.[73] In this regard, we see the extent to which the *Freie Wissenschaftliche Vereinigung* functioned as an important social setting for Jewish university students in the latter years of the Kaiserreich.

Eduard Isaac's claim that members of the F.W.V. had no interest in topics pertaining to Judaism is corroborated by organizational records as well. Even though the *Freie Wissenschaftliche Vereinigung* was populated almost exclusively by Jews, the organization never promoted a Jewish agenda. Between 1881 and 1914, the F.W.V. neither sponsored lectures devoted to topics of Jewish history, literature, or religion, nor mentioned the religious affiliation of its members within the pages of the *Monatsberichte des F.W.V.* (Monthly reports of the F.W.V.).[74] Examples of lectures presented by the organization include: "*Realismus in der Kunst* (Realism in art);" *"Rechtsfälle und deren Entscheidung* (Court cases and their decisions)"; *"Ehe und Syphlis* (Marriage and syphilis)", and *"Materialismus und Naturalismus* (Materialism and naturalism). There is absolutely no trace of any Jewish content within the pages of the F.W.V.'s monthly reports or the activities that it sponsored. If one ignored the surnames of the organization's membership lists, it would be nearly impossible to identify the "religious" composition of the membership.

Given, however, that after 1890 the *Freie Wissenschaftliche Vereinigung* was a self-proclaimed nondenominational student association comprised primarily of Jews, we need to recognize its important role in the process of identity formation for its members. The F.W.V.'s organizational structure and Jewish membership exemplify the "subculture" model of German Jewry delineated by David Sorkin wherein German Jews gained social cohesion from their use of the majority culture.[75] Moreover, the *Freie Wissenschaftliche Vereiningung's* academic agenda substantiates George Mosse's claim that "the concept of *Bildung* became for many Jews synonymous with their Jewishness," was accurate for members of the F.W.V.[76] But what about other students? Was the process of self-definition employed by Jewish students outside the orbit of the F.W.V. similar to or radically different from the version delineated above? Was *Bildung* central to the identity of all German Jewish students? Did most German Jewish students remain steadfast in their belief that self-cultivation was the entry ticket to German society, or did other loyalties and forms of Jewish expression develop in the years following the completion of the emancipatory process? To answer these questions, we need to examine the Jewish student organizations that appeared after the creation of the *Freie Wissenschaftliche Vereinigung* and evaluate the activities and social groupings of Jewish students who never joined a student association.

4

The Emergence of
Jewish Student Associations

In the decades after the creation of the *Freie Wissenschaftliche Vereinigung*, Jewish student organizations flourished at German universities. Historians, for the most part, have interpreted the creation of Jewish student associations in a manner similar to the way in which they have depicted the founding of the F.W.V.; as a response to antisemitism. The exceptions to this argument are provided by historians concerned specifically with the creation of Jewish nationalist student organizations who recognize that although antisemitism is central to the development of a Jewish national consciousness, its development is interpreted within the broader historical context of Jewish emancipation.[1]

The more traditional interpretive paradigm is exemplified by Ismar Elbogen's *Geschichte der Juden in Deutschland*.[2] He argues that the creation of the *Akademische Verein für jüdische Geschichte und Literatur* in 1883 and the subsequent founding of the *Kartell Convent deutscher Studenten Jüdischen Glaubens* (K.C.), the *Verein Jüdischer Studenten* (V.J.St.), and the *Kartell Jüdischer Verbindungen* (K.J.V.), were acts of "self-defense" and a means to protect the "honor" and "rights" of Jewish academicians. Given that Elbogen wrote at a time when Jewish existence in Germany was becoming increasingly precarious, his desire to cast a positive light on Jewish acts of resistance is understandable. Nevertheless, the portrayal of Jewish student groups as a dialectical response to antisemitism does not illuminate the distinct conditions that led to the creation of each of the groups discussed.

In his study of the *Kartell Convent,* Adolph Asch develops an argument very similar to Elbogen's. He posits that the founders of *Viadrina,* the Breslau University chapter of the K.C. established in 1886, became "aware of their Jewish inheritance" because of the antisemitic movement that gripped German universities.[3] Jehuda Reinharz perpetuates this line of interpretation by arguing that Jewish students responded to the rise of student antisemitism by forming their own organizations.[4] On the establishment of the *Kartell Convent* Reinharz writes that "the appearance of these fraternities [the Jewish organizations belonging to the K.C.], and especially of the *Viadrina,* introduced a radically new approach to antisemitism." He goes on to state that "almost ten years after the founding of the *Viadrina,* another Jewish student organization, the *Verein Jüdischer Studenten* (V.J.St.), was formed at the University of Berlin in reaction to antisemitism there." Although Reinharz recognizes that Jewish student organizations "sought to develop and defend a sense of Jewish consciousness," he presents the nascent associations as originating within the context of antisemitism.[5] All three scholars depict the manner in which German Jewish students positioned themselves in society and, hence, their identities, as being contingent upon antisemitism.

While it would be ludicrous and historically inaccurate to claim that antisemitism had nothing to do with the creation of Jewish student associations, there are two fundamental problems with the view that Jewish organizations emerged only or even primarily as a response to anti-Jewish activity. First, such an approach does not consider the internal dynamics of Jewish self-definition and the evolving nature of Jewish identity. From the onset of the Enlightenment to the granting of citizenship, Germany's Jewish populace continually negotiated a path between their Jewish and German heritages. With each succeeding generation, Jewish university students moved from the fringes of student society to its core. The emergence of Jewish student associations suggests that the process of identity formation continued to evolve, even after Jews became citizens of the Second German Reich. Second, by focusing on antisemitism, historians of Jewish student associations have blinded themselves to the fact that Jewish organizations emerged within an environment that produced a variety of new student groups. This latter problem accentuates the need to reassess the emergence of Jewish student associations during the Kaiserreich from a perspective that does not ignore the contemporary problems of antisemitism and exclusion but, rather, evaluates the appearance of Jewish organizations within the context of a German society that witnessed the proliferation of both student and general associations. Recognition of these problems does not change the fact that, as Shulamit Volkov accurately states, "from mid-century onward, restrictions on Jewish membership in a variety of social clubs and local associations caused the establishment of parallel Jewish bodies."[6] It does, however, call for an interpretation of this phenomenon that looks beyond the immediate impetus for the creation of Jewish organizations.

ANTISEMITISM, IDENTITY FORMATION, AND THE STUDENT *VEREINSWESEN*

Throughout the nineteenth century, Gentile proponents of Jewish emancipation were ambivalent about the perpetuation of recognizably distinct Jewish identities. Even after Jews were granted unconditional citizenship in 1871, many German liberals still anticipated the elimination of Jewish particularities. In his response to Treitschke's attack against the Jews, Theodor Mommsen argued that the preservation of Jewish identity served "no positive purpose at all." In a similar vein, Max Spangenberg openly espoused his view that intermarriage offered the best means to eliminate Jewish foreign characteristics. For more than a hundred years, from the era of Dohm and the early enlightened ideologues to the waning of German liberalism represented by Mommsen and Spangenberg, German liberals in favor of Jewish emancipation agreed that Jews had to abandon their religious and cultural particularism in exchange for German citizenship.[7]

For most German Jews, however, the bargain of emancipation did not necessitate such a trade-off. Members of the student association, the *Verein für Cultur und Wissenschaft der Juden*, attempted to modernize Judaism without stripping Jews of their Jewish identity. Although the organization failed to achieve its stated objectives, its efforts to deemphasize rabbinic Judaism in favor of a still somewhat nebulous form of Jewish nationalism heralded the arrival of the reform movement in Judaism. Religious reformers such as Samson Raphael Hirsch, Samuel Holdheim, Zacharias Frankel, and Abraham Geiger followed the path blazed by the *maskilim*, Jewish proponents of enlightened reform, and members of the *Verein für Cultur und Wissenschaft der Juden*. They altered religious Judaism in a way that enabled Jews to broaden their field of social and cultural activity beyond the environs of the Jewish community while still maintaining their religious identity.[8] Although their visions of emancipated Jewry differed significantly, Jewish reformers were unwilling to abandon their Jewishness in exchange for the right to participate in German society. In discussing the Jewish understanding of assimilation, a term closely connected to the parallel processes of emancipation and identity formation, David Sorkin writes that Jewish proponents of assimilation "thought [that] the continued existence of Jews and Judaism was beyond the bounds of the emancipation contract."[9] Only Jews who converted to Christianity, the so-called radical assimilationists, accepted the bargain of emancipation put forth by Gentile proponents of Jewish emancipation.

Herein lies the quandary of the emancipated German Jew and the paradox experienced firsthand by Jewish university students of the Kaiserreich. Throughout the nineteenth century German Jews deemphasized their Jewish heritage in favor of German cultural values. Synagogue attendance declined and for many Jews was limited to the High Holidays.[10] Some Jews went to great lengths to hide their Jewishness. As a Leipzig Jewish newspaper reported in 1843: "A Berlin Jew is blissfully happy when he is told that there is no longer anything Jewish about him."[11] The lack of Jewish organizations during the early Kaiserreich demonstrates that German Jews were acutely aware that separatist Jewish organizations violated the bargain of emancipation, which necessitated the public suppression of Jewishness.[12]

By the time the final emancipatory legislation was completed in 1871, the Jewish component of one's identity was relegated largely to the sphere of private life. Ismar Schorsch writes that "the tremendous pressure on the Jews to establish their German identity by repressing every religious, social, and ethnic distinctiveness had transformed being Jewish into a wholly internal matter."[13] Jewish religious traditions such as lighting the Sabbath candles on Friday evening and the celebration of Jewish holidays and lifecycle events took place in the home. Borrowing from the Hebrew poet Judah Leib Gordan, Marion Kaplan offers the following assessment of Jewish identity during the Kaiserreich: "Jews were men and women on the street and Jews at home. They displayed their Germanness while they privatized their Jewishness."[14] The privatization of one's Jewish identity was reinforced by the fact that Jews socialized largely with their fellow Jews. Although interaction with Gentiles on the streets and within the workplace was common, German Jews remained socially separate.[15]

Relegating one's Jewishness to the sphere of private and family life meant that German Jews experienced a sharp disjunction between their public and private identities. While this division was neither unusual nor inoperable, it did produce a dialectical state of tension. As long as German Jews retained the separation between their public and private identities and their Jewishness did not impinge on their activities within the public sphere, they preserved a precarious balance. Once Jewishness could no longer be contained within the realm of private identity and a German Jew's Jewish identity affected his or her range of activities within the public sphere, the resulting tension necessitated the construction of new paradigms. This is precisely the point where antisemitism and, especially, exclusion from associational life entered the picture.

Throughout the emancipatory process, German Jews tacitly understood that the bargain of emancipation did not mean that Jews would enjoy the same range of professional options as their Gentile co-nationalists, or that their social acceptance would be absolute.[16] German Jewish university students recognized that in spite of constitutional guarantees to the contrary, their range of career options would be restricted, with civil service positions being particularly difficult to obtain. Monika Richarz writes that "while most Christian university graduates found positions as clergymen, teachers and judges," all of which were civil service positions in Germany, Jewish university students pursued careers as private doctors, lawyers, and journalists.[17] It seems that German Jews accepted an unarticulated level of discrimination as long as they were able to actively participate in German society. In other words, so long as antisemitism did not circumscribe the activities of German Jews within the public sphere beyond a preconceived and variable notion of acceptable social and professional limitations, they tolerated what, in hindsight, appear to be pervasive anti-Jewish attitudes. When Jewish students began to be excluded from university organizations in which they had previously belonged, some students were compelled to reassess their self-defined images and determine whether the tension inherent in the disjunction between their public and private lives was worth tolerating. Students who joined Jewish associations rejected the terms of emancipation passed down to them by their parents and adopted public positions that accentuated their Jewishness.[18]

When evaluating the relationship between antisemitism and the establishment of Jewish student associations in the 1880s and 1890s, we must also consider the fact that Jews were not the only university students to create new organizations. In fact, the proliferation of voluntary associations, both within the university environment and within German society as a whole, was a fundamental feature of nineteenth-century Germany. The so-called *Vereinswesen,* or associational movement, began at the close of the eighteenth century and gained momentum throughout the nineteenth century.[19] As the number of voluntary associations increased, they actively sought to manipulate public opinion and affect the outcome of local and national elections. Large, highly organized national associations such as the *Bund der Landwirte* (The Farmers' League), the *Alldeutscher Verband* (Pan-German League), and a host of smaller special interest organizations, attempted to bring their influence directly to bear on the government.[20] By the beginning of the twentieth century, associational life was a defining characteristic of German society.

Although the dramatic increase in voluntary organizations reflects the growing strength of the German bourgeoisie, it also offers evidence for the segregationist tendencies of Wilhelmine German society. The most contentious issue, and the one primarily responsible for increasing tensions within German society, was German nationalism. According to Michael Hughes, the German populace held "widely differing and incompatible visions of the country's future and [entertained] bitter disputes about the exact nature of German national traditions rooted in starkly different versions of German history."[21] Foremost among the competing visions of German nationalism, and the one that had the greatest impact on university students, was *völkisch* nationalism.[22]

Völkisch nationalism idealized rural lifestyles, romanticized the past, and sought to return to a way of life that had theoretically existed at some nebulous point in the past. The *völkisch* movement rejected all aspects of modernity and was particularly disdainful of foreigners and foreign ideas. National minorities, Roman Catholics, Freemasons, and Jews were labeled by proponents of *völkisch* nationalism as "traitors to the nation" and were deemed unworthy of inclusion in the German *Volk*.[23]

The division of German society into "in" and "out" groups as delineated by *völkisch* ideology was exacerbated by Bismarck's method of political management. Bismarck's attacks against the power of the Catholic Church during the *Kulturkampf* (1874–80) and against the growing strength of German socialism, under the auspices of the Anti-Socialist laws (1878–90), were attempts by the *Reichskanzler* both to define his political enemies and to unify a disparate German society. By identifying these large groups of German citizens as "enemies of the Reich" (*Reichsfeinde*), Bismarck deepened the fissures within German society and provided state sanction for the outsider status bestowed upon Catholics and socialists by *völkisch* nationalists.[24] Moreover, governmental inflexibility on the question of linguistic autonomy for national minorities, the Poles, the Danes, and the French accentuated the exclusive nature of Wilhelmine society and perpetuated its segregationist tendencies. It was common during the Kaiserreich for groups identified as outsiders to create their own associations. Not only do we see the creation of Jewish organizations during the last two decades of the nineteenth century, but also of a wide variety of Catholic, socialist, and national minority associations. The founding of German Jewish organizations, therefore, must be recognized as the product of a divided society in which "out" groups sought to participate in Germany's active associational life.[25]

The formation of exclusive associations was a phenomenon well represented at German universities. The combination of the much-heralded freedom of German university students and the rise of new political and intellectual currents spawned a dizzying array of university student organizations during the last three decades of the nineteenth century.[26] In spite of the fact that the influence of the *Corps* began to wane in the 1880s and the *Burschenschaft* was plagued by divisive internal debates during the same decade, their influence was widely felt. The organizations' highly structured corporate codes and detailed rituals regarding drinking, duelling, and socializing served as models for other student associations.[27] The new *Landsmannschaften* of the Kaiserreich struggled to carve a niche for themselves within university corporate life by rejecting the *Burschenschaften's* political principle and adopting a more pluralistic attitude toward other students than the *Corps*. The *Turnerschaft* that emerged out of Germany's gymnastic associations in the 1880s also lacked a clearly articulated ideology, but, like the new *Landsmannschaften*, it was a color-carrying, duelling organization.[28]

A number of student organizations adopted the corporate structure pioneered by the *Corps* but rejected duelling as a matter of principle. Typical of these groups were the *Wingolfsbund*, a Christian student organization founded in the 1850s, the *Schwarzburgbund*, founded in 1887, and the *Cartell-Verband*, a Catholic counterpart to *Wingolf*, which first appeared at German universities in the 1860s. In addition to these highly structured student societies were the various *Vereine*, loose and flexible organizations that brought students together for a wide variety of purposes.[29] Although the *Vereine* at first avoided a tight-knit organizational structure, they, like virtually all student organizations and societies during the latter part of the nineteenth century, experienced a pronounced move toward corporatism. The move toward corporatism was so strong, in fact, that even the nonaffiliated students, or the so-called *Finkenschaften*, were compelled to establish their own organization. In 1896, the unaffiliated students of Leipzig created the first official *Finkenschaft* association, a group that was dedicated to giving "the majority of comrades who do not belong to any corporation that position in student life, that internal as well as external respect, and that valiant support of their rights which their number and importance deserve, but which have hitherto been denied." In the years that followed, *Finkenschaft* associations were founded at a number of German universities.[30]

It is within this matrix of an expanding and increasingly diversified student subculture that Jewish student organizations first emerged. While their appearance is undeniably related to the development of an organized and effective antisemitic movement, antisemitism alone does not explain the specific timing of each group's appearance or its attraction to the Jewish students who joined its ranks. It is essential, therefore, that we remain cognizant of the internal dynamics inherent within the process of Jewish self-definition and attuned to the larger social context in which Jewish student associations emerged as we assess the identities fashioned by members of Jewish student associations.

THE *AKADEMISCHE VEREIN FÜR JÜDISCHE GESCHICHTE UND LITERATUR*

In February 1883, nine students from the University of Berlin created an organization dedicated to the twin goals of increasing their knowledge of Jewish history and literature and establishing the critical study of Judaism as a legitimate field of academic discourse at German universities. The new student association was called the *Akademische Verein für jüdische Geschichte und Literatur* (the Academic Association for Jewish History and Literature, or simply, the AJGV). The founding members of the organization vowed to demonstrate their love of Judaism by studying Jewish history and deepening their knowledge of its literary expressions. Of the nine founders, eight were east Europeans and one was a native German; four were medical students and five studied philosophy. On February 22, 1883, the rector at the University of Berlin officially sanctioned the organization as a *wissenschaftliche Verein* (academic association).[31]

During the first decade of its existence, the fledgling association struggled to define its place among the myriad of student organizations. The main question confronting the members of the *Akademische Verein für jüdische Geschichte und Literatur* was "[were they] a Jewish association exclusively concerned with Jewish history and literature or [were they] an academic association that could just as well be occupied with different cultural traditions?"[32] A secondary problem was whether the organization intended to be comprised only of Jewish students or whether it meant to be a nondenominational association. At first the AJGV defined itself as a *wissenschaftliche Verein* that remained open, in theory, to both Gentile and Jewish members, but by the third semester of its existence, internal documents suggest that the confessional status of the organization was in doubt.

> We have gone too far to be simply an association of individuals with like minded professional and academic interests, or to adopt an exclusive position on religious and political matters. Our endeavor is much more absolute and singular and stems from our conviction that Jewish history and literature, along with their multi-faceted sources, are an essential, although not yet recognized component of universal history and general spiritual training.[33]

In this revealing self-appraisal, the Association for Jewish History and Literature argued that Jewish knowledge constituted an essential component of "universal history," and its author suggested that the day would come when Judaism and Christianity would be viewed as moral and intellectual equivalents. In a manner analogous to Heinrich Graetz and other proponents of the scholarly study of Judaism (*Wissenschaft des Judentums*), the AJGV advanced the position upon which the organization was founded: Judaism and the Jewish people should take their place alongside other cultural groups studied at German universities. Unfortunately, however, after Bismarck's break with the liberals in 1878 and the emergence of antisemitic political parties the following year, a universalistic and inclusive vision of German society was no longer applicable to the environment in which the Academic Association for Jewish History and Literature functioned. In spite of efforts by the *Freie Wissenschaftliche Vereinigung* to counter student antisemitism, student organizations increasingly defined themselves in exclusive terms.[34] Consequently, the call by the *Akademische Verein für jüdische Geschichte und Literatur* for the union of Christian and Jewish intellectual traditions fell largely on deaf ears. Only a few years passed before the members of the AJGV confronted the reality of this situation head-on.

As the associational landscape at German universities became increasingly segregated, the desire of the Academic Association for Jewish History and Literature to remain open to both Jewish and Gentile members proved untenable. According to a monthly report written in 1897, "Jewish organizations viewed the AJGV as *paritätisch*, or nondenominational, while the *paritätisch* organizations viewed it as Jewish."[35] The fact that most members were actively involved in the study of Judaism while enrolled at a university clearly reinforced the perception of the Academic Association for Jewish History and Literature as a Jewish organization. As long as the AJGV remained theoretically open to both Gentiles and Jews, members such as L. Finkenstein, who simultaneously attended lectures in philosophy and philology and studied Talmud at the *Hochschule für Wissenschaft des Judentums* under the guidance of Drs. David Cassel and Joel Müeller, struck a delicate balance between their commitments to *Judentum* and *Deutschtum*. Once the AJGV stipulated that being Jewish was a requirement for membership, the public posturing of the organization and the identities of its members underwent a subtle but important change.

Discussions of the organization's membership policy came to a head when a founding member of the association converted to Christianity and the active members had to decide whether or not to force one of their beloved *Alte Herren* (Old Boys) to resign.[36] If the organization were truly an academic association open to members of all religious persuasions, the fact that a member had converted from Judaism to Christianity would not affect his standing. It is clear, however, that the members of the Academic Association for Jewish History and Literature were not comfortable knowing that an *Alter Herr* had converted to Christianity. Acknowledging that such an individual should no longer remain active within the organization, twenty-one members of the AJGV and eight *Alte Herren* issued the following statement:

> We the undersigned members of the *Akademische Verein für jüdische Geschichte und Literatur* view the conversion to Christianity of one of our members, *in so far as he has converted without being completely convinced of the absolute truth of his new faith,* to be behavior opposed to our conception of honor and righteousness. We view such a change of faith, therefore, as damaging to the AJGV.[37]

Although the members who signed the statement did not address the issue of whether or not the Academic Association for Jewish History and Literature was an exclusively Jewish organization, the message to the recently converted member was clear. Upon hearing of the resolution, he resigned from the organization.[38] Evidently, even if the *Alter Herr* had embraced Christianity in a manner that demonstrated his conviction of "the absolute truth of his new faith," he still would not have been welcomed in the AJGV. The *Akademische Verein für jüdische Geschichte und Literatur* was a university student association comprised exclusively of Jewish students. By converting to Christianity, the former member had violated an unwritten but clearly understood requirement of membership and, as a result, he had to disassociate himself from the association.

Considerable insight into the identities fashioned by members of the *Akademische Verein für jüdische Geschichte und Literatur* is gleaned from its social and intellectual agendas. One member recalled that most midday meals were taken in the company of his associational brothers at a restaurant that was frequented by other

Jewish students. Given that the first Russian-Zionist students also frequented the same midday locale, it is reasonable to assume that the dining establishment may well have been a kosher restaurant and a common gathering place for Jews.[39] In the evening, the friends gathered together for friendly discussions, "a single glass of beer," and, when the occasion presented itself, they attended the local theater or went to hear a concert. On Sundays, members of the AJGV ventured out into the surrounding environs of Berlin and especially enjoyed taking a boat out on the Spree.[40] Together, members of the *Akademische Verein für jüdische Geschichte und Literatur* engaged in activities that were virtually indistinguishable from those of other university students, but they did so in a socially segregated coterie.

The biography of Marvin Warschauer, a philosophy student at the University of Berlin between 1890 and 1894 and a member of the AJGV, adds further definition to the emerging portrait of Jewish identity crafted by members of this student association.[41] Born in the town of Kanth, near Breslau, in 1871, Warschauer was reared in a traditional Jewish household. At age ten he was sent to Breslau to begin his *Gymnasium* studies. During the week Warschauer lived with his grandmother, but he journeyed back to Kanth on the weekends and holidays to be with his father and stepmother. When Marvin Warschauer entered the University of Berlin he simultaneously enrolled at the *Hochschule für Wissenschaft des Judentums* (College of Jewish Studies) to prepare for the rabbinate. While at the university, the young Warschauer attended the lectures of Heinrich Treitschke, Friedrich Paulsen, and other academic luminaries. It was at the *Hochschule,* however, that he received the greatest intellectual stimulation and eventually wrote his doctoral thesis.

During the first few years of his studies, Marvin Warschauer actively participated in AJGV and, before long, he was elected president of the organization. Ultimately, however, he became disenchanted with the organization's lack of commitment to its academic agenda. Apparently, his fellow members were more interested in making friends, playing cards, and drinking beer than they were in seriously pursuing the study of Judaism. Even though the *Akademische Verein für Jüdische Geschichte und Literatur* did not live up to the intellectual expectations of the young Warschauer, the organization provided a forum for him to establish friendships, many of which lasted throughout his life.[42]

In spite of Warschauer's misgivings about the academic commitment of his associational colleagues, the AJGV organized and sponsored numerous lectures.[43] For special celebrations, prominent members of the Jewish community, such as Dr. David Cassel (1818–93) of the *Hochschule für die Wissenschaft des Judentums* and Rabbi Immanuel Ritter (1825–90) of the Berlin reform community, were invited to deliver lectures to the organization and its guests. Most lectures, however, were given by active members of the Academic Association for Jewish History and Literature. Among the topics presented by the AJGV during the academic year 1895–96 were: "Jewish Activities in the Middle Ages," "Social Policies and Humanity in the Pentateuch," "An Overview of the History of Jewish Philosophy," The Reformation and the Jews," and "The Destiny of Spinoza's Life." All of the lectures concerned a critical evaluation of Jewish themes, and they either focused on an aspect of Jewish history and philosophy or offered a biographical sketch of an important figure within Judaism.[44]

By joining an organization that sponsored lectures on Jewish themes, members of the AJGV differentiated themselves from the vast majority of their coreligionists who either were completely disinterested in studying Jewish history and literature or did not have the interest and intellectual training to do so in any meaningful way. Although it is impossible to determine whether the familial background of the students who belonged to the Academic Association for Jewish History and Literature instilled these individuals with a knowledge and love for Judaica, or if joining the organization was a vehicle to strengthen the bond with their religious and cultural heritage, members of the AJGV joined a publicly identifiable Jewish student organization. In so doing, they defined themselves in a way that no longer relegated Jewishness to the private sphere.

The activities of the Academic Association for Jewish History and Literature resonated far beyond the university's walls. Throughout the 1890s, German Jews established a number of local *Vereine für jüdische Geschichte und Literatur*. These organizations, like their university counterparts, promoted the study of Jewish history and literature, sponsored lectures on Jewish topics, and published journals and newspapers to advance the critical study of Jewish history and literature among a populace distanced from its cultural heritage. Interestingly enough, these general Associations for Jewish History and Literature also adopted a theoretically open membership policy and, like the university organization, were comprised exclusively of Jews.[45]

If we were to extend our view beyond the political borders of Germany we would see that during the 1882 autumn semester, Jewish students at the University of Vienna founded an association to combat the assimilatory tendencies of Austrian Jewry and overcome the indifference of Austrian Jews to their Jewish heritage. Like the Academic Association for Jewish History and Literature in Berlin, which was founded by east European Jews and became an organization largely affiliated with indigenous Jews, the *Akademischer Verein Kadimah* developed in a similar manner.[46] *Kadimah* differed from the AJGV, however, in that it quickly shed its purely academic outlook in favor of a "Jewish nationalist" orientation. The pioneering role assigned to *Kadimah* derives from the fact while functioning as an outpost for Jewish nationalism within the Habsburg Empire, it rejected the loose format of the *Akademische Verein für jüdische Geschichte und Literatur* in favor of the more organized structure common to both the *Burschenschaften* and the *Corps*.[47] In the years following the creation of the AJGV, Jewish students in Germany created associations that were influenced by *Kadimah* and modeled after traditional student associations of the German *Kulturbereich*.

THE *KARTELL CONVENT DEUTSCHER STUDENTEN JÜDISCHEN GLAUBENS*

On October 23, 1886, twelve Jewish students at the University of Breslau issued an appeal to their coreligionists, calling for the creation of an "Association of Jewish Students [to] raise the badge of independent Jewry and . . . unite under its banner all those who are of the same mind."[48] Of the twelve founding members of the Jewish fraternity *Viadrina*, eleven studied medicine and one, Benno Jacob, was a rabbinical student. Like most rabbinical students of his day, Jacob simultaneously enrolled at a university and a theological seminary. In preparing for the rabbinate Benno Jacob followed in the footsteps of previous generations of his family, which had produced numerous rabbis and Jewish scholars.[49] Another founder, Alfred Goldschmidt, remained active in Jewish organizations long after he completed his university studies.

While there is little doubt that the founders of *Viadrina* were concerned about the perseverance of anti-Jewish attitudes and the exclusionary membership policies of traditional student societies, the organization's goals demonstrate a profound concern for the identity of German Jewry. Members of the first Jewish fraternity in Germany rejected the pattern of identity formation that either abandoned Judaism entirely or relegated Jewishness to the private sphere. In the words of the founders:

> This association by its mere existence will revive the almost extinguished consciousness that we are Jews, that we belong to a great community in the history of civilization and justified in its existence. It will show that there is no reason why our opponents should despise us and no reason why we should be ashamed of being Jews.[50]

The members of *Viadrina* lashed out against German Jews who denied their Jewishness. They argued that the denigration of Judaism not only caused many Jews to lose all self-respect but also legitimized the claims of antisemites who felt that Judaism was a morally debased and outmoded religion. "The man who has no self-respect, who denies his faith and descent, cannot be surprised if he loses the respect of his presumptuous opponents."[51] Claiming that *paritätisch* organizations ultimately became Jewish in all but name and reminding their coreligionists that Christian students had successfully organized their own exclusive societies, the founders of *Viadrina* established the following ideals for their Jewish student organization:

> We uphold, however, the principle that we can be Jews and good Germans at the same time, and we shall prove it by our behavior. We intend to educate ourselves to become men who will fulfill all demands that the state makes upon its citizens, with enthusiasm and a sense of duty. We want to work at the great tasks of our times together with our Christian countrymen. A union of Jews does not in any way mean seclusion, we shall not stop meeting our Christian fellow-students.[52]

Viadrina's members were acutely aware of the need to publicly express their Judaism in a way that was in complete harmony with the norms of German society. The elements of *Deutschtum* of the late nineteenth century that were incorporated into the identities fashioned by the twelve Breslau students later became the major tenet of the *Centralverein*.[53] This position stressed that becoming a German citizen and fulfilling the obligations of citizenship did not necessitate the abandonment of one's Jewishness. In other words, the founders of *Viadrina* refused to avoid all public declarations of Jewishness. Unlike the *Akademische Verein für jüdische Geschichte und Literatur*, which vacillated about the religious orientation of its membership, *Viadrina* vowed to be a student association that "openly and courageously [confessed the] descent of [its] members."[54] Although the self-conscious use of the word "descent" indicates that *Viadrina* no longer exclusively defined Jewishness in terms of religious affiliation, contemporary understanding of racial categories was seriously at odds with the view that one could be a German of the Jewish faith.

As to the practical aims of the organization, the members of *Viadrina* established the following agenda:

> Our association is to be, first of all, a place for physical training of every kind: gymnastics, fencing, rowing, swimming. We have to fight with all our energy the odium of cowardice and weakness which is cast on us. We want to show that every member of our association is equal to every Christian fellow-student in any physical exercise and chivalry. Physical strength and agility will increase self-confidence and self-respect, and in the future nobody will be ashamed of being a Jew.
>
> We hope to acquire a firm foundation for this self-respect and self-confidence by studying Jewish history, the deeds and sufferings of our ancestors.[55]

The physical characteristics of an idealized masculinity and the ability to defend one's honor by the sword are aspects of German student culture that date back to the eighteenth-century society known as the *Orden*. Throughout the nineteenth century, the tradition of duelling as a means to settle disputes between honorable university students was perpetuated by both the *Corps* and the *Burschenschaften*.[56] By the time of the Kaiserreich, the cult of masculinity and, especially, the maintenance of honor, pervaded the consciousness of German bourgeois society. In promoting physical conditioning and fencing as the primary tenets of its existence, *Viadrina* sought to overcome the stigma of Jewish physical inferiority and provide a setting for its members to function within German student society in a format identical to that of their Christian counterparts. For members of *Viadrina*, this meant defending one's honor in a duel, a right that had been curtailed in the early 1880s when Jewish students were excluded from some of the so-called *schlagende Verbindungen* (duelling societies) on the grounds that they were cowards and unworthy of defending their honor by the sword.[57]

Viadrina's subsidiary goal of educating its members about Jewish history was similar to the primary objectives of the *Akademische Verein für jüdische Geschichte und Literatur*. Both student associations recognized that the concomitant processes of emancipation and acculturation had denigrated the study of Judaism in favor of German cultural traditions. As a result, German Jews were deprived of the "self-respect" and "self-confidence" necessary to function as Jews within German society. Unlike the AJGV, however, *Viadrina's* commitment to the study of Jewish history and cultural traditions played second fiddle to the physical conditioning of its membership.

Sylvius Pick, an active member of *Viadrina* between 1889 and 1891, claimed that the association was not particularly interested in religious matters.[58] Born in Gleiwitz, a town that contained a Jewish community of some two thousand Jews, Pick went on to become a public health official. According to Pick, a typical weekly agenda went as follows:

> We had fencing training on a daily basis from 2:00 until 3:00. Our general meeting was on Monday evenings. We had gymnastic training under the direction of one of our sergeants on Tuesday and Friday. Saturday afternoons [were reserved] for swimming in the [River] Oder while Saturday evenings was our *Kneipe*, preceded by a general meeting of the *Fuxen* [initiates]. Sunday morning was *Frühschoppen* . . . while Sunday afternoons were utilized for a small outing to a Cafe or, possibly, a retreat to one's room.[59]

Pick's account of the weekly schedule reveals that *Viadrina's* rituals, social customs, and overall concerns emulated those of the *Corps* and *Burschenschaften*. The word *Kneipe* refers specifically to the association's formal drinking and singing sessions. These events were filled with beer, song, a certain amount of raucous behavior, and they epitomized the activities of the German fraternities. *Frühschoppen* designates a custom specific to traditional student corporations in Germany. Every Sunday morning during the semester, members of the various "color-carrying" associations would meet at their local drinking establishment dressed in full corporate uniform: hat, pins, and sash. After a few rounds of drinking and general merriment, the members would parade through the town, showing off their colors and demonstrating their elite status. As one might expect, this was a time when insults were hurled between members of the various organizations and fisticuffs often erupted. The exchanges of insults and blows provided the causes necessary for arranging duels. The routine outlined by Pick makes it clear that membership in *Viadrina* dominated one's social calendar. With activities scheduled on a daily basis, members shared many hours together in a social setting comprised exclusively of Jews. When we consider that Pick never mentions lectures on Jewish topics or offers evidence of a commitment to Jewish learning, it is evident that the process of identity formation employed by members of *Viadrina* conformed exactly to Sorkin's model of German Jewry as a "sub-culture."

The lack of a specific Jewish agenda within *Viadrina* is also addressed in Paul Posener's memoir/essay, "The Young Maccabees: A Historical Report on the First Armed Fight against Jew-Baiting in Germany, 1886–1898."[60] Even though Posener has serious misgivings about his years as a member of *Viadrina* and, therefore, one must read his memoir with caution, his comments on the organization's religious orientation are particularly illuminating. Contrary to his expectations that *Viadrina* would educate its members about Jewish history and literature, Posener found the actions and attitudes of his fraternal brothers to be seriously deficient.

> They [the members] were all Jews, all of them. But no[t] one of them was able to explain in clear and plain words what they meant by it. They were not pious. They did not understand Hebrew. They were disgusted when a word of Yiddish or Jewish Jargon was mentioned. They never showed their colours in the Synagogue; whereas Wingolf and Winfridia [two Christian organizations] made it a solemn service to go to church . . . *Viadrina*, at least during the time of my connection with it, did not believe in racialism or in Jewish nationalism. They only believed in the fact that Jews were treated as Jews but not as true German citizens.[61]

Posener's comments on *Viadrina's* religious indifference epitomize the enormously difficult task of remaining simultaneously
committed to two distinct cultural heritages. As the first generation
of German Jewish university students to openly proclaim their
Jewishness, members of *Viadrina* were hard pressed to define it
in meaningful terms. As highly acculturated individuals, they
had discarded the garments necessary to clothe themselves as
Jews. Traditional modes of identity formation such as religious
worship and study of Torah and Talmud were not part of their
cultural wardrobe. The vacuous content of *Viadrina's* Jewishness
is evidenced by the fact that lectures on topics of Jewish history,
literature, and religion were never presented by members of the
organization. Not only was there little Jewish "substance" to the
identities fashioned by members of *Viadrina*, but their activities
were profoundly influenced by Christian culture. According to
Posener, at Christmas "*Viadrina* never failed to have a Christmas
tree" and, when celebrating the final rights of passage into the organization, the membership of *Viadrina* hosted a "Beer-Baptism" at
which time initiates were "christened" with an official nickname.[62]

Despite the fact that *Viadrina* displayed a marked affinity for
German national customs and Christian symbolism, the organization provided an opportunity for its members to socialize with
fellow Jews in a secure and nurturing environment. Students who
joined *Viadrina* publicly functioned as Jews within the social setting
of German university corporate associations. In this regard, the
social function of identity formation took precedence over ideological concerns. One's Jewishness was defined by one's social
coterie.

During the 1890s, Jewish students at the Universities of Heidelberg, Berlin, and Munich established organizations that were
similar to *Viadrina*. In 1896, the three associations, *Badenia*, *Sprevia*,
and *Licaria*, together with *Viadrina*, formed the *Kartell Convent
deutscher Studenten jüdischen Glaubens* (the Association of German
Students of the Jewish Faith, or simply, the K.C.).[63] This newly
established interuniversity association adopted many of the positions delineated within *Viadrina's* founding manifesto. The *Kartell
Convent's* primary goals were to "fight for the full and formal
academic equality of Jewish students—meaning, the acceptance
of Jewish corporations as equal partners, capable of granting and
receiving satisfaction [and to] educate its members to become self-
confident Jews who will know through their historical, cultural,

and legal bonds [that] they are inseparably united with the German fatherland."[64] The raison d'être of the K.C. was to provide Jewish students with the opportunity to participate within traditional student corporate life and to promote a public identity in which being Jewish was placed on equal footing with being German. Toward this second goal, all members of the K.C. were required to align themselves with the Jewish community and to agree to raise their children as Jews. The *Kartell Convent* adamantly opposed all attempts to hide one's Jewishness and demanded that any former member who converted to Christianity remove himself from the ranks of the *Alte Herren*.[65]

The *Kartell Convent*'s emphasis on duelling and maintenance of its corporate character dictated the activities of the individual associations. During the final decade of the nineteenth century, the "Semester Reports" of *Badenia*, in Heidelberg, reveal the group's overwhelming preoccupation with duelling. Under the heading of "Internal Administration (*Innere Verwaltung*)," fencing was one of the first topics covered.

> The official fencing training took place daily between 7:00 and 8:00 in the evenings and it was regularly attended by all active members and *conkneipenen* [guests of the association who were allowed to participate in many, although not all, of its activities]. During the first half of the semester, a group of associational brothers also fenced in the mornings.[66]

The report also details the results of the numerous *Mensuren* held during the semester and comments on the association's relationship with other student organizations.

> During the course of the semester, the relationship of our association to others has not significantly changed. In regards to fencing, in the category of "heavy weapons," we have had ample opportunities to grant and receive satisfaction. In the category of "light weapons," we are in a situation wherein we receive satisfaction from all corporations except those belonging to the S.C. and D.C, although an ongoing and formal schedule of engagements has not yet materialized.[67]

The term *S.C.*, or *Senioren Convent*, refers to a set of rules and regulations regarding the conduct of individual associations, their members, and their activities. Within the *Badenia* report the term *S.C.* refers specifically to the *Corps*. All organizations desiring to arrange fencing matches with an association belonging to the *Corps* had to present themselves and their weapons for approval and obtain the status of *satisfaktionsfähig* (worthy of a duel). *Badenia* and most Jewish organizations were not regarded as *satisfaktionsfähig* and were unable to arrange matches with the *Corps*. The term *D.C.* stands for *Deputy-Convent*, the overriding body of the *Burschenschaften*. Most of the stipulations described for the S.C. also apply to the D.C. In short, *Badenia* could not schedule *Mensuren* with organizations that belonged to either the *Corps* or the *Burschenschaften*.

Badenia's leadership attributed its inability to arrange a fixed schedule of matches to the fact that older corporations had long since determined their opponents and were unable to schedule *Badenia* on a regular basis. In actuality, *Badenia*'s relations with other student associations remained on fragile footing throughout its existence, a situation that made it particularly difficult to arrange *Mensuren*. Between 1894 and 1898, *Badenia* held semiregular matches with the *freischlagende Verbindung* (free duelling association) *Salia*. As *freischlagende Verbindungen* were not tied to either the S.C. or the D.C., they were free to arrange duels with whomever they pleased. Unfortunately for *Badenia*, however, the group was compelled to discontinue its relationship with *Salia* when a member of *Salia* acted in a "dishonorable manner" at a *Mensur*.[68]

The Semester Reports of *Badenia* between 1895 and 1899 also reveal a long-running dispute with the *Burschenschaft* organization *Allemania*, a development that prevented *Mensuren* from being scheduled between the two associations. While the details of the dispute are not particularly noteworthy, it is interesting that although *Allemania* did not recognize *Badenia* as *satisfaktionsfähig*, *Allemania* utilized official channels to register complaints against the Jewish corporation and, in essence, legitimized *Badenia*'s corporate status. *Badenia*'s strained relationship with *Allemania* was an experience shared by its organizational brothers in Berlin and Munich. The *Semester Berichten* of both *Sprevia* and *Licaria* detail their troubled encounters with local *Burschenschaften* and document their inability to arrange matches with them.[69] It was no mere coincidence that the three Jewish fraternities were unable to engage in formal duels with members of the *Burschenschaften*. Unlike Austrian fraternal student organizations, which adopted a formal policy of exclusion,[70] the German *Burschenschaften* utilized special circumstances such as *Allemania's* dispute with *Badenia* to prevent *Mensuren* between its members and those of Jewish duelling associations.[71] The end result was that members of the K.C. were unable to arrange duels with their counterparts in either the *Corps* or the *Burschenschaften*.

While anti-Jewish attitudes may have provided the underlying rationale for the *Corps* and the *Burschenschaften's* unwillingness to take up swords with Jewish students, the refusal to arrange fencing matches with Jewish fraternities was not predicated on antisemitism alone. Rather, the increasing particularism of German student associations at the close of the nineteenth century resulted in the *Corps* and *Burschenschaften* becoming extremely selective with whom they would arrange duels and the weapons that could be used. Not only were Jewish and *paritätisch* organizations refused the "honor" of duelling with either the *Corps* or the *Burschenschaften*, but members of the *Corps* and *Burschenschaften* dueled mainly with one another. During the Wilhelmine era members of a given corporation were most likely to select their duelling opponents from organizations that occupied a similar position in the hierarchical ordering of student societies.[72]

Apart from members of the *Kartell Convent* being prevented from duelling with the more elite organizations at German universities, they took part in all official university functions. During the winter semester of 1895–96, *Badenia* participated in two official university ceremonies: one commemorating the establishment of the German Reich and the other celebrating the founding of Heidelberg University. In addition, every Semester Report from the summer of 1898 until the summer of 1900 claimed that "the association officially participated at all celebratory functions of the University."[73] The same holds true for *Licaria*. During the winter semester of 1896–97, its members took part in the official celebration of Kaiser Wilhelm I's one hundredth birthday and a torchlight parade in honor of the deceased rector of the university, Herr von Baur.[74] On July 12, 1898, three members of *Licaria* represented the association at a memorial service for Bismarck and, during the following year, *Licaria* reports that they, too, took part in all official university functions.[75] While the *Burschenschaften* and the *Corps* could discriminate against their Jewish counterparts when selecting duelling opponents, they were not able to exclude the chapters of the K.C. from taking part in university-sponsored events. By wearing the associational colors, hat, sash, and pin to these events, members of the *Kartell Convent* presented themselves to the university community as German students of the Jewish faith. Given that attending official university events was part of the process of self-definition employed by all officially sanctioned student societies, these students assumed a public position analogous to that of members of other student associations. The difference, of course, was that individuals who belonged to the K.C. participated in German student society in a manner that was openly and explicitly Jewish.

One activity that set the chapters of this Jewish fraternal organization apart from their Gentile counterparts was the desire to educate members about their Jewish heritage. Even though there were no regular discussions of Jewish history and literature, most *Semester Berichte* comment on the associations' attempts to organize *wissenschaftliche Abende* (academic evenings). *Badenia*'s report from the winter semester of 1894–95 comments on the active interest taken by the members in preparing for, and participating in, organizational discussions. Yet interest in academic evenings visibly waned in the years that followed. During the summer semester of 1899, the one *wissenschaftlicher Abend* sponsored by *Badenia* contained the lecture, "Why do we have academic evenings?"[76] *Sprevia*'s reports also indicate a general level of concern about the academic evenings, although members apparently lacked the energy for organizing them. One possible solution put forward by *Sprevia*'s leadership was to have its members attend the lectures of one of the local associations and avail themselves of the opportunity to hear "noteworthy speakers discussing important questions."[77] Only *Licaria*, it seems, remained actively involved in the study of Jewish topics. During the winter semester of 1896–97, members of *Licaria* presented two lectures on the subject of antisemitism[78] and, in the years that followed, regularly attended lectures sponsored by the Munich chapter of the *Verein für jüdische Geschichte und Literatur*.[79] Apparently, the common religious heritage of the two organizations and the probability that their members moved in overlapping social circles were sufficient to bring the two groups together for an occasional lecture.

The most important and distinguishing feature of the public position adopted by members of *Viadrina, Badenia, Sprevia,* and *Licaria* was their open display of Jewishness. The fact that they did not engage in duels with either the *Corps* or the *Burschenschaften,* or that the emphasis on fencing and physical fitness took precedence over the commitment to studying Jewish history, does not diminish the significance of belonging to an explicitly Jewish student association. Jewish students who joined a chapter of the *Kartell Convent* rejected an identity that eliminated all manifestations of Jewishness from the public sphere and chose, instead, to display their Jewishness honorably.[80] The willingness of students belonging to the *Kartell Convent* to openly proclaim their Jewish heritage clearly set them apart from both their unaffiliated coreligionists and members of the *Freie Wissenschaftliche Vereinigung*.

JEWISH NATIONALIST STUDENT ASSOCIATIONS

The *Kartell Convent* was not the only university association to establish a public Jewish profile. During the 1890 academic year, notices appeared on announcement boards at the University of Berlin calling for the creation of a "national-Jewish" student association on the model of the University of Vienna's *Kadimah*.[81] Unlike members of the *Kartell Convent*, who emphatically declared their allegiance to the Kaiserreich and postulated that they could be "German students of the Jewish faith," each member of *Kadimah* stated in writing that he undertook to combat assimilation, seal his commitment to the Jewish nation, and support the colonization of Palestine.[82] Although the attempt to establish a Jewish nationalist association at the University of Berlin failed in 1890, it was not long before such an organization came into being. By the following spring, they were ready to register their new association with the local authorities. On the evening of March 31, 1892, the student association *Jung-Israel, Jüdisch-nationaler Verein*, (Young Israel, Jewish National Association) held its first meeting.[83] Similar to the development of all Jewish student groups to date, Jewish students from eastern Europe greatly contributed to the creation of the first national Jewish student association in Germany. Many of the founding members of Young Israel had previously belonged to the *Russisch-jüdischer wissenschaftlicher Verein* (the Association for Russian-Jewish Academics), an academic student association comprised of Russian Jews and one native-born German Jew, Heinrich Loewe.

Born in the small town of Wanzleben, near Ackerbau, in 1869, Loewe came from a highly acculturated family. His father had participated in the revolutions of 1848 and was firmly committed to the idea of Jewish emancipation and integration into German society. As a child, Heinrich's circle of friends consisted of both Jews and Gentiles, for there were few other Jewish families in Wanzleben.[84] This situation changed significantly when the family moved to Magdeburg when Heinrich Loewe was fourteen years old. In Magdeburg Loewe was exposed to a large Jewish community, approximately one thousand souls, and introduced to Jewish religious worship and the study of Jewish history. Although educated in a church school and deeply interested in Christian religious history, Heinrich Loewe was befriended by one Rabbi Rahmer who introduced the adolescent to the history and religious practice of the Jewish people. Loewe's commitment to Jewish nationalism was sealed with an introduction to, and time spent with, Heinrich Graetz, the famous scholar of Jewish national history.[85] By the time that Loewe began his studies in history and oriental languages at the University of Berlin in 1889, he was already familiar with *Hoevei Zion*, the eastern European proto-Zionist organization. His commitment to Jewish nationalism and desire to interact socially with like-minded students brought him into contact with members of the Association for Russian-Jewish Academics.

Before the First Zionist Congress in 1897, *Jung-Israel* and a second Jewish nationalist student association called the *Humanitäts-gesellschaft* founded by German students at the University of Berlin in 1893 functioned as centers of proto-Zionist activity in Germany.[86] A poem composed for *Jung-Israel* by Heinrich Loewe offers poignant insight into the agenda of German Jewish nationalists:

Arise my folk, to noble deeds
For Battle you must arm.
No more can you just rest at ease
While foe intends you harm.
He plans, my people, to attack
Thus Judah rise and fight him back.
Courageous host,
With pride utmost
No foe, for sure, will set you back!

Freedom is the noble goal
Which Judah must entice.
His heart is beating hot as coal
To mark its sacrifice.
Proud eagle, soar up to the sky
Your chest so free, so clear your eye.
First, in battle din
Now . . . glorious win
A noble, stupefying high!

Arise my folk, my folk wake up
Your life has a new lift.
The sun will soon rise to the top
And tomorrow's noon will drift.
Wake up my folk and see the light
Which shatters into a thousand bites
To victory
My folk—You'll see
For honor, land and freedom fight.[87]

Set to the melody of the *Ma'oz Tsur Yeshuati* (Rock of Ages), a song that alludes to God's deliverance of the Jews from Egypt, Babylonia, Persia, and Syria and is traditionally sung after lighting the Hanukkah lights, Loewe's poem summons the memory of the legendary warrior Judas Maccabee to prepare his coreligionists for battle. At stake are Jewish honor and freedom, both of which have been besmirched by proponents of a Christian-Germanic society. Jews, according to Loewe, must reclaim their glorious heritage and call upon their noble past in order to arm themselves for the challenges of the day.

On July 4, 1895, members of *Jung-Israel* reorganized their association and changed its name to the *Vereinigung Jüdischer Studenten* (the Association of Jewish Students or, simply, the V.J.St.).[88] By calling their organization the V.J.St., the founders positioned themselves as a counterweight to the antisemitic, nationalist student organization, the *Verein Deutscher Studenten* (V.D.St.). Although the organization had at first avoided using the name V.J.St. for "fear of being regarded as the opposite pole to the antisemitic V.D.St.," Heinrich Loewe eventually convinced his fellow members that their organization should openly position itself as the counterpart to the V.D.St.[89] A poster designed to attract new members reveals the concerns of the V.J.St. and its programmatic objectives.

> Jewish Students! You will not be spared the hate and contempt that surrounds us because we are Jews. Your faith and heritage have been reproached, your parents have been insulted.
> Students! The word "Jew" hurled at you as an insult, should be worn by you as an honorable badge. . . . We Jews are proud of our past and our ancestors [*Stamm*], the first people to preach morality. [We are proud] of our ancestors [*Volk*] for introducing [the concept] of God into this world. [We are proud] of our fathers, who in times of furious persecution and deep humiliation, never denied their being!
> . . . Students! Help us protect these colors [the banner of Judaism]. Fight with us for our Judaism by cultivating [the study of] Jewish history and literature; by steeling [your] bodies; by raising the self-consciousness of our Jewish brothers! Join our circle! Struggle with us for our honor, for your honor![90]

The language of the above document attests to the fact that German Jewish university students were subjected to verbal abuse and racial epithets. Just as members of the *Akademischer Verein für jüdische Geschichte und Literatur* and the *Kartell Convent* created new public images when the dialectical state of tension between their private and public lives was disrupted by the continual degradation of their Jewishness, students belonging to the V.J.St. also rejected a public identity devoid of Jewish content.

The V.J.St.'s understanding of its Jewishness was encapsulated in an open letter to Jewish students written around the turn of the century by students at the University of Leipzig.[91] The letter begins with an organizational statement of purpose that, like the V.J.St. in Berlin, indicates that heightening Jewish self-consciousness was a primary goal of the association. According to the authors of the letter, Jewish students should be both aware of their Jewishness and proud of being Jews. To achieve this objective, the V.J.St. in Leipzig proposed to strengthen Jewish particularities by uniting all Jewish students within its organization, promoting the study of Jewish history and literature, and increasing the physical strength and dexterity of its membership.[92]

References to the physical regeneration of its membership and images of masculinity resonate throughout this letter. The following passage is but one of many examples.

By steeling our physical strength and increasing our dexterity, our bodies will be masculine and full of energy, ready to execute the orders of the mind. Today's Jews are not complete men for they lack unity, trust and equal development of the mind and the body.[93]

The V.J.St.'s image of a modern Jew was a physically fit male who was well versed in the historical and literary heritage of Judaism. Masculinity was inextricably intertwined with their vision of Jewishness.[94] The views of the V.J.St. closely resembled the ideas articulated by Max Nordau, the writer, philosopher, and Zionist who coined the phrase "Muscular Jewry." In an article entitled "Muskeljudentum," Nordau espoused the benefits of physical exercise and the need for Jews to become physically fit in order to lay to rest the charges of Jewish inferiority.[95] Not only were the V.J.St.'s attitudes about masculinity virtually identical to those of the *Kartell Convent*, they were no different from those employed by the *Corps*, the *Burschenschaften*, and all corporate student associations in Germany during the nineteenth century. All university corporate societies in Germany, be they Jewish or Gentile, defined the public sphere as a male domain. Furthermore, the masculine characteristics of self-discipline, courage, and bravery that were cherished by German corporate associations and passionately defended with the sword were also prized cultural values of nineteenth-century German bourgeois society.[96]

Even though university student associations incorporated idealized concepts of masculinity into their programmatic manifestos and participated in many common activities, the founding of Jewish student organizations must be understood as a response to the emancipatory process that had rendered Jewish university students unfamiliar with their Jewish heritage. Although a social history of German Jewry is still lacking, we know that the vast majority of German Jews had long since abandoned traditional modes of education and worship and only approximately 15–20 percent of German Jews of the Kaiserreich could be classified as traditional or Orthodox Jews.[97] Responding to a situation wherein they were neither fully accepted by the host society nor willing to live in cultural isolation from it, Jewish students founded an array of organizations that attempted to balance their commitment to both *Deutschtum* and *Judentum*. The *Akademische Verein für jüdische Geschichte und Literatur*, the *Kartell Convent*, and the *Vereinigung*

Jüdischer Studierender all promoted the study of Jewish history and literature as a means to overcome the ignorance of the Jewish student population toward its cultural heritage. The V.J.St. parted company with other Jewish student associations, however, with its commitment to Jewish nationalism and the preservation of the Jews as a distinct tribe and people [*Stamm* and *Volk*]. Unlike the *Kartell Convent*, which argued that its members could be "German students of the Jewish faith," the *Vereinigung Jüdischer Studierender* rejected the view that German Jews belonged to a German national entity. Instead, its members constructed a public identity that was imbued with a positive, national, Jewish consciousness. Although the V.J.St. did not initially call itself a Zionist organization, its position on Jewish nationalism put it at the forefront of the German Zionist movement.[98]

Not only did the V.J.St. offer a public profile of German Jewry that differed from those fashioned by the *Kartell Convent* and the *Akademische Verein für jüdische Geschichte und Literatur*, it is clear that the *Vereinigung Jüdischer Studierender* believed that its greatest adversaries were other Jewish student organizations.[99] A Semester Report of the Berlin V.J.St. written in 1897 demonstrates this concern.

> During this last semester as in semesters past, the V.J.St. has remained true to its program of promoting Jewish self consciousness. This, in spite of all the attacks against us, especially those emanating from the Jewish side. . . .
> We consider it our duty to counter, with all of our determination, the indifference that has developed during the last decade towards all Jewish questions, especially among educated Jews. . . .
> We will gain the attention of Gentiles—and *our opponents*—through open and honorable encounters with our Judaism.[100]

The reference to attacks "emanating from the Jewish side" and the distinction between "Gentiles" and "our opponents"—that is, Jews—reveals that the V.J.St. was already coming under fire from the *Kartell Convent*. The verbal sparring between the *Vereinigung Jüdischer Studierender* and the *Kartell Convent* marked the beginning of what became an intense and acrimonious debate between the two student organizations, one that heated up considerably in the decade before the First World War and paralleled, to a large extent, the growing animosity between the German Zionist Organization and the *Centralverein.*

By the close of the nineteenth century, a small group of Jewish university students had rejected public identities devoid of Jewish content and incorporated Jewishness into their public lives. This development led to the creation of three Jewish student associations: the *Akademischer Verein für jüdische Geschichte und Literatur,* the *Kartell Convent,* and the *Vereinigung Jüdischer Studierender.* Each of these groups publicly proclaimed their Jewishness and offered their members multiple opportunities to socialize openly with their coreligionists and learn about their much-neglected cultural heritage. While the existence of these Jewish student groups demonstrates that some Jewish university students of the Kaiserreich felt compelled to terminate the disjunction between their public and private identities, it reveals nothing about Jews who did not belong to one of these organizations. What types of identities did they construct? With whom did they socialize? In what activities did they engage? How did they define themselves within the university environment? Were there features of their identities peculiar to German Jews, or was the process of self-definition employed by these Jewish students indistinguishable from that of Gentile students who chose not to join a traditional student society? Although it is not possible to answer these questions for every Jewish university student who did not belong to one of the major Jewish student associations, we can sketch the identities of a small portion of this silent and overlooked majority.

III

DEFINING AND
REDEFINING
THE SUBJECT

5

Reconstructing Forgotten Jews:
Portraits of the
Noncorporate Student Body

German university students of the Kaiserreich operated in a social environment that was dominated by a highly organized and ritualistic corporate subculture. Students who joined traditional associations quickly established friendships with their fellow initiates and, before long, their daily routines were synchronized with the organization's activities. While one's commitment to an association's customs, traditions, and ideological platform varied from individual to individual, membership in a university student organization decidedly influenced the process of self-definition for those who joined its ranks. Yet, in spite of the seemingly ubiquitous presence of corporate associations, more than 50 percent of the student body remained unaffiliated.[1] The experiences of these students and the processes of identity formation that they employed were fundamentally different than those of the tradition-bound, duelling youths who joined corporate organizations.

For the unincorporated student, the rhythms and patterns of university life were negotiated on an individual and uniquely personal basis. In making the transition from the relatively protected environment of their childhood homes to the stimulating yet foreign atmosphere of German universities, independent students leaned heavily upon the familiar. Many journeyed to their university of choice with classmates from home, some called upon familial connections as their first social contacts, and others walked the streets of Berlin, Munich, and other university cities searching for a familiar face. In almost every case, one's background and place of origin influenced the early stages of one's university career. Once established at the university, the activities of unaffiliated students revolved around the quest for *Bildung*. They attended lectures, visited the theater and concert halls, and took excursions into the surrounding environs. Life as a university student presented a cornucopia of opportunities for intellectual and personal development.

To portray the lives of German Jews outside the orbit of organizational life, I have utilized the individual threads of memoirs to weave together the following narrative. Memoirs, by their very nature, allow us to evaluate how individuals functioned within the privacy of their homes, and they provide insight into how these individuals positioned themselves within the surrounding society.[2] The memoirs of German Jews, according to Monika Richarz,

> report vividly on childhood, school, and vocation, as well as community life, religious practice, culture and politics. These accounts testify to very diverse forms of Jewish identity and to the extraordinary variety of German Jewry. [They] also illustrate the relationship between Jews and their environment, cultural and social rapprochement, as well as denial of integration, and every level of antisemitic persecution.[3]

In addition, personal sources such as memoirs enable the historian to study the "drift and defection" of a Jewish community and evaluate the "forces that bound Jews to their ancestral community and those that worked to weaken traditional sympathies, pulling Jews into the larger society."[4] For Jewish university students outside the orbit of organizational life, autobiographical descriptions of their upbringing inform us that many, though not all, formed their closest friendships with fellow Jews and most operated within the university environment in a manner virtually indistinguishable from that of unaffiliated Gentile students. In other words, they luxuriated in the freedom of university life, valued time spent with friends, and did what was necessary to complete a university education before moving on to a professional career.

The following discussion is divided into four themes, each of which offers a unique vantage point from which to view the lives of Jewish students who were not affiliated with the major student organizations. The first, which I have called "Growing Up and Moving Out," juxtaposes the students' upbringings with their experiences at German universities. This section reveals the complex relationship between the identities instilled in people while they were young with those that they created as young adults. "The Importance of Time and Place"[5] demonstrates that as individuals move through life, even within the span of only a few months or years, their position in society and, hence, their identity, changes dramatically. The final two categories, "Forming a Social Coterie" and "All in the Pursuit of *Bildung*," highlight that making friends and becoming cultivated, educated adults were central to the lives of German university students, be they Jewish or Gentile. While the individual portraits presented in this section may not be statistically representative of German Jewish university students as a whole, they are suggestive of "larger social trends" among the Jewish student population.[6]

GROWING UP AND MOVING OUT

Born in 1851 in the town of Komsdorf, Eduard Silbermann spent the better part of his youth in the Franconian village of Bischberg, near Bamberg.[7] He was the son of a well-to-do merchant and small-scale farmer, and he was raised in a home environment steeped in traditional Jewish culture. According to Silbermann, "the Sabbaths and the holidays—all of which were strictly observed—brought the Jewish inhabitants [of the town] together, not only in the synagogue but also in many instances in the individual families. Every family event brought them together, one event the children, another the adults."[8] Eduard Silbermann's grade school education took place in both a German and a Jewish school, an arrangement necessitating that Silbermann journey back and forth twice daily between the two schools.[9] Silbermann's Jewish teacher "took great pains to impart a basic knowledge in religion, biblical history and the Hebrew language" and, by the time he was eleven years of age, he had sufficient command of Hebrew to translate the Prophets and the Pentateuch and understand all the prayers of the daily and Sabbath services.[10] As a youth, Eduard Silbermann's activities were influenced by both his Jewishness and his Germanness. His life at home and in the community resonated with Jewish culture and provided him with a clearly defined self-identity of being Jewish. Yet, Silbermann's education in both Jewish and German schools necessitated that he traverse the worlds of *Deutschtum* and *Judentum* and begin the art of synthesis central to the process of identity formation.

After completing his *Abitur* in 1871, Silbermann began his university education at the University of Würzburg in the spring of 1872. When he arrived in Würzburg before the semester started, Silbermann, like most first-term university students, utilized his free time to find living accommodations and to familiarize himself with the town. While strolling through the streets of Würzburg, he happened upon an acquaintance whom he knew from his *Gymnasium* in Bamberg and together they ventured to a Jewish restaurant for their midday meal. At the restaurant, Silbermann met a number of Jewish medical students with whom he would continue to have friendly, but not particularly close, personal relations throughout his time in Würzburg.[11] Having been raised within a predominantly Jewish social coterie, Silbermann's upbringing clearly affected the way in which he positioned himself as a new university student.

During the period of time before lectures started, Silbermann was recruited to join a fraternal student organization. Convinced that his time at the university should be devoted to his studies and that membership in a traditional, beer drinking and duelling society was nothing more than a social crutch, Silbermann chose not to join a corporate society.[12] He did, however, become a member of an academic society called *Harmonia,* an organization that attracted students from a variety of disciplines.[13] According to Silbermann, the advantage of this academic association was that "*Harmonia* had one large, and a number of smaller reading rooms filled with extensive periodical and other literature." Silbermann recalls that "he had hardly learned to read law when he came across the well known Seuffert Archiv, a collection of [legal] decisions written by the leading experts in Germany."[14] Being an energetic and conscientious student, Silbermann utilized the materials available to him as a member of *Harmonia* to familiarize himself with the German law code, its legal methods, and the types of questions that concerned legal experts. Given that Silbermann comments on neither the association's social activities nor on the other members, it appears that his membership in *Harmonia* was truly an academic affair.

As a university student, Eduard Silbermann took advantage of his independence and the multifaceted opportunities for intellectual growth and social interchange to break away from the traditional environment in which he had been raised. Reflecting on his religious observance, Silbermann comments that

> during my entire time at the university, my religiosity exercised itself very little. As the High Holidays always fell during a semester break, I was usually in Bamberg and attended synagogue there. For the most part, however, religious questions remained in the background.[15]

Although the pace and content of university life appealed to the young Silbermann and provided him an opportunity to experience life with Judaism "in the background," he writes that later in life, "I never completely broke with the traditions of my youth, even if at times there were periods of laxness. . . . I continued to be interested in Jewish writings, [and] my knowledge of these subjects has remained with me to this day."[16]

While studying at a German university, the extent to which Judaism influenced Eduard Silbermann's life was diminished but not eliminated. He temporarily constructed an identity that allowed him to function as a university student in a manner that deemphasized his commitment to religious Judaism. Later, outside the university environment, Silbermann redefined himself, with Judaism resuming a more central position than it had while functioning within the university environment. The memoir of Eduard Silbermann reminds us that identity formation is a lifelong process, and discussions of an individual's identity must be situated within a specific temporal and social context.

The degree to which Silbermann's life was influenced by his Jewish upbringing was not an experience shared by all of his coreligionists. The life of Joseph Gallinger (b. 1872) presents a contrasting picture of youth and the transition to student life. Like many German Jews of the nineteenth century, Gallinger's Jewishness manifested itself primarily among family and friends. His descriptions of the family's Sabbath celebration reveal how German Jews mediated between their German and Jewish heritages to create a distinctive cultural identity, one that was neither German nor Jewish, but both. "On every Friday evening," Gallinger writes, "the entire Fürther family [the family of his mother's parents, who resided in Fürth] gathered at [G]randmother's home. The men had their modest glass of beer while Aunt Malchen and Klara occupied their traditional spots on the sofa in the salon [*guten Stube*]." Gallinger's description of his family's Sabbath evening gatherings clearly demonstrates that the welcoming of the Sabbath Queen had lost its religious content. Sabbath rituals such as lighting the candles or reciting the Friday evening *Kiddush* are not mentioned at all. Rather, he comments on the types of refreshments served— *Torten, Glühwein,* and *Bierpunsch*—and the conversation, which ranged from aspects of general life (*Allgemeinheit*) to the activities of Eugen Richter (1838–1906) and the left-liberal political party, the *Fortschrittspartei*.[17] Although nearly three-quarters of German Jewry supported the National Liberals and Bismarck's policies before his break from the liberal wing of the party in 1878, once liberalism ceased to be a major power factor in German politics, the majority of German Jews turned to the *Fortschrittspartei*.[18] The rituals of Joseph Gallinger's family life reflect the German Jewish subculture of the Kaiserreich, a time when many German Jews had adopted the bourgeois lifestyle of German Gentiles and distanced themselves from the norms and practices of traditional Judaism, but continued to associate the Sabbath and Jewish festivals with opportunities for family gatherings.[19]

As a university student, Gallinger did not join a traditional association but preferred, instead, to stake out his own social network. His original circle of friends consisted primarily of Jews and two Christian students with whom he had studied at *Gymnasium.* Gallinger recalls that his Gentile colleagues were regulars at his coterie's *Stammtisch,* the group's reserved table at their local pub, until they decided to join a student organization that discriminated against Jewish students. After being initiated into the association, all social contact between Gallinger, his Jewish comrades, and the two Christians was discontinued, even though "both sides" would have preferred to remain friends.[20] Whereas religious differences had not prevented the youths from sharing a friendship while students at the *Gymnasium,* once the two Christians joined a corporate association that did not recognize Jewish students as social equals, the friendships had to be terminated. Gallinger's experience in this regard illuminates two features of life for young German Jews as they moved from childhood into the university environment. First, hometown friends were important pillars of stability during a moment in life when one's identity was in flux. Second, the decidedly exclusive social environment of German universities compelled Joseph Gallinger and his childhood friends to break off all social contact.

The experiences of Curt Rosenberg offer another window into the life of a German Jew as he negotiated the path from childhood to young adult. He was born in 1876 into a wealthy Berlin Jewish family. Rosenberg's father was a promoter of international art exhibitions and later owned a small chemical company.[21] Although he describes his parents as being "religiously indifferent," Rosenberg's mother insisted that he recite one of the following universalistic prayers before going to bed at night: "I am small and my heart is pure," or "When at night I go to sleep, the angels near me they do keep."[22] Rosenberg's grade school experience consisted of no formal Jewish education, yet he claims to have been very interested in the Bible and quite familiar with both the Old and New Testaments. All told, his childhood memories of Judaism are largely negative, a fact encapsulated by the following description of his grandmother reciting her morning prayers. "I remember thinking it odd to hear the sing-song tone of the incomprehensible Hebrew words which she recited." The entire routine reminded him of "the customs of an uncultivated tribe. It left me completely cold and spiritually empty."[23]

After completing *Gymnasium*, Curt Rosenberg enrolled in the University of Berlin in 1894. Following considerable reflection about his decision to become a lawyer and the various professors with whom he studied, Rosenberg's discussion of his student years turns to an encounter with a fellow student during the summer semester of 1895.

[One day], when I arrived late for a seminar, a colleague 'complained' about my being late. During the break I confronted him, and he challenged me to a duel. His name was Veigt and he was a member of the *Corps*. He may well have intended from the very beginning to produce a confrontation and he may have also been motivated by antisemitism. Of this, however, I cannot be certain.[24]

Upon being challenged by the *Corpstudent*, Rosenberg eagerly began taking fencing lessons from a well-known and respected teacher. He also secured "weapons" for the *Mensur* from the *Corps* Berussia. According to the rules of the *Senior Convent*, which regulated the duels fought by members of the *Corps*, all weapons had to be presented for inspection prior to a match and accepted as satisfactory. As we have already seen, by the time that Rosenberg was challenged to a duel, the *Corps* recognized only the weapons of rival *Corps* organizations and those of the *Burschenschaften* as acceptable. The securing of weapons from Berussia, therefore, was a formal prerequisite for Rosenberg, a Jew and not a member of an officially sanctioned organization, to engage in a duel with a member of the *Corps*. His intensive training notwithstanding, Rosenberg was overmatched. Although he took solace in the fact that the match lasted for twenty out of the twenty-two prescribed minutes, the *Mensur* ended in a decisive defeat for Rosenberg and left him with a scar that was clearly visible for many years.[25]

Although Rosenberg claims not to have been especially interested in Jewish questions during his student years,[26] he operated within the university environment in a manner that was clearly informed by his Jewishness. He admits that while courting a "beautiful and romantically inclined young Jewish woman," he began reading about Judaism and familiarizing himself with the works of Jewish authors.[27] As his knowledge of Jewish culture and heritage increased, his feelings for Zionism became more sympathetic, but not to the extent that he joined the Zionist movement. When discussing the position of Jews within German society with his friends, most of whom were outspokenly anti-Zionist, Rosenberg alone made positive remarks about Zionism.[28]

Although at first glance the memoir of Curt Rosenberg appears to contain conflicting information, when evaluated closely it illuminates a great deal about the society in which he operated and the way in which he positioned himself within that society. We learn that even though the *Corps* was a highly exclusive association, "social interaction" in the form of duels between its members and Jewish students still took place. Unlike the Austrian *Burschenschaften*, which explicitly prohibited its members from engaging in duels with Jewish students, the *Corps* retained its platform of religious neutrality and never officially adopted a policy of exclusion. As to Rosenberg's place within student society, the lively discourse about the relationship between *Deutschtum* and *Judentum,* his romantic involvement with a Jewish woman, and his sympathetic feelings for Zionism all indicate that "Jewish questions" influenced the formation of his private identity. Yet, in spite of the fact that he maintained a Jewish social coterie, he describes his university experiences as being no different than those of other unaffiliated students. While the discrepancy between Curt Rosenberg's descriptions of his student years and our reading of them suggests he was virtually blind to his own social reality, this disjunction accurately reflects the paradoxical condition of human existence wherein one's self-definition is often at odds with the way in which one is perceived by others.

THE IMPORTANCE OF TIME AND PLACE

When evaluating the process of identity formation employed by Eduard Silbermann, Joseph Gallinger, and Curt Rosenberg, the themes of "time" and "place" were clearly evident. The transition from the familial home to the university, from adolescence to young adulthood, altered their positions in society. The temporal specificity of identity is not only present at different stages of one's life, but also within a much narrower period of time. During the course of a given day, month, or year, individuals assume different roles, moving from the private sphere of the home environment to the public arena of school, work, and commerce. In a similar vein, as one journeys from location to location, the demands and dictates of a given environment influence how one functions within each setting. For Jewish students of the Kaiserreich, the contingencies of "time" and "place" are readily evident when reading the recollections of their lives.

Born in 1855, Ludwig Edinger belonged to the same generation as Eduard Silbermann. Unlike Silbermann's family, however, but similar to many German Jews of his era, Edinger's family went to synagogue only on the main Jewish holidays and did not observe the ceremonial functions of Judaism within the home. Although religious observance was largely absent from the household, Edinger describes his father as a "Spinozist," a reform-minded individual who detested all forms of orthodoxy but still believed that Judaism represented the highest religious ideal.[29]

In 1872 Ludwig Edinger enrolled at the University of Heidelberg as a student of *Naturwissenschaft* (Natural Science). During his second semester at Heidelberg, Edinger's closest circle of friends consisted of a group of students, most of whom emanated from the Frankfurt vicinity. In referring to his colleagues' activities, Edinger reflects on their tours through the beautiful environs of Heidelberg and the longer hikes through the local forests taken during periods of vacation. On the topic of their religious background, however, Ludwig Edinger remains absolutely silent. Hence, we do not know whether his friends were Jews, Gentiles, or a combination of both.[30]

After passing his first set of exams in the spring of 1874, Ludwig Edinger left Heidelberg and relocated to Strasbourg, where a new university had recently opened.[31] Following the culmination of the Franco-Prussian War in 1871 and the incorporation of the territories of Alsace and Lorraine into the newly created Second Reich, the German authorities transformed the old German secondary school in Strasbourg into the King Wilhelm University. Edinger's decision to change schools was typical of nineteenth-century German university students, who commonly attended more than one school during their academic careers. Once a German male *Gymnasium* student successfully completed his *Abitur*, he was qualified to attend the German university of his choice. No central bureaucracy dictated where a student would attend lectures.

While in Strasbourg, Edinger experienced the tensions associated with being an unwanted foreigner in a foreign land. Having only recently been incorporated into the German Reich, many native Alsatians were not entirely happy with their new nationality. The Jewish author and polemicist Alexandre Weill expressed the sentiments of many Jewish Alsatians when he composed the following verse.

> We Alsatians have always been a free people.
> We drink our own wine and we make our own beer.
> We are attached to the French like cockleburs.
> We speak German when we wish.
> But Moltke will never be our hero!
> The heavens would sooner crash down to earth
> Than see us become Prussians![32]

Ludwig Edinger viewed the animosity between Alsatians and Germans much like the poet Weill did. He quickly learned that "the populace clearly distinguished between the migrant German whose language was usually *allemanisch/alsatian* (German Alsatian) . . . and those who spoke only French. In many shops it was made clear to us [emigrant Germans] that we were not wanted."[33] The division between Alsatians and Germans was also perpetuated within the university environment. Edinger and his roommate, a foreign student from America, made it a point to avoid all social contact with Alsatians.

> We generally took our mid-day meal at a student cafeteria and, in the evenings, we would buy food to eat in our rooms. Normally, friends would join us, with their own food in hand, and afterwards we would venture off to a *specifically German Beerhall.* . . . We had no contact with Alsatian students other than in lectures where we kept our distance from them.[34]

The description of Ludwig Edinger's university years portrays an independent young man enjoying the freedom and carefree existence of a German university student. Like many of his colleagues, Edinger took particular pleasure in attending the theater and visiting the home of one of his professors when invited for a Sunday open house. During the lengthy semester breaks he traveled in typical student style, sleeping on the trains at night and staying with relatives when possible.[35] As a student in Strasbourg, tensions between native Alsatians and Germans accentuated Edinger's German identity and diminished the importance of his Jewishness. While in Alsace, Edinger was perceived as, and defined himself as, a German. Had he studied in Berlin or at some other German university with a large Jewish student population, Edinger's identity would most likely have been significantly different. The heightened sense of Germanness he experienced while in Strasbourg reveals that the process of self-definition is profoundly affected by one's environment.

The centrality of place to one's identity is a theme that resonates in the memoir literature of Jewish students who studied in Munich, especially if they spent time at more than one German university. For Arthur Czellitzer, the move from Breslau to Munich profoundly influenced how he positioned himself within student society.[36] During his first semester in Breslau, he was actively recruited by, and subsequently joined, a "free fraternity" by the name of *Alemannen*. Free fraternities like *Alemannen* rejected the dress code of the traditional corporations, which dictated that their members wear associational hats and bands bearing the group's colors, but emulated, to a large extent, the ritualized format of drinking. Czellitzer explains that most of *Alemannen's* activities centered around drinking: Wednesday nights were reserved for its formal *Kneipen,* and Sunday mornings were dedicated to the obligatory *Frühschoppen.* Since both events involved copious beer consumption and Czellitzer was not a "heavy drinker," he found these activities distasteful and began immediately looking for a way out of the association. As it turned out, the most convenient way to disassociate himself from *Alemannen* was to relocate to another university. After lengthy discussions with his family during the semester break about moving to Munich, Czellitzer arrived in the Bavarian capital in April 1890. Of his membership in a corporate society Czellitzer says that once he left Breslau, he "had nothing more to do with *Alemannen* and he never spoke of his experiences with them."[37] The decision to leave Breslau was a conscious decision to redefine his position within student society.

Arthur Czellitzer's first glimpse of life outside of Prussia left a deep and lasting impression on the young man.

> Munich was a new world for me. Everything in Bavaria was different, from the color of the postage stamps to the female street sweepers; from the four horse beer wagons to the numerous nuns and monks [*sic*] on all of the streets. In Prussia, [people of different] castes and ranks were clearly separated, but in Munich, people of all stations sit together when drinking beer.[38]

Clearly taken by the more fluid social hierarchy of Bavaria, Czellitzer found the environment intriguing and much to his liking. Although he went on to become a well-known ophthalmologist and founded the *Gesellschaft für jüdische Familienforschung* (the Society for Jewish Genealogical Studies), Czellitzer devoted more time to honing his skills at the billiard table than he did to pursuing his studies. After arriving in Munich with a few friends from Breslau, Czellitzer and his pals soon became acquainted with other students from northern Germany. Before long, this circle of university students turned into a regular but still loosely formed group that met weekly in a local pub.[39] Similar to Ludwig Edinger, who found himself more comfortable in the company of other native Germans when studying in Strasbourg, Arthur Czellitzer's closest comrades hailed from Germany's northern environs. Even though people of Munich from different "classes" may have shared a table while enjoying a fresh glass of Bavarian beer, meaningful social interaction and long-term friendships were significantly influenced by one's background and place of origin.

The impact of place on an individual's identity is also evident in the memoir of Georg Witkowski. Born in 1863, Witkowski attended the Universities of Leipzig and Munich before becoming a professor of literary history in 1896.[40] Shortly after arriving in Leipzig for his first semester of university study, Witkowski decided to join a scholarly association that, unlike traditional student organizations, did not concern itself with duelling.

> I immediately joined the *Neuphilologische Verein* [the New Philological Society], a group which I found to be the friendliest. There were about twenty members, almost all of whom were without substantial means and existed from stipends, *Freitischen* [free meals] and [wages] from private tutoring. Their lack of money, however, neither dampened their zest for life nor diminished their enthusiasm for study.[41]

Members of the New Philological Society met regularly to perform grammar exercises and sharpen their writing skills in German and the Romance languages. At the official meetings, the students listened to a scholarly lecture that was usually delivered by a member of the association, although occasionally a university *dozent* (lecturer) would do the honors. Lest one think that the associational gatherings were dedicated solely to the minutiae of German grammar and the mundane chore of improving one's expository writing, Witkowski is quick to point out that the *Neuphilologische Verein*'s academic endeavors were always followed by lively socializing and copious beer drinking. According to Witkowski, the beer-drinking sessions often proceeded "according to the *Comment* [the ritualistic code] of the duelling fraternities" and, like the corporate societies, the evening *Kneipen* operated under the tyrannical authority of the elders. When members of the association violated the well-established beer-drinking etiquette, they were fined either a "half or a whole beer," a penalty that meant they were required to drink the prescribed amount in one breath. If an offense were truly "serious," the offender would be banished from the table. When the level of drunkenness was sufficient, the younger members, Witkowski included, were sent out to the local marketplace to engage in a bit of sophomoric hooliganism. A favorite activity of Witkowski and his cohorts was to overturn the marketplace stalls that had already been set in place for the following day's business. The objective of this escapade was not to destroy property but to be apprehended by a local security guard and brought before the university court. A truly "successful" outing garnered the offender a few days' incarceration in the university jail or *Universitätskarzer*, a confinement that generally was spent in the company of friends, drinking beer and playing skat.[42]

In addition to holding scholarly discussions and engaging in ritualistic beer drinking, members of the New Philological Society attended the theater and the opera and staged their own performances. It was the custom of Witkowski's scholarly association to perform short plays in either English or French at all official celebrations. During the Christmas season they put on short musical pieces composed by members of the *Neuphilologische Verein* that lewdly parodied the mannerisms of their professors and fellow members.[43]

The New Philological society at the University of Leipzig was comprised of university students who shared an interest in literature and the study of language and a common desire to enjoy their student years to the fullest. Together they advanced their academic knowledge of philology, engaged in ritualistic beer-drinking sessions and pursued a variety of social activities. Witkowski's interest in literature and his enjoyment of a good time attracted him to this particular association, not his political views or his religious heritage. Evidently, the similar socioeconomic background of the associational members assumed greater importance in bringing the group together and cementing the bonds of friendship than the fact that Witkowski was a Jew. Once ensconced in Munich, however, the regional peculiarities of Bavaria and its different societal forces altered the composition of his primary social group.

Georg Witkowski's uninhibited nature and ability to establish friendships were character traits that served him well while studying at the University of Munich. Shortly after his arrival in southern Germany, Witkowski ventured to the theater for an evening's entertainment. While watching the play from the "standing" section of the theater, a location commonly filled with university students, he struck up a conversation with the student next to him. At the conclusion of the performance the young man invited Witkowski to meet his friends, a group of about a dozen students who, as Witkowski explains, were "all sons of good families" from the Rhineland region bordering France. In no time at all Witkowski was on good terms with members of the group, many of whom met daily for meals and rendezvoused in the evenings to drink beer and socialize. On their choice of eating establishments, Witkowski writes "that for a long time the entire group ate at a Kosher restaurant, an establishment that was almost devoid of Christians. For forty-five marks a month they received outstanding mid-day and evening meals."[44] Apparently Georg Witkowski had become friends with a group of Jewish students who shared his keen eye for an inexpensive meal and a predilection for evenings spent in Munich's convivial *Kneipen*. Whether the decidedly Catholic character of Bavaria compelled Witkowski to establish a Jewish social coterie is, unfortunately, difficult to determine.

The religious environment of Germany's large southern state, however, provided the backdrop for the university-sponsored costume balls of *Fasching*, Germany's pre-Lenten carnival season. For centuries German Catholics have celebrated the final days before the onset of Lent, the forty-day period that precedes Easter, with raucous celebrations. Although modern Mardis Gras festivities in New Orleans and Carnival in Rio de Janeiro are renowned for their sexual promiscuity and the presence of scantily clad individuals, the balls frequented by Witkowski were off-limits to women. While women were present at official university functions and formal dances, the topsy-turvy world of *Fasching* provided a perfect opportunity for male university students to engage in atypical social behavior. According to Witkowski, the rooms at these events would be

> teeming with male characters dressed in the clothing of the opposite sex, with a level of deception that was truly astounding. On one occasion when the theme of the ball was "Robbers and Bandits," brilliant fabrications had transformed the large, plain rooms [of the university] into a den of thieves. . . . It would have been difficult to recognize my young, handsome friend Nöther who was dressed as a bandit's wench in a low cut costume, had he not removed his breasts which he had fashioned out of a flesh painted rubber ball cut into two and, from time to time, juggled them.[45]

For another ball, Witkowski, with the help of "his landlady's night cream and a curly white wig," appeared as a woman and danced the night away with a young gentleman dressed as a suicide victim in "tails and a white neck-tie."[46] Even though *Fasching* and its accompanying festivities were intended to be outrageous events, the prohibition against female guests and the willingness of young men to not only dress but also act as women, suggests that German university students of this era were content to live their lives in a male environment, while their relationships with women were limited to traditionally defined gender roles. Not until the twentieth century would women be admitted to German universities and, in so doing, begin to challenge the roles constructed by men.[47]

The need for Georg Witkowski to reestablish himself in Munich demonstrates the historical contingency of one's identity. Relocating to a new university meant that students had to find new friends, establish new routines, and, in essence, redefine themselves. Although the main features of Witkowski's personality, his penchant for camaraderie, outrageous behavior, and beer remained relatively constant, the activities in which he engaged and the individuals with whom he associated were unmistakably conditioned by the location and temporal setting in which he operated. What remains unclear is whether environment or personality ultimately determines one's choice of friends. Absent a consensus on the relative importance of "nature versus nurture," the following discussion can only offer additional snapshots of Jewish students as they maneuvered within the university environment.

FORMING A SOCIAL COTERIE

Without a doubt, building a network of friends is of paramount importance to identity formation. Unlike students who joined Jewish fraternal associations and quickly established tight-knit social circles, unincorporated students utilized a variety of techniques to negotiate their way through the German university system. One strategy commonly employed by Jewish students was to join a *wissenschaftliche Verein*, or scholarly association.[48] By definition, these organizations were religiously neutral and generally not organized in a hierarchical manner. Although principally a venue for academic enrichment, the activities of Georg Witkowski suggest that many scholarly organizations also provided a forum for lively social discourse. In spite of the fact that the *wissenschaftliche Vereine* exerted little influence on the student body at large, especially in comparison to the *Corps* and the *Burschenschaften*, they played an important role in the lives, intellectual development, and process of identity formation for many Jewish university students.[49]

Adolf Heilberg's membership in an academic association vividly illuminates this reality. Born in Breslau in 1858, the high point of his university career was the year that he spent in Leipzig, from the winter of 1876 until the summer of 1877.[50] While in Leipzig, Heilberg belonged to an organization known as the *Akademischen volkswirtschaftlichen Verein* (The Academic Economic Association), a group that sponsored discussions and debates on contemporary political issues. Shortly after its founding, the association's evening discussions regularly drew more than one hundred students, who heatedly debated the policies of Otto von Bismarck's newly founded National Liberal Party and the emerging bitter campaigns of the Prussian government against the Social Democrats. Even though the Prussian police and the state prosecuting attorney attempted to clamp down on the Social Democratic press and the meetings of the SPD before the passing of the first "Socialist Law" in 1878, Heilberg and his comrades regularly attended gatherings arranged by the Social Democrats. They then would typically retire to a local pub for "ale-house" discussions on the pros and cons of social democracy. As Heilberg's self-defined political outlook was "left-bourgeoisie," he stood in opposition to both socialism and right-wing nationalism.[51] The profound interest in contemporary political issues suggests that, like many university students past and present, Adolf Heilberg's worldview expanded tremendously during his years in higher education.

As a student in Leipzig Adolf Heilberg's involvement in a *paritätisch* (nondenominational) scholarly association brought him into contact with a "lively and vibrant circle of students that consisted of Christians, Jews, native Germans and foreigners." He describes his fellow members as people with a wide range of views, individuals with whom he interacted at meals, during conversations in the pub, on walks, and on more extended journeys.[52] The engagement with students of different religious backgrounds and political opinions reveals that during this period of his life, Adolf Heilberg's identity, both private and public, was not greatly influenced by his Jewish heritage.

Curt Rosenberg, whom we have discussed previously, also joined a scholarly association during his tenure at the University of Freiburg.[53] According to Rosenberg's descriptions of the *sozialwissenschaftlichen Vereinigung* (social scientific organization) to which he belonged, he and his fellow members spent countless hours engaged in political discussions about social democracy and Marxism. Although most of his colleagues did not officially belong to a political party during their student years, many went on to become prominent members of the Social Democratic Party. Of those he mentions, Herr Frank became a member of the Bavarian Parliament, Kurt Rosenfeld was elected as a representative of the *Reichstag*, Herr Grumbach was selected as a representative from Alsace, and Oskar Meyer became the parliamentary state secretary during the Weimar Republic.[54] Participating in an academic association functioned as a crucial "formative experience" in the lifelong process of self-definition for Curt Rosenberg and his colleagues, an experience through which they gained exposure to events beyond the walls of the academic environment. Membership in a scholarly organization also provided the primary context in which Adolf Heilberg, Curt Rosenberg, Georg Witkowski, and countless other German Jewish university students developed their social coterie. Yet, as common as it was for both Jewish and Gentile students to become friendly with fellow members of their academic associations, there were alternate ways for unaffiliated students to establish friendships.

Students who did not associate with fraternal or academic organizations often moved within the circles of the so-called Free Students. We have already observed that in 1896, unaffiliated students at the University of Leipzig created the first *Finkenschaft*, or Free Students' association. In May 1900, the various free-student groups established the interuniversity association known as the *Freistudentenschaft* (Free Student Body).[55] Its goals were to promote the acquisition of *Bildung*, to represent the interests of the unaffiliated students, and to protect the "honor" of all free students. The *Freistudentenschaft* observed "the strict neutrality toward other student groups [by] offering as well as demanding tolerance" and under no circumstances did they "take a position on religious and political matters."[56] Given the Free Students' neutral stance on religion, it is not surprising that many Jewish students joined its ranks and became officers. Although the large contingent of Jewish officers caused resentment among some Gentile members, the issue was debated and put to rest with the following official statement: "It should be harmless and uncontroversial for Jewish comrades to participate in our offices. However, equal rights do not imply equal value. In the interest of the movement and the reconciliation between the races [greater] reserve is imperative."[57] Apparently, even the tolerant *Freistudentenschaft* was influenced by the ideas of race science that dominated western European academic discourse at the close of the nineteenth century.[58]

One German Jew who utilized the *Freistudentenschaft* as a primary base for social discourse was Moritz Goldstein (b. 1880). Before beginning his university studies, Goldstein had looked forward to joining a student corporate society. But while members of the *Corps, Burschenschaften,* and Jewish associations feverishly sought to enlist new members, Goldstein recalls that no one made the slightest attempt to recruit him.[59] Reflecting on his rejection, he writes that

"No, I was no true student. I was completely distanced from the pleasant, care-free existence [of other students]. . . . Since no student association had concerned itself with me, I participated in the life of the unincorporated students, the *Freien Studentenschaft*.[60]

Even though Goldstein joined the association of Free Students out of loneliness and a desire to overcome his isolation, during his three semesters as a member of the Berlin *Finkenschaft*, he formed no real friendships. Moritz Goldstein's memoir depicts the life of a quintessential loner, an individual, who in spite of his desire to interact socially with other students, had trouble making friends.

Throughout his student life Moritz Goldstein was prone to illness and, on the advice of a physician, he transferred to the University of Munich to take advantage of the warmer climate. Upon arriving in Munich, Goldstein looked forward to the pleasant hustle and bustle of the city. Unfortunately for Goldstein, however, the convivial ambiance of the famed Bavarian city could not overcome his predilection for sorrow and self-pity. On his first few weeks in Munich, Goldstein recalls that

for the time being, I was completely alone and without any social contact. . . . I knew nobody in Munich and no one knew me. I was so completely alone during my first weeks in Munich that apart from my old landlady with whom it really was not possible to have a conversation, I spent days without speaking a word. . . . As I did not want to spend the evenings alone in my depressing student accommodations, I went to a beer establishment [*Bierlokal*]. There, on one occasion, I got into a lively conversation with a man sitting at my table who claimed to be a painter. I took [this conversation] to be a turning point in my life . . . but I never saw the painter again.[61]

As the semester proceeded, Goldstein's landlady took in another boarder, a Catholic student from Posen. In spite of the lack of common interests between Goldstein and his fellow boarder, the two spent a great deal of time together. Later in the semester when Goldstein ran into a student whom he had known only in passing while studying in Berlin, he enthusiastically invited the man to join him and his housemate for a meal. After this first encounter, the unlikely threesome "were together almost daily throughout the semester." Yet, as Goldstein sadly admits: "I can not really say that we became friends."[62]

Moritz Goldstein did not experience the carefree existence and ubiquitous friendships common to most university students. He escaped his loneliness by writing articles and plays that offered refuge from a lonely and alienated existence. His position within student society was primarily informed by his melancholy personality. Questions of his religious heritage and its relationship to German nationalism were as foreign to him as the ability to engage in productive social discourse. The defining feature of Goldstein's public identity was his membership in the *Freistudentschaft*, an "organization" comprised of individuals who did not belong to a corporate or academic association. His entire student life was veiled in anonymity, a fact sadly attested to by the use of pseudonyms for his published articles.[63] Moritz Goldstein's description of his university career provides a glimpse into the life of an individual who is typically absent from historians' narrative descriptions of the period.

Not all students who joined the Free Students' association, however, were as socially inept and prone to melancholy as Goldstein. For some, the formality and pomp of fraternity life was simply not to their liking. Ernst Jolowicz's (b. 1883) experiences with a corporate student association convinced him that he was not suited for membership in a traditional student organization.

> Since my brother was one of *Alsatia's* (a *freischlagende Verbindung*) "old gentlemen" in Leipzig, I was invited to participate in their activities as a guest and a prospective member. Every Saturday night for several weeks I attended their beer drinking parties, where, as a guest, I was fortunately not compelled, as were the "foxes," to drink excessively. I did not enjoy it. Not that I had any scruples against enjoyment or even against drinking, but the formality, the pomp, the excessive ceremonials, all seemed to me to be senseless, and ridiculous, and what was worse, boring. . . . After about six weeks of this sort of trial period one of the officers came to my home, and formally and officially asked me whether I was interested in joining their fraternity. I replied that I would not join.[64]

Not only did Jolowicz refuse to join, but he also insulted the members of *Alsatia* by declaring that "the atmosphere of the meetings and the behavior of the individual members were not to [his] liking." Only the fact that his brother was an esteemed *Alter Herr* saved him from having to defend his honor in a series of duels with the three ranking officers of the organization.[65]

After his experience with *Alsatia*, Jolowicz joined the *Freistudentenschaft*. As a member of the literary section of the Leipzig Free Students' association, Ernst Jolowicz "participated actively in discussions, presented one or two lectures [himself], and took part in some dramatic productions by directing, dancing and acting."[66] On one occasion, he played a minor role in a semiprofessional production of Schiller's "Die Rauber" that made a short European tour. The troupe's travels through Germany and Holland were a high point of Jolowicz's university career, a twenty-day period that he describes as being "full of gaiety and camaraderie."[67]

Ernst Jolowicz's theatrical activities stemmed directly from his association with the literary section of the *Freistudentenschaft*. Unlike Moritz Goldstein, who joined the Free Students' association as a refuge from isolation and rejection, Jolowicz was neither a loner nor a social recluse. For him the organization simply provided a vehicle to pursue his love of theater and make friends.[68] As members of the *Freistudentenschaft*, both Goldstein and Jolowicz fashioned public identities that accentuated their roles as university students and were entirely devoid of religious characteristics. The memoirs of Moritz Goldstein and Ernst Jolowicz provide no evidence that being Jewish had any impact on how they positioned themselves within student society. The segregated nature of German universities notwithstanding, the experiences of Goldstein, Jolowicz, and students who joined academic associations suggest that many Jewish students were not compelled to develop social coteries that consisted entirely of fellow Jews. Apparently, the "burning" issues of *Deutschtum* and *Judentum* did not inform the process of identity formation employed by every German Jew in Imperial Germany.

ALL IN THE PURSUIT OF *BILDUNG*

One aspect of student life that was consistent from university to university and virtually indistinguishable between Jewish and Gentile students was the commitment to the pursuit of *Bildung*. The emphasis on self-cultivation meant that a student's experience outside of the classroom was as important to one's education as knowledge gleaned from lectures. The raison d'être of traditional corporate associations was to facilitate the process of character formation. Duelling, ritualized beer drinking, and the ability to conduct one's self in an honorable manner were integral to this process. For the noncorporate student, the pursuit of *Bildung* was carried out by attending the theater, symphony, and opera, and by exploring the environs of Europe. Even hiking, an activity generally associated with recreation, was thought to develop a sensitivity toward the natural environment and a respect for a higher spiritual authority that characterized the cultivated individual. This is not to say that members of student fraternities did not partake in these activities, but students who did not have access to a predefined format for acquiring *Bildung* engaged in these extracurricular activities with particular zeal.

Ernst Herzfeld's experiences epitomize the efforts of many nonaffiliated Jewish university students to acquire *Bildung*. Born in Posen in 1874 to an upper-middle-class Jewish family, Herzfeld studied law at the Universities of Freiburg, Munich, and Berlin.[69] Following the completion of his *Abitur*, Herzfeld and two *Gymnasium* colleagues departed for Freiburg to inaugurate their academic careers. For Herzfeld, the trip to Freiburg was only the second time in his life that he had ventured beyond the borders of his native Posen. Having traveled at night to save the expense of hotel accommodations, Herzfeld and his two traveling companions arrived in Freiburg at 5:00 A.M. On the differences between Posen and the southwest region of Germany, Herzfeld remarks that although "winter had already begun in [my] northeastern homeland, the *Glycinien* [*sic*] and lilacs were blooming in the fields of southern Germany and brilliant, warm sunshine brightened up the world."[70]

Upon arrival at the train station, Herzfeld and his companions were greeted and actively recruited by members of a local chapter of the *Burschenschaften*. According to Herzfeld, the young men

took our bags and showered us with so much attention and kindness, that we inexperienced youths were not prepared to refuse their assistance. Although we were not really looking for a hotel, we were nevertheless escorted to one and assisted to bed. When we appeared for breakfast, our mentors were there [to greet us]. They accompanied us as we looked for living accommodations and with their assistance, we achieved rather rapid success. Now, at this point, I alone was questioned whether perhaps one of my friends was Jewish. My reply was apparently not the expected response for when I said that in fact all three of us were Jewish, it brought an immediate conclusion to what up until that moment had been a truly warm relationship.[71]

Subsequent recruiting attempts were cut short when Herzfeld promptly declared to all interlocutors that he and his friends were Jewish. Ernst Herzfeld's experiences in Freiburg demonstrate two salient features of life for Jewish university students. First, many individuals made the transition from home to the university in the company of *Gymnasium* colleagues. And, by the mid-1890s, Jewish university students were largely excluded from both the *Corps* and the *Burschenschaften*.

Apart from the fact that Herzfeld's traveling companions were Jewish, the manner in which he conducted himself within the public sphere and eagerly pursued the acquisition of *Bildung* was not particularly influenced by his being Jewish. Traveling, hiking, and theatergoing were central to his university experience. Herzfeld comments that during the summer semester of 1894, "[his] studies demanded little of [him]." After listening to a number of "hairsplitting" lectures on the distinction between "property" (*Eigentum*) and "possession" (*Besitz*), it quickly appeared to Herzfeld and his friends that the "Black Forest was incomparably more important and interesting than the university." Consequently, the young men spent countless days rambling through the local forest, exploring its streams, trails, and hills.[72]

The following semester brought Ernst Herzfeld to Munich for the continuation of his university career. Much like Arthur Czellitzer, Herzfeld found the atmosphere in Bavaria to his liking, especially the openness with which the native population socialized with people from all walks of life.[73] In Munich, as in Freiburg, socializing with friends and attending the theater assumed a prominent position in Herzfeld's life. Even though university students were able to purchase theater tickets at a reduced price, one had to have the wherewithal to negotiate the hurdles of purchasing tickets in order to take advantage of the student discount. Herzfeld's description of his theatergoing elucidates its time-consuming nature.

> To obtain an inexpensive gallery ticket, a student had to arrive at the box office very early in the morning and stand in line. In the gallery, there was seating for only about a third of the spectators and to acquire a seat, one had to arrive two hours before the beginning of the performance and wait for an hour and a half, tightly squeezed between iron gratings, until the doors opened. As soon as they finally opened, a race up five flights of stairs began immediately. The remaining half hour before the beginning of the performance was hardly sufficient to recover [one's composure] and consume the buttered bread that one had brought with them.[74]

Obviously, the pursuit of *Bildung* was a full-time commitment that required ample patience and fortitude.

Throughout the nineteenth century, exploring the European countryside was an integral component of one's university experience and central to the acquisition of *Bildung*. By the end of the century, students could still travel in a relatively inexpensive manner, provided they took full advantage of discounted rail tickets and low-cost sleeping accommodations available to university students. Arthur Czellitzer's account of his student years reveals that traveling and, especially, hiking were his true passions. Portions of his memoir read more like an enticing travel guide than a description of university life. He says that his deep-seated "wanderlust" prompted him to utilize every spare moment to ramble through Europe's beautiful mountain regions. His mountain excursions ranged from pleasurable day hikes to two-week hiking vacations through the Italian and Swiss Alps.[75]

In preparation for the trips, Czellitzer and his traveling companions sketched out detailed agendas, planning the appropriate train connections, locating the least expensive accommodations, and selecting the desired trails. Their days typically began at 4:00 A.M., when they caught the earliest train to their hiking destination and hiked throughout the day. Czellitzer and his friends used every minute of daylight to explore the selected location, and they often arrived at their predetermined destination in time for only a light supper and some convivial conversation recalling the day's adventures and sights before retiring to bed.

Hiking, for Arthur Czellitzer, was by no means exclusively a summertime event. On one particularly rain-soaked outing he explains that "the trail was still heavily covered in snow and, [consequently,] we climbed with great effort and difficulty until we reached our overnight destination." When Czellitzer and his friends arrived at the inn, they discovered that they were not the only students on the trail that particular day, for the restaurant was filled with a number of university-aged young men who had also endured the harsh weather.[76] The pleasure of negotiating a challenging, snow-packed trail, experiencing the satisfaction and relief that comes with arriving at one's destination after an arduous experience in the outdoors, and then reliving the day's adventures and mishaps with one's comrades by the warmth of an evening fire are experiences that leave an indelible impression on one's character.

Arthur Czellitzer's most memorable excursions were those that he shared with his uncle, Max Schlesinger. Czellitzer's excitement at having received an invitation from Uncle Max to accompany him on a two-week tour of the Dolomite region in the Italian Alps inspired him to write the following postcard to his mother.

Who is the luckiest soul under the sun? I who am now sitting in [lecture]. Tonight I am going to hear [Wagner's] "Walkuere" at the Hoftheater. On Sunday I will travel to the blue Königsee and, in eight days, I will be in the Dolomites, speaking Italian with Uncle Max. Hurrah![77]

After sixteen days of touring with his uncle in a style considerably more luxurious than that a student could normally afford, Czellitzer returned to Munich a bit "spoiled" but ready to resume his student routine. He writes, "I enjoyed the last six weeks in Munich to the fullest: evenings in the Hofthrater [sic], Beerhall concerts and Billiards—The days were filled with hiking and [viewing] the international art exhibit."[78] Only after the conclusion of the summer semester did Arthur Czellitzer assume a more studious routine. Following the cessation of lectures, he returned to his parents' home in Breslau and spent the entire semester break preparing for his first round of state examinations. The life of a German university student and the acquisition of *Bildung* dictated that students worked when necessary but recreated as often as possible!

The memoirs of Ernst Herzfeld, Arthur Czellitzer, and the other noncorporate students that we have examined provide highly personal and informative descriptions of the lives of German Jewish university students. The activities depicted in their memoirs portray an overwhelming concern with life's extracurricular activities and the pursuit of *Bildung*. Regardless of one's socioeconomic background, political outlook, or religious heritage, the drive for self-improvement and a commitment to a diverse and carefree lifestyle were hallmark features of the identities fashioned by German university students in the nineteenth century.

The shared commitment to *Bildung* notwithstanding, the university experience for nineteenth-century German Jews was not identical to that of their Gentile cohorts. Whether one participated in corporate student life or chose not to join one of these associations, it was impossible to escape the anti-Jewish sentiment that pervaded the universities of the Second Reich. Exclusion, derogatory comments about Jews, and, at times, outright aggressive behavior confronted all German Jews within the university environment. Although members of Jewish student associations responded to anti-Jewish animosity by adopting explicitly

Jewish public identities, antisemitism did not predetermine the paradigms of self-definition for all Jewish students. As the memoirs of noncorporate Jewish university students reveal, it was possible to be a Jew in a socially exclusive environment without letting antisemitism become the focal point of one's identity.

6

A Coat of Many Colors:
German Jewry on the Eve of
World War I

At the dawn of the twentieth century, Germany was a nation on the move. The demographic balance had shifted from the rural environs to the cities, industrial production surpassed that of Britain, and Emperor Wilhelm II launched an aggressive campaign to secure Germany's position as a world power. Central to the Kaiser's *Weltpolitik* was a nationalist program to ameliorate the political and ideological divisions endemic to German society. The goal of the *Sammlungspolitik* was to strengthen "Germany's position abroad while cementing an antidemocratic status quo at home."[1] Not only did the imperial government fail to realize its objectives, but its policies exacerbated tensions already present within a deeply fractured society. One result of this failed policy was that differences became increasingly pronounced within the paradigms of self-definition fashioned by all Germans.

In the decade and a half before the outbreak of World War I, German Jews added new flourishes and greater definition to an already rich and vibrant tapestry of German Jewish identity. Their handiwork was prominently displayed at German universities as religiously observant Jewish students established their own organizations and nationalist student associations competed for the support of the Jewish student body. In constructing their identities

Jewish nationalists employed concepts of race, religion, and national origin to distinguish themselves from both their coreligionists and their Gentile colleagues. Religious Jews, on the other hand, focused exclusively on *Halakhah*, or Jewish law, to set themselves apart from nonobservant Jews and determine the criteria for membership in their organizations. For the first generation of female university students, gender rather than nationality or religious heritage largely determined their social groupings. Members of each group, however, drew from the cultural wellsprings of both *Deutschtum* and *Judentum* as they secured their positions within student society.

WOMEN AT GERMAN UNIVERSITIES

Beginning in 1896, women were allowed to audit courses at German universities. Previously they had been dependent upon the good will and talents of university *dozenten* (unpaid lecturers) for their instruction. In 1901 Baden was the first state to officially enroll women. Bavaria followed Baden's example in 1904, and Prussia, never known for its progressive policies, followed suit in 1908. By 1914 women accounted for approximately 7 percent of all German university students; Jewish women comprised 12.9 percent of the female student body.[2]

Breaking into a clearly defined male environment was no easy task. Nathan Stein, a student at the University of Berlin, recalls one professor of psychiatry who "tolerated" the presence of women at his lectures for the first time during the winter semester of 1899/1900.[3] Walter Heinemann relates that when a professor in national economics at the University of Berlin began his lecture with the greeting, "Ladies and Gentlemen" (*Meine Damen und Herren*), the students voiced their disapproval. Each time the professor began his lecture with this greeting he was met with the same vocal response. When he altered his introduction and simply stated *"Meine Herren,"* he was interrupted once again, but this time with thunderous applause.[4]

As difficult as it was for female students to make their way within the university environment, the memoir literature of Jewish women suggests that their experiences were, in many ways, similar to those of their male counterparts. Making the transition from home to the university, forming social coteries, and acquiring *Bildung* are themes that resonate within the descriptions of university life found in these sources. Although gender clearly shaped their identities, the societal norms of German universities also influenced how Jewish women positioned themselves within this segment of German society. To illuminate this situation and highlight the types of identities fashioned by Jewish women who studied at German universities before World War I, the following discussion focuses on the lives of three women: Rahel Straus, Frieda Hirsch, and Käte Frankenthal. While their experiences are neither typical nor statistically representative, they do offer insight into the daily routines and the process of self-definition employed by Jewish women who attended German universities.

Rahel Straus was the first female student permitted to study medicine at the University of Heidelberg. Born in Karlsruhe in 1880, Straus was unique among Jewish women university students in that she came from a traditional Jewish home, received a thorough Jewish education, and became an avowed supporter of Zionism before she began her university studies.[5] Her decision to study at university, therefore, necessitated that she strike an extremely delicate balance between her commitment to religious Judaism and her desire to become a physician. Although the centrality of Judaism to her identity distinguishes Straus from most female Jewish students, the difficulties that she faced were shared by others.

On her first semester at the University of Heidelberg in the fall of 1899, before she was officially matriculated, Straus writes that

> naturally Ernst [her brother] was a proper academic citizen [university student] while I was only an auditor. Due to my shyness, this situation caused all sorts of problems. For each lecture that I wanted to attend, I had to seek out the professor in his office and ask him permission to audit [his course]. They were all quite nice and friendly to me, but each one inquired somewhat astoundedly about my age—I was nineteen at the time—and asked why I had begun my university studies at such a young age. I quickly discovered that I was much younger than the other female auditors whom I encountered at lectures.[6]

An additional burden for Straus was that, as a female auditor, she was not eligible to purchase discounted railway tickets. As a result, her daily commute between Mannheim and Heidelberg was significantly more expensive than it was for her brother Ernst.[7] Even after women received the right to matriculate at German universities, they confronted a system that was ill-prepared to accept them on an equal basis. As Marion Kaplan astutely observes, "in the first decade in which women enrolled in the universities, Jewish women were keenly aware that sexism, rather than anti-Semitism, was the predominant obstacle in their paths."[8]

To succeed at German universities, female students had to be resilient, resourceful, and determined to overcome the numerous barriers placed in front of them. The challenge for women who wanted to become doctors was particularly daunting. The study of medicine was considered to be an exclusively male domain and most women avoided the extreme anti-female bias of the medical faculty by majoring in the humanities.[9] Rahel Straus's desire to become a doctor, however, propelled her into the heart of this male-dominated environment. After securing the financial support necessary to study medicine, Straus met with the dean of the medical faculty, hoping to obtain permission to switch majors in the middle of the semester.[10] During this meeting, she was not only denied the right to alter her course of study but also told that "she had no idea of the colossal demands that the study of medicine placed on one's body and soul, head and heart." The intimation was that women could not endure the stress and strain of the medical profession and that Straus should select a course of study "more suitable" to a female.[11] When, after successfully completing two and a half years of her medical studies, Straus entered the dean's lecture hall, he reminded her that he had not expected to see her again and stated, in front of the class, "I know women [and] none of them can endure this!" Straus's rejoinder of, "Yes, you know women, but mostly when they are sick," engendered a laugh from the professor and, from that moment on, the two of them "were good friends."[12]

Outside the lecture halls, women faced additional challenges. Having rejected their traditional roles, female university students had to counter charges of being "anti-female" and "unnatural," and they were conscious of the need to act as "proper bourgeois ladies."[13] The romanticized lifestyle of drinking and dueling, cherished and sought after by many male students, was not an experience shared by women. As Else Croner, a contemporary of Rahel Straus, recalls, an unbridgeable gap [exists] between male and female students. . . . For male students this period of study is a precious thing in and of itself. They are delighted. . . . They enjoy every day. . . . The women students that I have met [are] earnest and conscientious. . . . Their student years are not the golden time of freedom, but only a transition period to reach their goals.[14]

In spite of the obstacles faced by women, their experiences were not entirely different from those of men. In striking similarity to male university students, the first generation of women students, shortly after entering the university environment, formed their own organizations. Rahel Straus comments that since the universities were already divided into groups, it was "no wonder that the desire surfaced among women [students] to come together in such a manner."[15] In their early stages, women's student groups were organized differently than those of their male counterparts. Having battled family expectations and societal norms to enter the university, the first generation of female students was an independent and a strong-willed group of individuals. Consequently, they would not tolerate regulations that dictated their behavior and mode of social intercourse.[16] As Rahel Straus explains,

We made our female student group as free as possible: one was not compelled to do anything and one came when they wanted. There was no *Commers* [ritualistic celebrations]. Neither *Fuchse* [initiates] nor *Bursche* [full-fledged members], neither exams nor political orientation. All female auditors, regardless of their nationality or religion, could become members. These conditions remained in effect until ultimately we became a proper female student association. . . . I look back fondly at our stimulating evenings in which interesting women sat together and *participated in the construction of a new female identity* [*beteiligt am Aufbau eines neuen Frauendaseins*].[17]

Straus's observations reveal the centrality of gender in her, and her female colleagues', public identities.

Following Straus's graduation, however, women students began to distinguish themselves from one another on the basis of nationality and religion. Only a few weeks after the members had thrown her a warm and beautiful going away party, Rahel Straus's organization disbanded. The new generation of female university students that succeeded her and her associates "was already inclined to present themselves completely differently." According to Straus: "They wanted a true student association . . . one from which foreigners and Jews were excluded. Our entire group, including myself as the only female Jewish student, withdrew from the new group."[18] Within a span of only five or six years, the pressures of a highly segregated society profoundly altered the manner in which Jewish women positioned themselves within the university environment.

Frieda Hirsch (1890–1965) belonged to the second generation of female students to attend German universities. She was the third of six children born to a economically comfortable and religiously observant Karlsruhe family. Describing the centrality of Judaism to her childhood identity, Hirsch states that she and her siblings went to synagogue every Saturday and that the family's closest friends were other Jews.[19] Her father's desire to provide his children with a well-rounded education, however, meant that Frieda's social circle extended beyond an exclusively Jewish milieu. When she enrolled at a local *Gymnasium* for girls, she was the only Jew in her class. Although Frieda received special permission to be absent from classes on Saturdays and Jewish holidays, she does not mention being ostracized from her classmates or having difficulties establishing friendships. Frieda's upbringing and educational program conditioned her to navigate between Jewish and Gentile social circles at a very young age.[20]

After completing the *Abitur* in 1907 but before entering the University of Heidelberg as a full-time student in the fall of 1908, Frieda Hirsch lived at home, helped out with household chores in the morning, and attended lectures at the university in Karlsruhe in the afternoon. In spite of being unofficially engaged to Berti Hirsch, a confirmed Zionist, Frieda engaged in frequent social activities with other men. During her first year at the University in Karlsruhe, she befriended a non-Jewish university student and member of the *Burschenschaften* by the name of "B." Together the two young friends listened to lectures in philosophy and psychology, went cross-country skiing in the Black Forest, and attended concerts held in the local opera house. Although Hirsch claims that her parents got along quite well with the young man and enjoyed his company, it was clear to her from the outset that her father would never tolerate an "Aryan son-in-law." Even though the two young friends parted dramatically in the summer of 1908, they remained on good terms and corresponded frequently until Frieda's departure from Germany in 1933.[21]

In September 1908, Frieda Hirsch traveled unaccompanied to Heidelberg to search for a place to live and to prepare for the upcoming academic term. After spending six hours looking for suitable accommodations, she found what she wanted: "a spacious room with a bed, sofa, table, chairs, wardrobe and a chest of drawers with a marble top" on which she could place her alcohol stove. The room was illuminated with a petroleum lamp and heated with a coal oven. Compared to other student accommodations, Hirsch considered her quarters to be "opulent."[22]

While in Heidelberg, Frieda nurtured the hope of becoming a physician and attended lectures in the school of medicine. During this same period, Berti, her future husband, was also in Heidelberg completing the clinical rotations that were part of one's medical training. Each day the young couple took their midday meal at a kosher restaurant run by two brothers from Hungary. Here, they interacted with a small group of fellow students, both men and women, all of whom were close in age and from similar socioeconomic and religious backgrounds. Together, according to Frieda, they comprised a relaxed and amicable social group that engaged in friendly chatter typical for university students.[23]

For a short period of time Frieda Hirsch attended meetings of a women's organization. Although her memoir does not refer to the name of the organization or its primary focus, its unifying features were the gender of the membership and the desire to preserve the independence and equal status of female students. Toward this end the organization frowned upon activities such as male students assisting women with their coats but it encouraged its members to preserve their femininity. While a group of this sort provided valuable support for women as they confronted the well-defined masculine environment of German universities, Frieda soon relinquished her membership in the organization. As she puts it, "I already had sufficient company and diversion." The preestablished social coterie afforded by membership in a university association was something that the outgoing and gregarious Frieda neither needed nor desired. Between her fiancée and the regulars at her lunch table, she had established a well-defined and supportive Jewish coterie.[24]

Hirsch returned to Karlsruhe to continue her studies after spending only one year in Heidelberg. With two younger sisters in *Gymnasium*, her parents could no longer afford the luxury of maintaining an apartment for Frieda. Unlike in Heidelberg, where she dined daily with fellow Jews and spent her free time with her fiancée, Hirsch formed a "pure Aryan circle of friends" while living in Karlsruhe.[25] The close-knit group of young men and women met weekly in the Hirsch home for musical evenings, attended concerts, read and discussed the latest literature, and utilized Sundays for short trips to study art and architecture. The acquisition of *Bildung* occupied their every waking hour, with time spent outdoors assuming a preeminent role in their quest for self-cultivation.

Raised only a short distance from the Black Forest, Hirsch enjoyed cross-country skiing with a passion. As members of an academic ski association, she and her friends participated in numerous weekend ski adventures. Recalling the solitude and beauty of her trips, Hirsch writes that "the snow-covered terrain, the ice-clear air, the delicate silhouettes of evergreen trees blanketed in snow and the holy silence" that one encounters when gliding through a forest deep in its winter sleep made the ascent up the mountain a joy. The strain of rising early and skiing with heavily laden backpacks dissipated in the company of friends and vanished entirely when the group arrived at the "ski-hotels" ubiquitous in the Black Forest. Once ensconced in their "student" quarters and warmed by the heat of a roaring wood fire, the young friends reflected on the day's journeys and revitalized themselves with coffee and cake.[26] Frieda Hirsch, a Jewish women from Karlsruhe, luxuriated in this winter ritual in the company of friends, most of them Gentiles. Although raised in a self-consciously Jewish family and engaged to a confirmed Zionist, she enjoyed intimate social discourse with both Gentiles and Jews. Her experiences indicate that even individuals whose Judaism remained central to their private identity were capable of establishing meaningful friendships with people of different religious heritages. For Hirsch and many Jews of her era, the process of self-definition did not produce rigid categories of identity. Rather, remaining adaptable was critical to functioning successfully within the social environment of Wilhelmine Germany.

The memoir of Käte Frankenthal (1889–1976) suggests that close relations between Gentiles and Jews were not unique to Frieda Hirsch. Although Frankenthal attended a preparatory school for girls with fifteen other Jewish students, her childhood friends included both Jews and non-Jews.[27] Throughout her university career, she continued to move within non-Jewish circles.

After completing the *Abitur* in 1909, Käte Frankenthal began her medical studies at the university in Kiel. Similar to Frieda Hirsch, who remained at home during her first year of university study, Frankenthal's lifestyle did not conform to that of the carefree student until she went to Heidelberg in 1910. In preparation for her second year of university, Frankenthal's father journeyed to Heidelberg with his daughter and rented her a "small two-bedroom apartment." Not wanting to squander the family's money, Käte explained to her father that the "typical student digs" consisted of only a single room. Her father, however, was of the opinion that a female student needed a two-room apartment. He could not fathom the idea of his daughter entertaining male colleagues in her bedroom. According to Frankenthal, this was the last time that her father attempted to influence her moral behavior.[28]

The importance of place in the process of identity formation is readily apparent when reading Käte Frankenthal's descriptions of Heidelberg. She refers to Heidelberg as a "typical German student city" wherein the fraternal organizations dominated the social landscape and the professors, "most of whom were *Alte Herren* of the associations, engaged in friendly social relations with the students." The city, according to Frankenthal, was ideal for young people making the transition from *Gymnasium* to the university. Unlike *Gymnasium* students who live under the watchful eyes of their parents, university students are free to "squander away their time, ruin their health and run up debts in their father's name."[29] Nestled along the Neckar River and situated peacefully in the shadow of the majestic castle above, the old city of Heidelberg provided the perfect ambiance for such a lifestyle.

Käte Frankenthal's student career brought her to six universities in ten semesters. Her social relations were punctuated by close friendships with men, most of whom were non-Jews, and a curious lack of intimacy with women. While in Heidelberg, she befriended a young man from working-class origins with whom she had her first discussions of socialism. In spite of his hatred for the propertied classes that had made his social ascent so difficult, the desire to distance himself from his proletarian background propelled Frankenthal's companion into the ranks of the *Burschenschaften*.[30] Although the two university students' religious and socioeconomic statuses differed dramatically, they spent two years together and communicated frequently throughout the First World War. The bonding agent of their friendship may well have been the desire to transcend the traditional boundaries of their respective positions within society and the shared belief that a university education offered the means to do so. Their friendship dissolved when Frankenthal became active within the Socialist Party following the war and the political landscape of the Weimar Republic became increasingly polarized.[31]

During the time that Frankenthal was a student, she witnessed significant changes in the position of women students at German universities. During her first semester in Kiel, female students were still something of a novelty. By the time she concluded her studies, however, women comprised 10–15 percent of the students in her courses. According to Frankenthal, male students neither treated women with hostility nor gave them special consideration.[32] Accepting women within the halls of academia was easier for students than it was for professors, especially those within the medical faculties. Frankenthal recalls with unrestrained joy an exchange that transpired between herself and a professor of anatomy. Unable to answer a question in class on the topic of human genitalia, the professor requested that she come to see him in his office. When the professor asked Frankenthal if "the anatomical differences between the sexes was clear to her," her sense of humor was immediately piqued. "No, Herr Professor," she replied. Frustrated by her continued negative responses to questions regarding the physical makeup of men and women, the embarrassed young professor showed Frankenthal an anatomical drawing and queried, "Now is it clear?" After coyly replying that she thought so, the professor suggested that she take time to do some further reading on the subject.[33] With this, the playful interchange between professor and student came to a close.

From the beginning of the twentieth century until the outbreak of the First World War, Jewish women established their presence at German universities. Although the process of self-definition differed with each individual, the lives of the women examined here suggest some common experiences. First, the transition from home to university was carried out under the watchful eye of the family. Frieda Hirsch and Käte Frankenthal lived at home during their first year of university, while Rahel Straus lived with her brother and remained in close contact with her extended family. Moving into a segment of German society traditionally dominated by men necessitated caution. A second theme that resonates within the memoir literature of these women is the determinant influence of place. Frieda Hirsch formed dramatically different social coteries in Karlsruhe than she did in Heidelberg and Käte Frankenthal's frequent moves necessitated that she constantly reposition herself within student society. Remaining in Heidelberg allowed Rahel Straus to set down deep roots and construct an unusually stable identity for a university student. Central to the lives of each of these women was the quest for *Bildung*. Whether immersing themselves in their studies, going to the theater and symphony, or enjoying the outdoors, the desire for self-cultivation was intense. Regardless of one's socioeconomic background, religious heritage, or gender, one's university experience was a time for personal and intellectual growth.

RELIGIOUS JEWS AT GERMAN UNIVERSITIES

While Jewish women struggled to secure their positions within university society, a student organization emerged at the University of Berlin that positioned religious Judaism at the core of its identity. The *Vereinigung Jüdischer Akademiker* (V.J.A.) was founded in 1903 by Jewish students who remained true to the dictates of Jewish law (*Halakhah*) and desired to associate with fellow observant Jews. Members were drawn from all faculties and, in contrast to other student associations that distinguished between active members and *Alte Herren*, the V.J.A. was open to both matriculated students and graduates. This organizational arrangement distinguished the *Vereinigung Jüdischer Akademiker* from "true" student associations, which, according to university policy, could be comprised only of registered students.[34] In June 1906, the *Vereinigung Jüdischer Akademiker* of Berlin joined forces with the newly established chapters of the V.J.A. at the Universities of Munich (1904) and Strasbourg (1905) to create the *Bund Jüdischer Akademiker* (the Association of Jewish Academics), or the B.J.A.[35]

The *Bund Jüdischer Akademiker's* commitment to religious Judaism was clearly articulated within the organizational statutes.[36] In the words of Isaac Breuer, an important figure within the Orthodox community and a founding member of the B.J.A., the Association of Jewish Academics was "an inter-university federation of

Jewish academic students who in theory and practice conformed to the spirit of the Torah."[37] Although loyal to the dictates of *Halakhah*, the B.J.A. adopted a pragmatic approach to Judaism consistent with Samson Raphael Hirsch's neo-Orthodoxy, which "sought to make peace with modernity" so that observant Jews could participate in a secular civil society. As one member of the B.J.A. explained, "the association that only knows tradition and remains ignorant of progress, is doomed to fail."[38] In spite of the fact that members of the B.J.A. pursued their studies within the university environment, they remained steadfast to their religious views, even when in conflict with modern science. To help students reconcile the worlds of *Wissenschaft* and traditional Judaism, each member was assigned a faculty mentor with whom he could discuss the conflicts that invariably arose between a Jewish world-view and what was taught at the university.[39]

The distinctive feature of the identity constructed by the Association of Jewish Academics was the creation of an all-encompassing Jewish world. To ensure that students remained committed to religious Judaism, members were required to attend daily study sessions in Bible and Talmud. The *Bund Jüdischer Akademiker* also discouraged social interaction between its members and Gentile students. Toward this end, the association arranged "communal gatherings," at which lectures on Jewish subjects were presented, and organized social events to ensure that members were not "lured away by the attractions of modern town life."[40] In spite of its efforts to create a Jewish enclave within student society, the B.J.A. was greatly influenced by the environment in which it operated. Not only did the organization imitate the highly regimented format and activities of the corporate associations, but it also displayed a profound predilection for song, drink, and the creation of lifelong friendships.[41] Its activities in this regard reveal the synthetic nature of identity formation. Even religious Jews who preferred to socialize among themselves were not immune to the sway of the larger cultural environment in which they operated.

Students who joined the *Bund Jüdischer Akademiker* engaged in a process of self-definition similar to that of members of the *Verein für Cultur und Wissenschaft der Juden* of the previous century. Members of both groups found the contemporary status of Judaism and Jewish identity in dire need of revision and created new Jewish identities. The two associations differed, however, in that the *Verein für Cultur und Wissenschaft der Juden* pioneered the effort to diminish the religious component of Jewish identity, whereas members of the B.J.A. rejected the de-Judaized versions of Jewish identity fashioned throughout the nineteenth century and expressed their religious Judaism in their public as well as their private lives. The *Bund Jüdischer Akademiker*'s efforts to create a public identity imbued with religious Judaism indicate that the definition of one's Jewishness remained open to debate long after Jews had been formally emancipated.

CONSOLIDATION AND GROWTH OF STUDENT ZIONISM

The *Bund Jüdischer Akademiker* was not the only student group in pre-World War I German society that incorporated Jewishness into its public identity. The *Verein Jüdischer Studenten* (V.J.St.) had promoted Jewish nationalism since its founding in 1895 and, on January 16th, 1901, the chapters of the V.J.St. at the Universities of Berlin, Leipzig, Breslau, and Munich created an umbrella organization known as the *Bund Jüdischer Corporationen* (B.J.C.). The program of the B.J.C. stated:

1. The B.J.C. is the rallying point of all Jewish students who feel themselves consciously as Jews and desire to participate in a living Judaism.
2. The B.J.C. strives to educate Jewish students to be enthusiastically sympathetic towards Jewish life and to equip them with the spiritual qualities necessary to assume a position on academic, political and social questions concerning Judaism.
3. The B.J.C. will assist in the physical training of its membership and work towards the physical regeneration of the Jewish people.
4. The chapters of B.J.C. will look after and represent the interests of Jewish students [at their respective universities].
5. The B.J.C. will promote its viewpoints within the widest Jewish circles.[42]

The *Bund Jüdischer Corporationen*'s objectives were consistent with those articulated by the V.J.St. They sought to promote a new, positive Judaism through Jewish learning and to counter the tendency of German Jewish students to suppress all external manifestations of their Jewishness. The goal to provide all associational brothers a "Jewish philosophy of life" (*jüdische Lebensanchauung*) required that all initiates study the complete range of Jewish history, from the founding of the religion to the development of modern national Judaism.[43]

In spite of its lofty goals, the B.J.C.'s conception of Jewish nationalism was initially quite vague.[44] In a poll taken during the winter semester of 1900/1901, members of the association replied positively to the questions of whether the Jews were a people (*Volk*) united by origin and historical development, and whether they were aware of the national character of Judaism.[45] Subsequent questions, however, of whether the organization itself was "founded on a national basis" and whether it should "stress its national Jewish character" received more ambivalent responses. Fourteen members declared that the organization was founded on a national basis, while eleven said that it was not and three were undecided. Only thirteen respondents felt that the *Bund Jüdischer Corporationen* should stress its national character, whereas fourteen members said that it should not and one was undecided.[46]

Between 1902 and 1907 the pages of the organization's monthly journal, *Der Jüdische Student*, served as an open forum for members of the *Bund Jüdischer Corporationen* to hammer out a working definition of the terms "people" and "nationalism." An article entitled "Unser Verhältnis zum Judentum" (Our relation to Judaism) offers the following observations:

> We [are] Jews, both in spirit as well as in body. Our fathers, forefathers, and all of our relatives are Jews that have been raised in a Jewish house. We descend from one people (*Volk*) whose development is unique in the history of the world. The religions of more than 600 million people are based on the most Jewish of all Jewish books, the Bible.[47]

Further efforts to clarify the B.J.C.'s position on Jewish nationalism focused on the term "Judaism" itself. The author of the essay, "Sind die Juden eine Religionsgemeinschaft?" (Are the Jews a religious community?) argued that being Jewish was a matter of origin rather than choice and that there was more than one type of Judaism.

> It is not possible to speak of a single religious community that consists of Hassidic Rabbis on the one side and followers of

the Berlin Reform community on the other. . . . Ashkenaz and Sephardic Rabbis share as little in common with Professors Lazarus and Cohen as did Baruch Spinoza with his contemporary, Shabbatai Zevi.[48]

The crux of the author's argument is clear. Judaism is a multi-faceted religious phenomenon that contains divergent and even antithetical ideas within it. The belief in one God cannot serve as the sole criterion for a religious community. Being a Jew is not dependent on religion but on descent. After all, even "nonbelieving Jews" (*ungläubigen Juden*) are still considered Jews.[49]

Emil Cohn's article "Das nationale Bewusstein," (National consciousness) offered further clarification of the B.J.C.'s position on Jewish nationalism. Cohn's essay starts with the premise that "the basis of all human activity is the desire for unity and harmony."[50] It then proceeds to explain that humans cannot obtain both unity and harmony and, in fact, only unity is within the grasp of humankind. According to Cohn, the desire for unity produces the beginning of a "national consciousness," a development that ultimately allows one to say,

> This tribe, these peoples' life is my life. Their history with its events and tribulations is my history. Their past with all its spiritual and intellectual creations, with its scholarship and art—in short, their entire culture is my past.[51]

Although Cohn never mentions Jews, Jewish nationalism, or Zionism, his article defines the constituent features of a Jewish national identity. By placing a people's entire cultural heritage at the core of their national consciousness, Cohn lays the basis for a Jewish identity that features race, religion, and national origin as its primary features.

By 1907, the move toward a Zionist definition of Jewish nationalism was gathering support among the ranks of the *Bund Jüdischer Corporationen*. Although there was still opposition to an explicitly Zionist platform, and three years would pass before the organization formally adopted one,[52] the activities of the B.J.C. between 1901 and 1907 demonstrate its understanding of and commitment to Jewish nationalism. During this period, members of the Association of Jewish Students presented numerous lectures on the history of the Jews and their position within German and

European society. A few examples of the lectures given are: "On Assimilation and Nationality," "Jews in Modern Literature," "The Meaning of Dietary Laws," "The Jewish Racial Question," and "Hess's Rome and Jerusalem."[53] These lectures, their accompanying discussion evenings, and the essays published in *Der Jüdische Student* helped the *Bund Jüdischer Corporationen* crystallize its views on Jewish nationalism. Two additional developments, however, aligned the B.J.C.'s definition of a Jewish national identity closer with that offered by German Zionists. One was the emergence of an explicitly Zionist student organization and the other was a generational change of leadership.

The first Zionist student association in Germany was founded at the University of Berlin in 1902. The driving force behind the establishment of *Hasmonaea* was Egon Rosenberg, a Jew whose commitment to Zionism was well established before he began his university studies in Berlin. The most important objective of *Hasmonaea* was to train its members to be committed Zionists. Only "distinguished" (*vornehme*) men with like-minded views could become associational brothers. In 1906, *Hasmonaea* united with *Jordania*, a student Zionist organization founded in Munich in 1905, to create the *Kartell Zionistischer Verbindungen* (K.Z.V.). The following year, *Ivria* of Freiburg joined the K.Z.V.[54]

The activities of the organizations belonging to the *Kartell Zionistischer Verbindungen* are discussed by Walter Fischer (b. 1889), a former member of *Hasmonaea*.[55] Fisher was raised in an "assimilated Berlin family" and had little exposure to Jewish tradition before attending university. He first heard of Theodor Herzl and the Zionist movement at the time of Herzl's death in 1904. Shortly thereafter he became devoted to the Zionist cause. After joining the *Berliner Zionistischen Vereinigung* in 1906, he attended a celebration at which members of *Hasmonaea* were present. Fischer recalls seeing this "group of well dressed young men, all of whom wore a gold-embroidered star of David on their breasts" and being asked to join them at their table. In the weeks that followed he was a guest at their *Kneipen*, at which he became acquainted with the "strange ritual of the *Bierkomment*" and participated in the raucous singing sessions. Upon graduating in the summer of 1907, Fischer became an official member of *Hasmonaea*. According to Fischer,

the student life of *Hasmonaea* consisted not only of *Kneipen* and dueling, but the Zionist training was also seriously pursued.

We had outstanding instruction in Zionism from Elias Auerbach [b.1882], a twenty-five-year-old doctor. We received excellent lessons in Jewish history from Eugen Täubler who later became a full professor [*Ordinarius*] of ancient history in Heidelberg. I became acquainted with the actual problems of Zionism through [my friendship] with Auerbach and [Richard] Lichtheim [1895–1963].[56]

The public identity fashioned by members of the K.Z.V., like that of all Jewish student organizations of the Kaiserreich, was a synthetic construction. Ritualistic beer drinking, dueling, and the wearing of associational uniforms were ornaments of German student culture. The study of Jewish history and the commitment to Zionism were tools of self-definition employed by individuals who desired to create a conscious link to their Jewish past.

The activities of the K.Z.V. served a dual purpose. They were designed not only to "promote the Zionist idea" but also to create a well-disciplined and loyal cadre of Zionists. The association's ruling body demanded "unconditional" acceptance of its decisions and, most importantly, demanded that all "differences of a personal and a specific nature" be set aside for the good of the entire organization.[57] On the training of its members, Richard Lichtheim wrote that "the discipline of the K.Z.V. is especially important. Without a doubt it is stricter than that of either the B.J.C. or the K.C. . . . Due to the unusual nature of our ideology (*Tendenz*), however, discipline is not enforced by sharp commands, but through a union of the external with the internal (*durch eine Verbindung des Aeusserlichen mit dem Innerlichen*)."[58] In other words, members of the K.Z.V. willingly acted on the knowledge that to be a good Zionist one must be completely loyal and dedicated to the Zionist cause. The demands for discipline were so stringent and of such paramount concern that they took priority over all other organizational goals. As Egon Rosenberg candidly admitted, "*Hasmonaea's* spiritual possession of Jewish values was certainly not richer, and probably poorer than that of the Jewish foundations of the B.J.C."[59]

A second development that influenced the *Bund Jüdischer Corporationen*'s move toward Zionism and contributed to its eventual fusion with the *Kartell Zionistischer Verbindungen* was the emergence of a new generation of leaders. The dominant figure within this group was Kurt Blumenfeld (1884–1963). Born to a "Jewish family of German culture," Blumenfeld was raised in an environment devoid of Jewish culture. His parents' social circle was comprised of non-Jews who shared similar intellectual and musical interests. Blumenfeld's closest childhood friend was Catholic and, as a student at a confessionally mixed *Gymnasium*, he immersed himself in the study of German political and national culture.[60] There is nothing within Kurt Blumenfeld's descriptions of his childhood to suggest that he would one day place Zionism at the center of his public and private identities. By the time that he entered the university in 1904, however, he openly defined himself as a Zionist.[61]

Zionism, for Blumenfeld, was the path by which Jews who had been "thoroughly Europeanized" could find their way back to the Jewish people. Although he believed that German Jews were obligated to support the German state, Blumenfeld rejected the notion that German Jews were "German citizens of the Jewish faith." The sooner that Jews denounced their identification with the German *Volk*, Blumenfeld argued, and accepted the fact that they belonged to a Jewish people, the easier it would be to resolve the misunderstandings, (i.e. antisemitism) between Jews and Germans.[62]

In spite of his Zionist convictions, Blumenfeld joined the nationalist but not yet officially Zionist organization, the *Verein Jüdischer Studenten*. Within this group, Blumenfeld used his powerful rhetorical skills and leadership ability to influence the ideological development of the *Bund Jüdischer Corporationen*. As a student in Königsberg, he resuscitated the local V.J.St. chapter by recruiting new members who were loyal Zionists.[63] On returning to Berlin in 1906, Blumenfeld and fellow student Arthur Biram (1878–1967) founded the *Maccabaea*, the first V.J.St. organization to define itself as Zionist. As a committed Zionist organization, *Maccabaea* constituted a "radical national-Jewish" element within the *Bund Jüdischer Corporationen*. Although *Maccabaea's* members claimed that they were not looking to transform the B.J.C. but simply wanted to live out its character in pure form, the Berlin *Maccabaea*, along with the V.J.St. in Königsberg, spearheaded the movement that culminated in the B.J.C.'s adoption of an explicitly Zionist platform.[64]

From 1907 to 1910, the *Bund Jüdischer Corporationen* engaged in an internal struggle over the organization's relationship to Zionism. Under the influence of Blumenfeld, who had since graduated from the university and become actively involved in the *Zionis-*

tischer Vereinigung für Deutschland (the German Zionist Organization), the B.J.C. moved closer to the Zionist ideology. At the B.J.C.'s *Kartelltag* (party congress) in 1910, Blumenfeld adroitly outmaneuvered his opponents and garnered the support necessary to pass a pro-Zionist resolution. The resolution stated that the V.J.St. was to prepare its members to "lead the fight for the future of the Jewish people," and it called on the chapters of the *Verein Jüdischer Studenten* to "put decisive emphasis on the Zionist development of their members."[65] Although a special congress convened in May retracted Blumenfeld's resolution, the B.J.C. was effectively allied with Zionism.[66]

As the ideological differences between the B.J.C. and the *Kartell Zionistischer Verbindungen* narrowed, the two organizations discussed a merger.[67] When members of the K.Z.V. and the B.J.C. had first explored the topic of creating a single student association in 1907, differences between the two groups had been too great to allow for their union.[68] Competition for new recruits had heightened tensions between the two nationalist associations and the debate over which organization produced better and more committed Zionists had exacerbated these ill feelings.[69] Ultimately, however, once members of both the *Kartell Zionistischer Verbindungen* and the *Bund Jüdischer Corporationen* recognized that not only did the two associations share common objectives but they were also fighting a common enemy, the *Kartell Convent,* they cast aside their differences.

According to the presidium of the K.Z.V., the K.C. "had transformed itself from an organization dedicated to the struggle against antisemitism to an organization dedicated to the struggle against Zionism. As a result, it had become a force to be reckoned with."[70] The increasing strength of the "anti-Zionist" movement in general and the *Kartell Convent* in particular, awakened members of the K.Z.V. and the B.J.C. to the realization that as long as there were two distinct Jewish nationalist organizations at German universities, neither association could wage an effective counteroffensive against the *Kartell Convent.* Instead of splitting the loyalties of students sympathetic to the cause of Jewish nationalism, it was time to merge the *Kartell Zionistischer Verbindungen* and the *Bund Jüdischer Corporationen.*[71]

Negotiations for a union between the two groups began in earnest in May 1914. The main obstacles facing the negotiators were the name of the new organization and its platform. While both groups agreed that the new student association would be Zionist in orientation and that a new name was imperative, differences emerged over its precise wording. The leaders of the B.J.C. argued that incorporating Zionism within the name would serve to make the group a target for anti-Zionist forces and alienate potential recruits who had only heard negative comments about Zionism. The K.Z.V.'s presidium, on the other hand, declared that as a Zionist organization it was incumbent on the new association to pronounce itself as such.[72] After lengthy and intense debates, the representatives of both organizations reached an agreement.

On July 19, 1914, the *Kartell Zionistischer Verbindungen* and the *Bund Jüdischer Corporationen* united under the banner of the *Kartell Jüdischer Verbindungen.* (K.J.V.) The new Jewish nationalist student organization issued the following statement:

> The K.J.V. strives to educate its members as men who will be conscious of the national unity of the Jewish people and are resolved to stand up for a renewal in Eretz-Israel which will be worthy of its history.[73]

Although the new association neither called itself Zionist nor claimed to be a student branch of the German Zionist organization, it was loyal to the Zionist cause. Nineteen years after the founding of the *Verein Jüdischer Studenten,* German Jewish university students had created an interuniversity organization that articulated and adhered to a nationally defined German Jewish identity. In so doing, they rejected the argument that Jews were a religious confession rather than a national entity, and they vehemently opposed those who claimed that German Jews were simply German citizens of the Jewish faith.

THE RHETORICAL DANCE

Central to the process of identity formation employed by all Jewish associations was a rhetorical dance wherein each association defined itself in opposition to the other groups. At issue were the parallel concerns of Jewish integration into German society and the perpetuation of a distinct and viable Jewish cultural heritage. Not only did members of the *Kartell Convent* and the two Jewish nationalist student organizations go head to head over these issues, but each Jewish student association defended its version of a Jewish identity against accusations from the other organizations. No Jewish student association was above the fray.

The attacks against the *Kartell Convent* by the Jewish nationalist associations were particularly vicious. Articles in *Der Jüdische Student* called the K.C. "the first step towards conversion," and members of the B.J.C. regularly chastised the alcoholic tendencies of the *Kartell Convent*.[74] Richard Lichtheim, a leader of the K.Z.V., depicted the K.C. as the "mortal enemy" of the *Kartell Zionistischer Verbindungen*.[75] A second member argued that the *Kartell Convent* had outlived its usefulness and that the K.C. was "completely different than that of earlier times." Whereas members of the K.C. had formerly emphasized their Judaism and fought against antisemitism, they now accentuated their "Germanness (*Deutschtum*) and attempted to outdo the beer-drinking habits (*Biergewohnheit*) of Aryan students."[76] The vacuous Jewish content of the *Kartell Convent* was a theme emphasized time and again by both the B.J.C. and the K.Z.V. In addition, the *Kartell Convent*'s alleged similarities to traditional student associations prompted Friederich Loewenthal to claim that the K.C. "would become superfluous if the S.C. [the *Corps*] and the *Burschenschaften* would once again accept Jews."[77]

The *Kartell Convent* responded by pointing out the inaccuracies in the charges rather than by engaging in an escalating exchange of insults. Employing a format befitting of future lawyers, members of the K.C. dissected the accusations that maligned the character of the membership and their organization, and they offered reasoned retorts to each charge. In an article entitled "K.C. und B.J.C.," Max Mainzer discussed the *Bund Jüdischer Corporationen's* decision to target the *Kartell Convent* for attack, and he viewed the B.J.C.'s subsequent renunciation of its call to arms a tactic "typical of the press polemics employed by the presidium of the B.J.C."[78] In a second article entitled "K.C. und B.J.C.," Ludwig Holländer reminded his readers that it was the K.C. who had unilaterally decided not to respond to the attacks published in *Der Jüdische Student*, before reiterating his previous charge that the B.J.C. had employed defamatory accusations against the K.C. while wooing new recruits.[79] Continuing to demonstrate the aggressive and disingenuous tactics of the *Bund Jüdischer Corporationen*, Karl Löwenstein juxtaposed the *Berichtigung* (correction) issued by the B.J.C. that denied any wrongdoing and all aggressive behavior on its part, with the original articles that accused the K.C. of "assuming a vile fighting style" and possessing "improper intentions."[80] Löwenstein's article, along with the others presented here, effectively demonstrate the offensive posture employed by the *Bund Jüdischer Corporationen* as it attempted to undermine the *Kartell Convent*'s credibility and challenge its ability to represent the interests of the Jewish student body. As the larger of the two organizations, the K.C. could comfortably assume a moral high ground in the battle with its arch-rival, the B.J.C.

The war of words between the *Kartell Convent* and the two Jewish nationalist student associations paralleled the increasing animosity between the *Centralverein* (C.V.) and the *Zionistischen Vereinigung für Deutschland*. Marjorie Lamberti argues persuasively that "peaceful coexistence between the Zionists and non-Zionists in the German-Jewish community broke down after 1910 because of changes in the Zionist organization" that brought Blumenfeld's influence to the fore. Blumenfeld and other young German Zionists "wanted to make the Zionist organization a radical Jewish nationalist party," and they argued, accordingly, that accommodation with the *Centralverein* was not in the best interests of the Zionist organization.[81] Among the student population, the verbal strife between the Jewish nationalist organizations and the *Kartell Convent* not only distinguished the groups from one another but, even more importantly, provided an open forum for members of these associations to elucidate their versions of Jewish identity. As Stuart Hall reminds us, group identities are defined in relation to the "other."

Although the *Kartell Convent* served as the negative image of modern Jewry constructed by Jewish nationalist students, members of the *Bund Jüdischer Corporationen* also utilized the *Freie Wissenschaftliche Vereinigung* (F.W.V.) and the *Bund Jüdischer Akademiker* (B.J.A.) for a similar purpose. In an article purported to evaluate the recently published *F.W.V.er Taschenbuch*, a member of the B.J.C. claimed that the *Freie Wissenschaftliche Vereinigung* was nothing more than "a refuge from reality," and that the organization served "as a wall against the incredible cultural distractions of our time."[82] According to the B.J.C., the F.W.V.'s lack of realism was evident in its use of the same defensive standpoint as that used by educated Christians who claimed to oppose antisemitism but, nevertheless, harbored serious misgivings about the idiosyncrasies of "Jewish spiritual, moral and physical qualities."[83] The contemptuous attitude of the *Bund Jüdischer Corporationen* toward the F.W.V. resonated throughout the discourse crafted for university elections. In the campaign for the directorship of the *Akademische Lesehalle* (Academic Reading Hall) at the University of Berlin, the *Verein Jüdischer Studenten* argued that in spite of the fact that the *Freie Wissenschaftliche Vereinigung* was comprised almost exclusively of Jews, "only men who openly declared their Jewishness" were worthy of representing the interests of Jewish students.[84]

The war of words between the *Bund Jüdischer Akademiker* and the *Bund Jüdischer Corporationen* was complicated by the overlapping features of their identities. In contrast to the majority of German Jews who defined their Judaism as a matter of faith rather than descent, both organizations emphasized the historical uniqueness of the Jewish people and rejected the notion of Jewish integration or amalgamation into German society. The similarities between their ideological and social platforms were so great that during the first few years of the *Bund Jüdischer Akademiker*'s existence a number of students belonged to both associations. Ultimately, however, the exclusive character of German student society and the exacting nature of identity formation compelled the B.J.A. to pass a resolution prohibiting dual memberships.[85]

In challenging the Association of Jewish Academics, the *Bund Jüdischer Corporationen* emphasized the "clear social separation" between the two groups and vehemently complained about the tenacious recruiting efforts of the *Bund Jüdischer Akademiker*. Apparently, a student by the name of Bachrach became a point of contention between the two organizations when, contrary to the desires of his father, he attempted to join the Strasbourg chapter of the B.J.C. rather than the *Verein Jüdischer Akademiker* in Heidelberg. Upon hearing of his son's arrival in Strasbourg, the father, together with an Orthodox rabbi and the president of the V.J.A. in Heidelberg, employed strong-arm tactics to convince the young man to return to Heidelberg. Although Bachrach succumbed to the pressure and took up his studies in Heidelberg, he refused to join the association of Orthodox students and remained in contact with Jewish nationalist students. Not only were Bachrach's refusal to join the V.J.A. and his commitment to Jewish nationalism held up as positive examples for new initiates of the B.J.C., but the entire affair was presented as proof of the strenuous struggle between the two organizations and the danger of the Association for Jewish Academics for the cause of Jewish nationalism.[86]

Zeroing in on the deficiencies of a Jewish identity that focused exclusively on religious Judaism, the B.J.C. opined that the maintenance of *Halakhah* would not ameliorate the contemporary condition of German Jewry.

> What makes this type of orthodoxy such an ardent foe for us is the knowledge that here is a broad based organization that seeks to arouse in its members the idea that Judaism can be saved by the strict application of its religious tenets and, . . . [in so doing], evade the burning problems of Jewry.[87]

Jewish nationalists not only rejected a religious paradigm of self-definition, but they also believed that adherence to the stipulations of traditional Judaism would do nothing to solve the existential question of Jewish self-definition in Wilhelmine Germany.

The *Bund Jüdischer Akademiker* was not a passive foe. In its assessment of the *Bund Jüdischer Corporationen* the B.J.A. recognized that Jewish nationalist students "had rediscovered faith in the future of its people and rekindled a feeling of enthusiasm for its common ancestry."[88] Recognition of the common concerns of the two organizations notwithstanding, the *Bund Jüdischer Akademiker* took issue with its national coreligionists on a number of specific points. In a speech delivered to a group of Jewish students just prior to the start of their university careers, a representative of the B.J.A. warned his audience of "false prophets who, in the name of freedom," present new arrivals to the university "with choices." Claiming that other Jewish organizations hid their Jewishness and denied their peculiarities, the speaker admonished his audience to remember that "the Jewish people are nothing without the Jewish religion." Although he never mentioned the name of a single student association, the speaker's message was clear: the *Bund Jüdischer Akademiker* was the organization of choice for Jewish students who desired to publicly express their Judaism.[89]

In an article entitled "Jüdische Studentenverbindungen," the B.J.A. continued its war of words with the *Bund Jüdischer Corporationen*.[90] The Association of Jewish Academics charged that the B.J.C. was created largely in response to antisemitism and that the primary concern for the young Jewish nationalists was "steeling their bodies" in preparation for the fencing matches that were central to the organization's reason for existence.[91] Of grave concern to the Association of Jewish Academics was the *Bund Jüdischer Corporationen*'s "silence" about the Jewish religion. According to the author of the article, "law biding Jews must completely dismiss [the agenda of] the B.J.C. . . . because of the danger that it poses for religious Jews."[92] As a political movement, the B.J.C. had no interest in religious practice. Jewish consciousness was acquired through the study of history and the adoption of a social position wherein members proudly proclaimed their Jewish heritage and demanded the right to defend their honor with the sword. For religious Jews, knowledge of one's Jewishness could never be achieved without a deep understanding of classical texts. The intimate connection between religious instruction and Jewish consciousness was central to the programmatic agenda of the B.J.A. Not only was the "religious nihilism" of the Jewish nationalists offensive to the Association for Jewish Academics, so too was its approach to Jewish history. After all, there was a "world of difference between the history of [Heinrich] Graetz and [Jehuda] Halevy." A critical approach to Judaism could never be condoned by an organization bound by the dictates of *Halakhah*. For the B.J.A., biblical history, the development of the oral tradition, and the writings of Maimonides were fundamental to its definition of Jewishness.[93] By challenging the religious indifference of the B.J.C. and accentuating its deficient understanding of Jewish history, the *Bund Jüdischer Akademiker* defined itself in a manner favorable to Jewish university students who remained committed to the dictates of *Halakhah*.

The rhetorical campaigns of Jewish student organizations were part of the larger phenomenon of identity formation in which all Jews of the German Kaiserreich participated. By the eve of World War I, German Jewish identity had become increasingly variegated. Much like the weaver who begins by laying out the warp, or foundation, of the cloth and then proceeds to embellish the fabric with the strands of the weft, German Jewish university students added new flourishes and increasing definition to an already rich and vibrant tapestry of German Jewish identity.

In many respects, German Jewish identities were similar to custom-made clothing. What appealed to one group of German Jews was often rejected and chastised by another. Whether they proclaimed their support for Jewish nationalism, remained religiously observant, or emphasized other aspects of their cultural heritage, German Jewish university students constructed a mul-tifarious array of well-defined identities that enabled them to participate within the social setting of German universities. Their activities in this regard underscore the variety of ways in which German Jews adapted to their environment and created a vibrantly colored coat of German Jewish identity in which religious, na-tional, and cultural definitions of Jewishness were woven together into a fashionable yet functional garment.

Conclusion

From the end of the Napoleonic era until the opening salvos of World War I, the enticing prospect of increased educational opportunities lured Jews from their secure but separate cultural environs and paved the way for unprecedented social interaction between Jews and Gentiles. The theory of emancipation posited that once government officials removed the onerous economic and legal restrictions that had burdened Jews for centuries, Jewish particularism would vanish and Jews would become more like their Christian neighbors. Proponents of emancipation, however, neither imagined the contours of modern Jewish identities nor provided Jews with a reliable blueprint for the future.

The task of refashioning Judaism was not unique to the nineteenth century. Following the destruction of the Second Temple in 70 C.E., Jews adjusted to the contingencies of *Galut*, or exile, by developing a religious tradition in which the temple no longer functioned as the centerpiece of Jewish religious ritual. Throughout the common era, Jews had adapted to conditions dictated by their host societies and adjusted their paradigms of self-definition accordingly. The novel feature of modernity and, specifically, emancipation, was that Jews no longer lived in a world bounded by the homogeneous community and defined by Jewish law. Once German Jews discarded the protective veil of *Halakhah* and transcended the boundaries of their autonomous communities, they redefined what it meant to be a Jew.

Jews who attended German universities before 1871 constructed identities that allowed them to remain Jews, yet participate in German society. Members of the *Verein für Cultur und Wissenschaft der Juden* were the first Jewish university students to recast Judaism from a religious to a national construct. The vague and tenuous conception of Jewish nationalism proffered by members of the *Verein* explains why many who belonged to the association ultimately converted to Christianity. Had the organization developed a more articulate and, ultimately, successful image of modern Jewry, the conversionary impulse would not have been as significant.

Once the *Verein* disbanded, sixty years passed before Jewish university students established their own organizations. During this period, Jews gradually made their way from the margins of student society to its center. The most direct path, one chosen by a minority of Jews, was joining a German fraternal organization. Membership in either the *Corps* or *Burschenschaften* supplied Jewish university students with ready-made public identities that offered them direct access to the heart of German bourgeois culture. The cost, however, was typically quite high: separation from one's Jewish heritage via the baptismal font.[1] The gap between *Deutschtum* and *Judentum* was still too great to bridge in a single step.

Jewish university students of the Kaiserreich confronted the realization that emancipation did not ensure equality or social acceptance. Raised with the expectation that they would enjoy the full benefits of citizenship, Jewish students in the 1870s continued the pattern of identity formation that relegated Jewishness to the private sphere. Once it became clear, however, that even the private expression of one's Jewishness was at odds with the dominant national culture, Jewish university students began to rearrange their public images.

The emergence of Jewish student associations in the 1880s and throughout the Kaiserreich represents a significant paradigmatic shift in the process of Jewish identity formation. Founded in 1881, the *Freie Wissenschaftliche Vereinigung* was a nondenominational association that attempted to play down all external manifestations of its Jewishness. Nevertheless, by 1890 the organization was comprised exclusively of Jews and had become a vehicle for highly acculturated Jewish students to participate in student society within the context of a Jewish social coterie. The *Akademische Verein für Jüdische Geschichte und Literatur,* the *Kartell Convent,* the *Bund Jüdischer Corporationen,* and the *Bund Jüdischer Akademiker* not only provided a forum for Jewish students to come together as Jews, but each association also articulated a public identity that was self-consciously Jewish. All Jewish student organizations, however, were imbued with sufficient German cultural characteristics to enable members to function as German university students.

Even though many Jews joined student organizations, an equally large group of German Jewish university students utilized alternate means to determine their social groups. While some participated in the subgroups of the *Freistudentenschaft* and others formed their own social circles, the public identities of noncorporate students served the same purpose as those fashioned by members of Jewish student organizations; they were the means to function within the university environment. The key difference between the two processes of identity formation, however, was that most noncorporate Jewish students sublimated their Jewishness in favor of other concerns and interests and, consequently, their public identities were quite similar to those of unincorporated Gentile students. This pattern of identity formation was also evident among the first generation of female Jewish university students, whose positions in student society were, at first, unaffected by their religious heritage.

German Jewish identity formation was a dynamic phenomenon. What began under the rubric of emancipation and employed the concept of *Bildung* as a guiding metaphor later blossomed into a variegated array of patterns. Members of the *Freie Wissenschaftliche Vereinigung* adhered to paradigms of self-definition modeled on *Bildung* and crafted what might be called a "non-Jewish, Jewish identity." While the organization defined itself as nondenominational, its primarily Jewish membership meant that it was viewed by contemporaries as a Jewish association. In many ways, nonaffiliated Jewish students operated in an analogous manner. Firmly committed to the principles of self-cultivation and reluctant to publicly proclaim their Jewishness, the social coteries of nonaffiliated Jewish students often consisted of fellow Jews.

Whereas the identities created by members of the *Freie Wissenschaftliche Vereinigung* and unaffiliated students perpetuated the project of *Bildung*, the Jewish associational movement of the 1890s reflects a shift in cultural reference points. Students who joined the *Kartell Convent* and Jewish nationalist organizations defined their Jewishness according to the gender specific concept of honor that was pervasive in fin de siècle central European society. The norms of an idealized masculinity replaced the acquisition of *Bildung* as the centerpiece of their German Jewish identity. Further evidence of a paradigmatic shift in identity formation is witnessed by the insistence on parity between Jewish public and private identities. Students who joined a Jewish organization refused to relegate their Jewishness to the private sphere.

Jewish university students of the nineteenth century fashioned patterns of self-definition that were unique to their time and place. The identities of German Jews on the eve of World War I differed radically from those constructed by previous generations. The combined effect of advancing time and the evolving concept of the German "place" altered how Jews positioned themselves in society. Although German Jewish identities were often riddled with paradox and fraught with tension, they enabled their creators to function in German society. Given the centrality of time and place to identity formation, however, it is not reasonable to assume that the identities crafted by German Jews before the First World War would be functional in the fundamentally different environment of the Weimar and Nazi eras. Avoiding teleological readings of history requires that we remain focused on the temporal and social contexts in which our historical actors perform.

Notes

PREFACE

1. For the purposes of this study the term "Germany" refers to the territory of the German Kaiserreich of 1871, not the entire German *Kulturbereich*.

2. Robert Seltzer, *Jewish People, Jewish Thought. The Jewish Experience in History* (New York: Macmillan, 1980), 515.

3. Ismar Schorsch, *Jewish Reactions to German Anti-Semitism, 1870–1914* (New York: Columbia University Press, 1972); and Jehuda Reinharz, *Fatherland or Promised Land. The Dilemma of the German Jew, 1893–1914* (Ann Arbor: University of Michigan Press, 1975).

CHAPTER 1

1. While Stanislawski makes this comment in reference to the Jews of Poland and Russia in the twentieth century, I find it quite fitting for Jews who lived west of the Elbe River during the nineteenth century. The quote is found in Stanislawski, *For Whom do I Toil. Judah Leib Gordon and the Crisis of Russian Jewry* (New York: Oxford University Press, 1988), 5.

2. *Childhood and Society* (New York: W.W. Norton and Co., 1950).

3. The major exceptions are Stephen Poppel, *Zionism in Germany 1897–1933: The Shaping of Jewish Identity* (Philadelphia: Jewish Publication Society, 1977); and Michael Meyer, *Jewish Identity in the Modern World* (Seattle: University of Washington Press, 1990).

4. "Ethnicity: Identity and Difference," *Radical America* 23, no. 4 (June 1991): 15; and "Cultural Identity and Diaspora," in *Identity: Community, Culture, Difference.* Jonathon Rutherford, ed. (London: Lawrence and Wishart, 1990), 222–37.

171

5. Hall, "Cultural Identity and Diaspora," 222.

6. Joan Walloch Scott, *Gender and the Politics of History* (New York: Columbia University Press, 1988), 42.

7. Hall, "Ethnicity," 11.

8. Emphasis mine. "Identity Complexes in Western Europe: Social Anthropological Perspectives," in *Inside European Identities. Ethnography in Western Europe*, Sharon Macdonald, ed. (Providence: Berg Publishers, 1993), 6.

9. A. L. Epstein, *Ethos and Identity* (London: Tavistock Publications, 1978), 101.

10. Anthony P. Cohen, "Culture As Identity: An Anthropologist's View," *New Literary History: A Journal of Theory and Interpretation* 24, no. 1, (winter 1993): 195–209.

11. David Sorkin, "The Impact of Emancipation on German Jewry: A Reconsideration," in *Assimilation and Community. The Jews in Nineteenth-Century Europe*, Jonathan Frankel and Steven Zipperstein, eds. (Cambridge: Cambridge University Press, 1992), 178. For a more detailed exposition of German Jewry as a subculture see his *The Transformation of German Jewry, 1780–1840* (New York: Oxford University Press, 1987).

12. Sorkin, "Impact of Emancipation," 193.

13. Quoted in Simon N. Herman, *Jewish Identity: A Social Psychological Perspective* (Beverly Hills: Sage Publications, 1977), 31. Originally found in H. C. Kelman, "The Place of Jewish Identity in the Development of Personal Identity." A working paper prepared for the American Jewish Committee's Colloquium on Jewish Education and Jewish Identity, November 1974.

14. Marion Kaplan's work on German Jewish women convincingly demonstrates the need to move beyond exclusively male models of Jewish identity when evaluating the identity of German Jews. *The Making of the Jewish Middle Class: Women, Family and Identity in Imperial Germany* (New York: Oxford University Press, 1991).

15. Milton M. Gordon, *Assimilation in American Life. The Role of Race, Religion, and National Origins* (New York: Oxford University Press, 1964), 31–32.

16. Marion Kaplan, "Gender and Jewish History in Imperial Germany," in *Assimilation and Community. The Jews in Nineteenth Century Europe*, Jonathon Frankel and Steven J. Zipperstein, eds. (Cambridge: Cambridge University Press, 1992), 198–224.

17. Perry London and Alissa Hirshfeld, "The Psychology of Identity Formation," in *Jewish Identity in America*, David M. Gordis and Yoav ben Horin, eds. (Los Angeles: University of Judaism Press, 1991), 32–41.

18. Hall, "Ethnicity," 10.

19. Ilene Philipson, "What's the Big I.D.? The Politics of the Authentic Self," *Tikkun* 6, no. 6 (Nov/Dec 1991): 51.

20. For example, see the memoir of Simon Hayum, ME 560, 24.

21. Jacob Katz, *Out of the Ghetto: The Social Background of Jewish Emancipation, 1770–1870* (New York: Schocken Books, 1978), 20–26.

22. The first medical degree awarded by a German university to a Jew was in 1721. Guido Kisch, *Die Universitäten und die Juden: Eine Historische Betrachtung zur Fünfhundertjahrfeier der Universität Basel* (Tübingen: J.C.B. Mohr, 1961), 16–18; and Monika Richarz, *Der Eintritt der Juden in die Akademischen Berufe* (Tübingen: J.C.B. Mohr, 1974), 24–27.

23. Jacob Katz, *Tradition and Crisis: Jewish Society at the End of the Middle Ages* (New York: Schocken Books, 1961), 189–91.

24. Ibid., 191–94.

25. Mordechai Eliav, "Jüdische Erziehung in Deutschland im Zeitalter der Aufklärung und der Emanzipation," *Bulletin des Leo Baeck Institut* 3 (1960): 207.

26. A translation of the text appears in *Readings in Modern Jewish History*, Ellis Rivkin, ed. and Helen Lederer, trans. (Cincinnati: Hebrew Union College, 1957). An abridged version is found in *The Jew in the Modern World. A Documentary History*, Paul Mendes-Flohr and Jehuda Reinharz, eds. (New York: Oxford University Press, 1980), 27–34.

27. Dohm, "Über die bürgerliche Verbesserung," Mendes-Flohr and Reinharz, *The Jew in the Modern World*, 30.

28. Ibid., 32–33

29. The document is published in Alfred Pribram, *Urkunde und Akten zur Geschichte der Juden in Wien* (Vienna, 1918), 1:494–500 and is found in Raphael Mahler, ed. and trans., *Jewish Emancipation: A Selection of Documents by R. Mahler*, Pamphlet Series, Jews and the Post–War World, no. 1 (New York: American Jewish Committee, 1942). For an abbreviated text of the Edict of Toleration see Mendes Flohr and Reinharz, *The Jew in the Modern World*, 34–36. Joseph issued separate edicts for Bohemia, Moravia, Lower Austria, and Galicia, the provisions of which varied between locations. For further comments on the Edicts' impact on Jewish society in these regions see, Hillel J. Kieval, "Caution's Progress: The Modernization of Jewish Life in Prague, 1780–1830," in *Toward Modernity. The European Jewish Model*, Jacob Katz, ed. (New Brunswick: Transaction Books, 1988), 71–105.

30. "Edict of Toleration," *The Jew in the Modern World*, 35.

31. Naphtali Herz Wessely, *Divrei Shalom ve'Emet* (Warsaw, 1886), 6–7. For an abridged translation of this work see Mendes-Flohr and Reinharz's *The Jew in the Modern World*, 62–67.

32. Katz, *Out of the Ghetto*, 66–69 and 124–26; and Sorkin, *Transformation of German Jewry*, 54–57.

33. The text of the Hebrew manuscript was published by Louis Lewin in "Aus dem jüdischen Kulturkampfe," *Jahrbuch der jüdisch-Literarischen Gesellschaft* 12 (1918): 182–94. An English translation is found in Mendes-Flohr and Reinharz, *The Jew in the Modern World*, 67–68.

34. Sorkin, *Transformation of German Jewry*, 208–9; and Mordechai Eliav, *Jewish Education in Germany in the Period of Enlightenment and Emancipation* (in Hebrew) (Jerusalem: Hebrew University, 1960), 71–141.

35. Eliav, "Jüdische Erziehung," 211–13.

36. Charles E. McClelland, *State, Society and University in Germany, 1700–1914* (Cambridge: Cambridge University Press, 1980), 107–49.

37. McClelland, *State, Society and University*, 106–11; and Rudolf Vierhaus "Bildung," in *Geschichtliche Grundbegriffe. Historisches Lexikon zur politisch-sozialen Sprache in Deutschland*, Otto Brunner, Werner Conze, and Reinhart Koselleck, eds. (Stuttgart, 1972), 1:508–51.

38. David Sorkin, "Wilhelm von Humboldt: The Theory and Practice of Self-Formation (*Bildung*), 1791–1810," *Journal of the History of Ideas* 44, no. 1 (1983): 55–73.

39. Wilhelm von Humboldt, *The Limits of State Action*, J.W. Burrow, ed. (Cambridge: Cambridge University Press, 1969), 81.

40. Sorkin, "Wilhelm von Humboldt," 62–64. A sampling of Humboldt's letters dealing with *Bildung* are found in W. H. Buford, *The German Tradition of*

Self-Cultivation. Bildung From Humboldt to Thomas Mann (Cambridge: Cambridge University Press, 1975), 1–28.

41. This definition is given in *Der Grosse Brockhaus,* a standard encyclopedia published between 1928–1935, and quoted in Fritz K. Ringer, *The Decline of the German Mandarins* (Cambridge: Cambridge University Press, 1969), 86–87.

42. Ringer, *Decline of the German Mandarins,* 24–32; and Friedrich Paulsen, *The German Universities and University Study,* Frank Thilly, trans. (New York: C. Scribner's Sons, 1906), 280.

43. Ringer, *Decline of the German Mandarins,* 33.

44. Ibid., 34–35.

45. Ibid., 15–16.

46. Avraham Barkai. *Die Jüdische Minderheit und Industrialisierung. Demographie, Berufe und Einkommen der Juden in Westdeutschland, 1850–1914* (Tübingen: J.C.B. Mohr, 1988), 58–73.

CHAPTER 2

1. The inability to give an exact count of Jewish students during this era results from the lack of data. Many universities did not indicate the religious affiliation of their student body before 1880. The numbers given here are for the period 1805–1845 and they are found in Monika Richarz, *Der Eintritt der Juden in die Akademischen Berufe* (Tübingen: J.C.B. Mohr, 1974), 92.

2. Siegfried Ucko, "Geistesgeschichtliche Grundlagen der Wissenschaft des Judentums. (Motive des Kulturvereins vom Jahre 1819)," *Zeitschrift für die Geschichte der Juden in Deutschland* 5 (1935): 1–42; H. G. Reissner, "Rebellious Dilemma: The Case Histories of Eduard Gans and Some of His Partisans," *Leo Baeck Institute Yearbook* 2 (1956): 179–93; Michael A. Meyer, *The Origins of the Modern Jew: Jewish Identity and European Culture in Germany, 1749–1824* (Detroit: Wayne State University Press, 1979), 157–82; and Ismar Schorsch, "Breakthrough into the Past: The *Verein für Cultur und Wissenschaft der Juden,*" *Leo Baeck Institute Yearbook* 33 (1988): 3–28.

3. Richarz, *Der Eintritt der Juden,* 100–101.

4. Schorsch, "Breakthrough into the Past," 4.

5. Ucko, "Geistgeschichtliche Grundlagen," 9–12. This translation is found in Paul Mendes-Flohr and Jehuda Reinharz, eds., *The Jew in the Modern World: A Documentary History* (New York: Oxford University Press, 1980), 186–87.

6. Ibid., 186.

7. The emphases are found within the translation provided in Mendes-Flohr and Reinharz. Ibid., 187.

8. The entire text is found in Ucko, "Geistgeschichtliche Grundlagen," 13–20. This translation is from Albert Hoschander Friedlander, "The Wohlwill-Moser Correspondence," *Leo Baeck Institute Yearbook* 11 (1966): 270.

9. Ibid., 214–16.

10. S. Rubaschoff, "Erstlinge der Entjudung," *Der Jüdische Wille* (1918–19): 36–41, 108–21, and 193–203. The translation of Gans's speech is found in Mendes-Flohr and Reinharz, *The Jew in the Modern World,* 190–93.

11. Mendes-Flohr and Reinharz, *The Jew in the Modern World,* 192.

12. Meyer, *Origins of the Modern Jew,* 182.

13. Wolfgang Hardtwig, "Strukturmerkmale und Entwicklungstendenzen des Vereinswesens in Deutschland, 1789–1848," in *Historische Zeitschrift Beiheft #9:*

Vereinswesen und bürgerliche Gesellschaft in Deutschland, Otto Dann, ed. (Munich, 1984), 17–23.

14. Thomas Nipperdey, "Verein als soziale Struktur in Deutschland im späten 18. und frühen 19. Jahrhundert. Eine Fallstudie zur modernisierung I," in *Gesellschaft, Kultur, Theorie. Gesammelte Aufsätze zur neueren Geschichte* (Göttingen: Vandenhoeck and Ruprecht, 1976), 174–85.

15. Hardtwig, "Strukturmerkmale und Entwicklungstendenzen," 39–43.

16. Manfred Studier, *Der Corpsstudent als Idealbild der Wilhelminischen Ära. Untersuchnungen zum Zeitgeist 1888 bis 1914* (Würzburg: Gemeinschaft für deutsche Studentgeschichte,1990), 15 and 24–28; and *Studentenwörterbuch 4: Überarbeitete und erweiterte Aufluge.* Friedhelm Golücke, ed. (Würzburg: Gesellschaft für deutsche Studentgeschichte, 1987), 100.

17. *Was sind und wollen die Corps? Entwurf einer Zusammenstellung der allgemeinen deutschen Corps Principen* (Göttingen, 1869), 8.

18. *Constitution der Rhenania zu Heidelberg* (1802). Quoted in Studier, *Der Corpsstudent,* 29.

19. This principle was introduced by the *Corps,* but later adopted by a variety of university student associations. On the use of weapons to defend one's honor see *Was sind und wollen die Corps,* 10–12; *Die Corps der deutschen Hochschulen. Nebst einer eingehenden Darstellung studentischer Verhältnisse. Anhang: Die modernen Burschenschaft* (Leipzig, 1870), 49–75; and, Studier, *Der Corpsstudent,* 30–31. For contrasting interpretations of the significance of the duel see Kevin McAleer, *Duelling: The Cult of Honor in Fin-de-Siecle Germany* (Princeton, N.J.: Princeton University Press, 1994); and Ute Frevert, *Ehrenmänner. Das Duell in der Bürgerlichen Gesellschaft* (Munich: C. H. Beck, 1991).

20. *Constitution der Franconia zu Leipzig von 1811, Capital 3,* quoted in Studier, *Der Corpsstudent,* 32.

21. Albin Angerer, "Die Entwicklung des Toleranzgedankens in Studentischen Zusammenschlüssen. Eine Studie aus dem Institut für Hochschulkunde in Würzburg," *Einst und Jetzt. Jahrbuch des Vereins für corpsstudentische Gesichtsforschung* 3 (1958): 93. One must read Augerer's assessment of the religious equality within the *Corps* with a certain amount of caution, for he was an "old boy" of the organization and committed to the ideal of religious toleration.

22. Studier, *Der Corpsstudent,* 31–32.

23. Wolfgang Hardtwig, "Studentische Mentalität Politische Jugendbewegung: Nationalismus, Die Anfänge der deutschen Burschenschaften," *Historische Zeitschrift* 242 (1986): 585–90; Karl-Georg Faber, "Student und Politik in der ersten deutschen Burschenschaft," *Geschichte in Wissenschaft und Unterricht* 21, no. 2 (1970): 68–72; and Konrad Jarausch, "The Sources of German Student Unrest: 1815–1848," in *The University in Society, Vol. 2: Europe, Scotland, and the United States from the 16th–20th Century,* Lawrence Stone, ed. (Princeton, N.J.: Princeton University Press, 1974), 536–38. A somewhat uncritical history of the organization's early development is Paul Wentzcke, ed., *Geschichte der deutschen Burschenschaft. Vor und Frühzeit bis zu den Karlsbader Beschlüssen,* vol. 1 (Heidelberg: Carl Winter, 1919), 95–224.

24. Hardtwig, "Studentische Mentalität," 590; and Jarausch, "Sources of German Student Unrest," 538.

25. Hardtwig, "Studentische Mentalität," 590–91.

26. Jürgen Schwarz, "Deutsche Studenten und Politik im 19. Jahrhundert,"

Geschichte und Wissenschaft und Unterricht 20, no. 2 (1969): 75–77; and Faber, "Student und Politik," 69–73.

27. Richarz, *Der Eintritt der Juden*, 91; Faber, "Student und Politik," 70–71; and Schwarz, "Deutsche Studenten und Politik," 79. Exact figures for membership between the years 1815 and 1818 are problematic since most members of *Burschenschaft* organizations at this time had previously belonged to the *Corps*, and there was not always a clear distinction between the membership lists of the two organizations. See Bernhard Sommerlad, "Wartburgfest und Corpsstudenten," *Einst und Jetzt* (1979): 16–42.

28. On the *Corps'* belief that *Wissenschaft* was central to *Bildung*, see *Was sind und wollen die Corps*," 8–9; and "Über das Wesen der Corpsverbindungen auf den deutschen Universitäten," *Akademische Zeitschrift. Organ für die gesammten Interessen der deutschen Hochschulen* 2 (1868): 21–24. For a rebuttal of this position see "Über das Wesen der Corpsverbindungen auf den deutschen Universitäten (Entgegnung)," *Akademsiche Zeitschrift* 4/5 (1868): 55–57; and *Das gegenwärtige deutsche Studententhum, Seine Partien und die Grundzüge Seiner Entwickelung. Dargelegt in der Form einer Erwiderung auf die Schrift: Was sind und wollen die Corps?* (Göttingen, 1869). For further elaboration on the *Burschenschaften's* understanding of politics as central to the acquisition of *Bildung* see *Was will und soll die Burschenschaften? Ein Wort zur Aufklärung* (Breslau, 1864).

29. *Handbuch der deutschen Burschenschaft: Herausgegeben vom Hauptausschuß der deutschen Burschenschaft im Geschäftsjahr 1981/82* (Bad Neuheim, 1982), chap. 2, p. 3; and Jarausch, "Sources of German Student Unrest," 537.

30. Schwarz "Deutsche Studenten und Politik," 76–79.

31. James Sheehan, *German Liberalism in the 19th Century* (Chicago: University of Chicago Press, 1978), chap. 1; and Reinhard Rürup, "German Liberalism and the Emancipation of the Jews," *Leo Baeck Institute Yearbook* 20 (1975): 59–68.

32. Oskar Franz Scheuer, *Burschenschaft und Judenfrage. Der Rassenantisemitismus in der deutschen Studentenschaft* (Berlin: Verlag Berlin-Wien, 1927), 14–32; Friedrich Schulze and Paul Ssymank, *Das deutsche Studententum von den ältesten Zeiten bis zur Gegenwart* (Leipzig: R. Voigtländers Verlag, 1910), 192–94; Jarausch, "Sources of German Student Unrest," 536–40. Bruno Weil, on the other hand, claims that "from the beginning, the *Burschenschaft* was established on Christo-Germanic principles" *(Juden in der deutschen Burschenschaften. Ein Beitrag zum Streit und die Konfessionelle Studentenverbindung* [Straßburg, 1905], 14, 16–18. He is supported by Karl-Georg Faber, "Student und Politik," 72.

33. Scheuer, *Burschenschaft und Judenfrage*, 9; and Weil, *Juden in der deutschen Burschenschaften*, 13.

34. Scheuer, *Burschenschaft und Judenfrage*, 10–12; Weil, *Juden in der deutschen Burschenschaften*, 16–18; and Schulze and Ssymank, *Das deutsche Studententum*, 193.

35. George W. Spindler, *The Life of Karl Follen. A Study in German-American Cultural Relations* (Chicago: University of Chicago Press, 1917), 7–76.

36. Scheuer, *Burschenschaft und Judenfrage*, 12–13.

37. Quoted in Hartmut Reichold, "Dr. jur. David Morgenstern. Juden in der Burschenschaft des Vormärz," *Israelistische Kultusgemeinde Fürth* (September 1983): 15.

38. Scheuer, *Burschenschaft und Judenfrage*, 34.

39. Wentzcke, *Geschichte der deutschen Burschenschaft*, 311–67; Schulze and Ssymank, *Das deutsche Studententum*, 176–89.

40. Scheuer, *Burschenschaft und Judenfrage*, 32–33; *Handbuch der deutschen Burschenschaft*, chap. 2, p. 5.

41. My analysis is based on the university matriculation records, *Die Matrikel der Universität Heidelberg*. Gustav Toepke, ed., vols. 5 and 6 (Heidelberg: Carl Winter's Universitätbuchhandlung, 1904), and the comprehensive membership lists of the major student organizations. Only the organizations that remained in existence from the time of their establishment until at least 1871 were utilized for this case study. Consequently, a number of groups identified as part of the early *Burschenschaft* movement at Heidelberg, such as *Teutonia*, are not incorporated into the data on Jewish membership that I have compiled.

42. These words of a Dr. Fick are quoted in George Morey Miller, *Alt Heidelberg and its Student Life* (Heidelberg: Otto Peters, 1911), 6.

43. Hans Dietrich Graebke, "Der Heidelberger Seniorenconvent (SC) vom beginn des 19. Jahrhunderts bis Heute," 17–36, and Ernst Wilhelm Wreden, "Die Heidelberger Burschenschaft 1814–1986," 45–67, in *Weiland Bursch zu Heidelberg. Eine Festschrift der Heidelberger Korporationen zur 600-Jahr-Feier der Ruperto Carola*, Gerhart Berger and Detlev Aurand, eds. (Heidelberg: Heidelberger Verlagsanstalt u. Druckerei, 1986).

44. The origins of the word itself are obscure, but it is peculiar to the vocabulary of German university students. Frevert, *Ehrenmänner*, 133 and McAleer, *Duelling*, 120–26.

45. For a description of the garb worn by students in the 1840s, see William Howitt, ed., *The Student-Life of Germany. From the Unpublished Manuscripts of Dr. Cornelius* (London: Longman, Brown, Green and Longmans, 1841), 127–28. For a more modern description that includes eye protection, see Lee Knowles, *A Day With Korps-Students in Germany. Being an Account of Some Heidelberg Duels* (Heidelberg, 1908), 16–17.

46. In his analysis of Czech Jewry, Hillel Kieval points to the acquisition of a universal education, industrialization, and urbanization as indices of acculturation. *The Making of Czech Jewry. National Conflict and Jewish Society in Bohemia, 1870–1918* (New York: Oxford University Press, 1988), 3–7. See also, Richarz, *Eintritt der Juden*, 88–89.

47. Jacob Katz, *Out of the Ghetto: The Social Background of Jewish Emancipation, 1770–1870* (New York: Schocken Books, 1978), 1–80.

48. Ernst Wilhelm Wreden, "Die Heidelberger Burschenschaft 1814–1986," *Weiland Bursch zu Heidelberg*, 45–67.

49. Ernst Wilhelm Wreden "Burschenschaft Allemania," *Weiland Bursch zu Heidelberg*, 124–26; and *Geschichte der Burschenschaft Allemania zu Heidelberg, 1856–1906* (Heidelberg,1906). On Frankonia see *Die Burschenschaft Franconia zu Heidelberg, 1856–1886. Eine Festgabe zum dreißigjährigen Stiftungsfest* (Heidelberg, 1886); and Torsten Locher, "Burschenschaft Frankonia in der DB," *Weiland Bursch zu Heidelberg*, 127–31.

CHAPTER 3

1. Konrad Jarausch, *Students, Society and Politics in Imperial Germany: The Rise of Academic Illiberalism* (Princeton, N.J.: Princeton University Press, 1982), 27–31; *Deutsche Studententum 1800–1970* (Frankfurt am Main: Suhrkamp Verlag, 1984), 71–80, and "The Social Transformation of the University: The Case of Prussia, 1865–

1914," *Journal of Social History* 12 (1979): 609–36. See also C. E. McClelland, *State, Society and University in Germany, 1700–1914* (Cambridge: Cambridge University Press, 1980), chaps. 6 and 7.

2. Norbert Kampe explains the term "over-representation" as conveying a "notion of an ideal situation of balance, . . . between different religious groups in institutions of higher education." See "Jews and Antisemites at Universities in Imperial Germany (I) Jewish Students: Social History and Social Conflict," *Leo Baeck Institute Yearbook* 30 (1985): 358–59, note 5.

3. The most comprehensive statistical data available detailing the religious affiliation of the German student body during the Kaiserreich comes from the matriculation records of the Prussian universities. This data does not provide information on the religious affiliation of the student body until 1886 and, consequently, statistical discussion of Jewish university students of the Kaiserreich cannot account for the religious affiliation of students before 1886. The figures cited here are from Norbert Kampe's monograph on the "Jewish Question" at German universities, *Studenten und "Judenfrage" im Deutschen Kaiserreich: Die Entstehung einer akademischen Trägerschlicht des Antisemitismus* (Göttingen: Vandenhoek and Ruprecht, 1988),79.

4. Jarausch, *Students, Society and Politics*, 35.

5. Ibid., 35–40.

6. Friederich Paulsen, "Die Entwicklung der Realschule zum Realgymnasium in Preußen," *Das Gymnasium in Geschichte und Gegenwart*, Hermann Röhrs, ed. (Frankfurt a.M.: Akademische Verlagsgesellschaft, 1969), 14–41; and Fritz Ringer, *Education and Society in Modern Europe* (Bloomington: Indiana University Press, 1979), 70–81.

7. Kampe, "Jews and Antisemites (I)," 360.

8. These figures are derived from Kampe, "Jews and Antisemites (I)," 388, table 2b.

9. These dates are given in Marion A. Kaplan, *The Making of the Jewish Middle Class: Women, Family and Identity in Imperial Germany* (New York: Oxford University Press, 1991), 277, note 1.

10. Jarausch, *Students, Society and Politics*, 37, and "Social Transformation of the University," 618–19.

11. Kaplan, *Making of the Jewish Middle Class*, 138.

12. Ibid., 137.

13. Jarausch, *Students, Society and Politics*, 38.

14. Kampe, "Jews and Antisemites (I)," 389, table 3.

15. Jack Wertheimer, "The Ausländerfrage at Institutions of Higher Learning. A Controversy Over Russian-Jewish Students in Imperial Germany," *Leo Baeck Institute Yearbook* 27 (1982): 187.

16. During the academic year 1912–13, there were 2,350 Russian students studying at German institutions of higher learning and, of this group, Jews accounted for 1,845 of them, or 78.5 percent. These figures are derived from Wertheimer, "Ausländerfrage," 212, table 2.

17. Jack Wertheimer, "Between Tsar and Kaiser. The Radicalisation of Russian-Jewish University Students in Germany," *Leo Baeck Institute Yearbook* 28 (1983): 329–38.

18. Usiel O. Schmelz, "Die Demographische Entwicklung der Juden in Deutschland von der Mitte des 19. Jahrhunderts bis 1933," *Bulletin des Leo Baeck*

Instituts 83 (1989): 15–62; and Abraham Barkai, "German Jewish Migrations in the 19th century, 1830–1910," *Leo Baeck Institute Yearbook* 30 (1985): 301–18.

19. Monika Richarz, *Jewish Life in Germany: Memoirs from Three Centuries*, Stellan and Sidney Rosenfeld, trans. (Bloomington: Indiana University Press, 1991), 6; Barkai, "German Jewish Migrations," 305–11; and Schmelz, "Die Demographische Entwicklung," 31–36.

20. Steven Aschheim, *Brothers and Strangers: The Eastern European Jew in German and Jewish Consciousness, 1800–1923* (Madison: University of Wisconsin Press, 1982); and Jack Wertheimer, *Unwelcome Strangers: East European Jews in Imperial Germany* (New York: Oxford University Press,1987).

21. Kampe, "Jews and Antisemites (I)," 379–83.

22. Paul W. Massing, *Rehearsal for Destruction: A Study of Political Anti-Semitism in Imperial Germany* (New York: Harper, 1949), 21–50; Peter G. J. Pulzer, *The Rise of Political Anti-Semitism in Germany and Austria* (New York: John Wiley and Sons, 1964), 88–103 and 249–50; Michael Meyer, "Great Debate on Antisemitism. Jewish Reaction to New Hostility in Germany, 1879–81," *Leo Baeck Institute Yearbook* 11 (1966): 142–45; Werner Jochmann, "Struktur und Funktion des deutschen Antisemitismus," *Juden im Wilhelminischen Deutschland, 1890–1914* (Tübingen: J.C.B. Mohr, 1976), 411–29; and Ismar Schorsch, *Jewish Reactions to German Antisemitism, 1870–1914* (New York: Columbia University Press, 1972),36–39 and 54–63.

23. Norbert Kampe, "Jews and Antisemites at Universities in Imperial Germany (II): The Friedrich-Wilhelms-Universität of Berlin: A Case Study of the Students' Jewish Question," *Leo Baeck Institute Yearbook* 30 (1987): 46. See also Adolph Asch, *Geschichte des K.C. (Kartell jüdischer Studenten) im Lichte der deutschen kulturellen und politischen Entwicklung* (London, 1964), 31–32; and Pulzer, *Rise of Political Anti-Semitism*, 248–50.

24. For an excellent discussion of the function of language within antisemitic rhetoric see Shulamit Volkov, "Antisemitism as a Cultural Code: Reflections on the History and Historiography of Antisemitism in Imperial Germany," *Leo Baeck Institute Yearbook* 23 (1978): 25–46. For a copy of Stöcker's treatise, entitled "What We Demand of World Jewry," see Massing, *Rehearsal for Destruction*, 278–87.

25. Quoted from Massing, *Rehearsal for Destruction*, 283–87.

26. Kampe, "Jews and Antisemites (II)," 45–46; Asch, *Geschichte des K.C.*, 31–32; Pulzer, *Rise of Political Anti-Semitism*, 243–44; and Hans Liebeschütz,"Treitschke and Mommsen on Jewry and Judaism," in *LBI Yearbook* 7 (1962): 172–73. The essay, in its entirety, is contained in Walter Boehlich, ed., *Der Berliner Antisemitismusstreit* (Frankfurt am Main: Insel Verlag, 1965), 7–14, and can be found in English in Ellis Rivkin, ed., *Readings in Modern Jewish History*, Helen Lederer, trans. (Cincinnati: Hebrew Union College, n.d.), 1–7.

27. Rivkin, *Readings in Modern Jewish History*, 3.

28. Emphasis mine. Ibid., 2.

29. Liebeschütz, "Treitschke and Mommsen," 158–59.

30. Volkov, "Antisemitism as a Cultural Code," 42–44.

31. "A Word About Our Jewry," *Readings in Modern Jewish History*, 7.

32. The entire text of this essay can be found in Boehlich, *Der Berliner Antisemitismusstreit*, 212–26. For English translations I have utilized the abridged version located in Paul Mendes-Flohr and Jehuda Reinharz, *The Jew in the Modern World: A Documentary History* (New York: Oxford University Press, 1980), 284–87.

33. "Another Word About Our Jewry," *The Jew in the Modern World*, 286–87.

34. Ibid., 286. For a discussion of Mommsen's view of the Jews in German society see Liebeschütz, "Treitschke and Mommsen," 175–82.

35. Pulzer, *The Rise of Political Anti-Semitism*, 250.

36. Ibid., 94–96.

37. Emphasis mine. Reinhard Rürup, "The European Revolutions of 1848 and Jewish Emancipation," in *Revolution and Evolution: 1848 in Jewish History*, Werner E. Mosse, Arnold Paucker, and Reinhard Rürup, eds. (Tübingen: J.C.B. Mohr, 1981), 42.

38. Pulzer, *Rise of Political Anti-Semitism*, 96; and Massing, *Rehearsal for Destruction*, 39–40.

39. Massing, *Rehearsal for Destruction*, 442.

40. *Die Judenfrage als Racen—Sitten—und Culturfrage* (Karlsruhe and Leipzig, 1881), 3–4. In English see, Mendes-Flohr and Reinharz, *The Jew in the Modern World*, 273–74.

41. Kampe, *Studenten und "Judenfrage,"* 23–51

42. Kampe, "Jews and Antisemites (II)," 48–50. For more detailed discussion of the petition itself and support for it by university students see L. Quidde, *Die Antisemitenagitation und die deutsche Studentenschaft* (Göttingen: Verlag von Robert Peppmüller, 1881); and Kampe, *Studenten und "Judenfrage,"* 23–29.

43. Student supporters of the petition met on November 22 and December 10, 1880, to discuss the petition and proposed limitation of Jewish rights. A record of the speeches given at these meetings is found in *Die studentische Petition als Annex der allgemeinen Petition betreffend die Einschränkung der jüdischen Machtstellung. Reden gehalten in dem am 22. Nov. u. 10. Dec. zur Besprechung der Frage in Tritschlers Saal u. der Central-Halle privat abgehaltenen Versammlungen* (Leipzig, 1881). Kampe discusses these meetings in "Jews and Antisemites (II)," 49.

44. Quoted in Kampe, "Jews and Antisemites (II)," 50. Three different editions of the student petition were issued. For references to them see Kampe's footnote #38 found on page 50.

45. Ibid., 51 and Kampe, *Studenten und "Judenfrage,"* 31.

46. Kampe, *Studenten und "Judenfrage,"* 31.

47. Ibid., 51, and especially note #75 page 58.

48. Ibid., 35–42.

49. Ibid., 51.

50. The text of Hahn's speech at the opening of the Kyffhäuserfest is contained in Kampe, *Studenten und "Judenfrage,"* 48. On Hahn's continued involvement in conservative politics, see George Vascik, "The German Peasant League and the Limits of Rural Liberalism in Wilhelminian Germany," *Central European History* 24, no. 2 (1991): 147–75.

51. Friedrich Schulze and Paul Ssymank, *Das deutsche Studentum von den ältesten Zeiten bis zur Gegenwart* (Leipzig: R. Voigtländers Verlag, 1910), 328–29.

52. Not only is there very little secondary source information about the *Freie Wissenschaftliche Vereinigung*, but even primary sources are scarce. Those that do exist are the group's monthly reports, which are merely a chronicle of events and activities of the association, and pamphlets about the F.W.V. written by the members of the organization. Although rather uncritical, the best source of information for the F.W.V. is the *Freie Wissenschaftliche Taschenbüche in zwei Bearbeitung*, published by the Alte Herren der Freien Wissenschaftlichen Vereinigung an der Universität Berlin, Berlin 1931.

53. Richard Jutrosinski, "Die Entstehung der Freien Wissenschaftlichen Vereinigung," in *Freie Wissenschaftliche Taschenbüche in zwei Bearbeitung*, 29.

54. Max Spangenberg, "Unsere Ziele. Gründungsrede von 4 Juli, 1881," in *Freie Wissenschaftliche Taschenbüche in zwei Bearbeitung*, 14–15; Schulze and Ssymank, *Das deutsche Studentum*, 331; and Jarausch, *Students, Society and Politics*, 271. These sentiments are echoed by other members of the F.W.V. in their articles on the establishment of the group. For example, see also Jutrosinski, "Der Entstehung," 27–28.

55. Spangenberg, "Unsere Ziele," 14–17. A good overview of the corporate subculture of student associations is given in Jarausch, *Students, Society and Politics*, 234–62. See also Prof. Aschaffenburg's, "Der Student und die Alkoholfrage," in *Neudeutsches Studentenbrevier. Aufsätze zur Einführung ins akademische Leben der Gegenwart*, Paul Ssymank, ed. (Munich: Breyslag, 1912), 116–20; and "Die Studentische Kultur von 1850 bis zur Gegenwart," in Schulze and Ssymak, *Das deutsche Studententum*, 422–59.

56. Heinz Herz,"F.W.V. und Nation," 53; and Ernst Bein,"F.W.V. und Wissenschaft," in *Freie Wissenschaftliche Taschenbüche in zwei Bearbeitung*, 41.

57. Spangenberg,"Unsere Ziele," 9.

58. Franz von Liszt,"Organisation und Organisationsformen in studentischen Leben," in *Freie Wissenschaftliche Taschenbüche in zwei Bearbeitung*, 22–23.

59. George Mosse,"Jewish Emancipation: Between *Bildung* and Respectibility," in *The Jewish Response to German Culture From the Enlightenment to the Second World War*, Jehuda Reinharz and Walter Schatzberg, eds. (Hanover: University Press of New England, 1985), 1–16; George Mosse, *German Jews Beyond Judaism* (Bloomington: Indiana University Press, 1985), 1–20; and David Sorkin, *The Transformation of German Jewry, 1780–1840* (New York: Oxford University Press, 1987), 13–40.

60. The text of this speech was published along with Spangenberg's initial address to the F.W.V. in *Der Standpunkt der Freien Wissenschaftlichen Vereinigung an der Universität Berlin: Zur Judenfrage und zur Wissenschaft; zwei Reden an seine Vereingenossen gehalten am 4. Juli 1881 und 30. October 1882*, Berlin 1882, 17–35 and is also reproduced in the *Freie Wissenschaftliche Taschenbüche in zwei Bearbeitung*, 86–98.

61. Spangenberg, *Der Standpunkt*, 23–24.

62. Ibid., 24–25. On Auerbach see David Sorkin,"The Invisible Community: Emancipation, Secular Culture, and Jewish Identity in the Writings of Berthold Auerbach," in *The Jewish Response to German Culture From the Enlightenment to the Second World War*, Jehuda Reinharz and Walter Schatzberg, eds. (Hanover: University Press of New England, 1985), 100–119 and Nancy A. Kaiser, *Social Integration and Narrative Structure: Patterns of Realism in Auerbach, Freytag, Fontane and Raabe* (New York: Lang, 1986).

63. Spangenberg,"Unsere Ziele," 26.

64. Ibid., 27–28.

65. James Sheehan, *German Liberalism in the 19th Century* (Chicago: University of Chicago Press, 1978), 159–60.

66. Spangenberg,"Unsere Ziele," 32–33.

67. Ibid., 33.

68. Alan Levenson,"Jewish Reactions to Intermarriage in Nineteenth Century Germany" (Ph.D. diss., Ohio State University, 1990), 125; and Michael A. Meyer,

Response to Modernity: A History of the Reform Movement in Judaism (New York: Oxford University Press, 1988), 62–100.

69. Herz,"F.W.V. und Nation," 50–51. These figures are found in Kampe, *Studenten und "Judenfrage,"* 155.

70. Memoir of Eduard Isaac, ME 326.

71. Ibid., 12.

72. Ibid., 22–24.

73. Ibid., 24–25

74. An extensive, but incomplete collection of the *Monatsberichte des Bundes Freier Wissenschaftlicher Vereinigung* (Berlin, December 15, 1887–January 1928) is located in the Leo Baeck Institute Library, New York.

75. Sorkin, *Transformation of German Jewry,* 6.

76. Mosse, *German Jews Beyond Judaism,* 4.

CHAPTER 4

1. For example see Walter Gross, "The Zionist Students' Movement," *Leo Baeck Institute Yearbook* 4 (1959): 143–64; Stephen M. Poppel, *Zionism in Germany 1897–1933: The Shaping of Jewish Identity* (Philadelphia: Jewish Publication Society, 1977); and Moshe Zimmermann, "Jewish Nationalism and Zionism in German-Jewish Students' Organizations," *Leo Baeck Institute Yearbook* 27 (1982): 129–53.

2. (Berlin: Juedische Buch-Vereinigung, 1935). See especially 294–97.

3. Adolph Asch and Johanna Philippson, "Self-Defence at the Turn of the Century: The Emergence of the K.C. (Kartell-Convent)," *Leo Baeck Institute Yearbook* 3 (1958): 132–33; and Adolph Asch, *Geschichte des K.C. (Kartell jüdischer Studenten)im Lichte der deutschen kulturellen und politische Entwicklung* (London,1964).

4. Jehuda Reinharz, *Fatherland or Promised Land. The Dilemma of the German Jew, 1893–1914* (Ann Arbor: University of Michigan Press, 1975), 29–30.

5. Ibid., 32–35. See also Thomas Schindler, *Studentischer Antisemitismus und jüdische Studentverbindungen, 1880–1933* (Gießen: Schriftenreihe der Studenten-geschichtlichen Vereinigung des CC, 1988).

6. Shulamit Volkov, "The Dynamics of Dissimilation: *Ostjuden* and German Jews," in *The Jewish Response to German Culture From the Enlightenment to the Second World War,* Jehuda Reinharz and W. Schatzberg, eds. (Hanover: University Press of New England, 1985), 198–99.

7. David Sorkin labels this phenomenon as an "illiberal tradition of liberalism." "Emancipation and Assimilation: Two Concepts and their Application to German-Jewish History," *Leo Baeck Institute Yearbook* 35 (1990): 20. Ismar Schorsch writes that "both the opponents and the advocates [of emancipation] desired conversion or, at the very least, the abandonment of Judaism. They differed only on the question of timing." *Jewish Reactions to German Antisemitism, 1870–1914* (New York: Columbia University Press, 1972), 3.

8. Michael A. Meyer, *Response to Modernity: A History of the Reform Movement in Judaism* (New York: Oxford University Press, 1988), 62–99.

9. "Emancipation and Assimilation," 21. For further discussion of the Jewish position on emancipation see Robert Liberles, "Was There a Jewish Movement for Emancipation in Germany?," *Leo Baeck Institute Yearbook* 31 (1986): 35–49.

10. Monika Richarz, ed., *Jewish Life in Germany. Memoirs from Three Centuries,*

Stella P. Rosenfeld and Sidney Rosenfeld, trans. (Bloomington: Indiana University Press, 1991), 19.

11. Quoted in Schorsch, *Jewish Reactions*, 6.

12. The *Detusch-Israelitischer Gemeindebund* was founded in 1869 and brought together the official communal organizations of German Jewry. In 1881, the organization succumbed to pressure from the Saxon government and disbanded. On the *Gemeindebund* see Schorsch, *Jewish Reactions*, 23–52.

13. Schorsch, *Jewish Reactions*, 12. Shulamit Volkov also discusses the phenomenon of Jews preserving their Jewishness within the "intimate culture" of family life rather than in the public sphere. "The Dynamics of Dissimilation," 195–211.

14. Marion A. Kaplan, *The Making of the Jewish Middle Class: Women, Family and Identity in Imperial Germany* (New York: Oxford University Press, 1991), 11.

15. Ibid., 10., and Richarz, *Jewish Life in Germany*, 2 and 24.

16. Sorkin, "Emancipation and Assimilation," 20–21.

17. Richarz, *Jewish Life in Germany*, 14. On the limits of Jewish occupational choices during the Kaiserreich see Ismar Schorsch, "The Religious Parameters of Wissenschaft. Jewish Academics at Prussian Universities," *Leo Baeck Institute Yearbook* 25 (1980): 3–19; Peter Pulzer, "Religion and Judicial Appointments in Germany: 1869–1918," *Leo Baeck Institute Yearbook* 28 (1983): 185–204; and Werner T. Angress, "Prussia's Army and the Jewish Reserve Officer Controversy Before World War I," *Leo Baeck Institute Yearbook* 17 (1972): 19–42.

18. Ismar Schorsch argues that "the formation of the *Centralverein* in 1893 signaled the beginning of a Jewish revision of the terms of emancipation." *Jewish Reactions*, 12.

19. Thomas Nipperdey, "Verein als soziale Struktur in Deutschland im späten 18. und frühen 19. Jahrhundert. Eine Fallstudie zur modernisierung I," in *Gesellschaft, Kultur, Theorie. Gesammelte Aufsätze zur neueren Geschichte* (Göttingen: Vandenhoek and Ruprecht, 1976), 174–205; and Wolfgang Hardtwig, "Strukturmerkmale und Entwicklungstendenzen des Vereinswesens in Deutschland, 1789–1848," in *Historische Zeitschrift Beiheft #9: Vereinswesen und bürgerliche Gesellschaft in Deutschland,* Otto Dann, ed. (Munich: R. Oldenbourg Verlag, 1984), 11–50. For the later period see Nipperdey's *Deutsche Geschichte 1866–1918. Zweiter Band. Machtstaat vor der Demokratie* (Munich: C. H. Beck, 1992), 576–94.

20. Michael Hughes, *Nationalism and Society. Germany 1800–1945* (London: Edward Arnold, 1988), 138–139.

21. Ibid., 156–57.

22. Norbert Kampe, *Studenten und "Judenfrage" im Deutschen Kaiserreich: Die Entstehung einer akademischen Trägerschicht des Antisemitismus* (Göttingen: Vandenhoek and Ruprecht, 1988), 33–51 and 139–51; Konrad Jarausch, *Students, Society and Politics in Imperial Germany: The Rise of Academic Illiberalism* (Princeton, N.J.: Princeton University Press, 1982), 266–71, 353–56, and 384–85; and George Mosse, *The Crisis of German Ideology. Intellectual Origins of the Third Reich* (New York: Grosset and Dunlap, 1964), 190–203.

23. The literature on the *völkisch* movement and *völkisch* nationalism is considerable. Hughes offers a concise and informative summary in *Nationalism and Society,* 142–48. Fritz Stern evaluates the writings of the movement's primary ideologues, Paul de Lagarde and Julius Langbehn, in *The Politics of Cultural Despair. A Study in the*

Rise of the Germanic Ideology (Berkeley: University of California Press, 1961), while George Mosse provides an excellent analysis of the movement's intellectual and ideological components in *The Crisis of German Ideology*, 13–148. The movement as a response to modernization is discussed by Shulamit Volkov in *The Rise of Popular Anti-Modernism in Germany 1873–1893. The Urban Master Artisans* (Princeton, N.J.: Princeton University Press, 1978).

24. Hughes, *Nationalism and Society*, 153–57. On the *Kulturkampf* see David Blackbourn, *Class, Religion and Local Politics in Wilhelmine Germany. The Centre Party in Württemberg Before 1914* (New Haven: Yale University Press, 1980).

25. On Jewish organizations see Schorsch, *Jewish Reactions;* and Reinharz, *Fatherland or Promised Land.* For an overview of Catholic associations see Blackbourn, *Class, Religion and Local Politics;* and R. J. Ross, *The Beleaguered Tower. The Dilemma of Political Catholicism in Wilhelmine Germany* (Notre Dame: University of Notre Dame Press, 1976). On socialist societies, see Vernon L. Lidtke, *The Alternative Culture: Socialist Labor in Imperial Germany* (New York: Oxford University Press, 1985) and Guenther Roth, *The Social Democrats in Imperial Germany* (Totowa, N.J.: Bedminster Press, 1963).

26. The best guide to the complicated corporate subculture of German universities is Paul Seiffert, *Geschichte und Entwicklung der studentischen Verbände* (Breslau, 1913).

27. Jarausch, *Students, Society and Politics,* 248–62.

28. Ibid., 253–54.

29. Among the more organized *Vereine* were the Catholic *Studentvereine* which coalesced into the *Kartell-Verband* in 1866, and the various *wissenschaftliche Vereine* that grew out of study and reading groups in the 1850s and 1860s and into national associations in the 1870s, 1880s, and 1890s. An overview of these organizations is given by Jarausch in his *Students, Society and Politics,* 256–62.

30. The quotation is found in ibid., 277. For further discussion of the *Finkenschaft* movement see Paul Ssymank, *Die Finkenschaftsbewegung: Ihr Enstehen und ihre Entwicklung bis zur Gründung der "Deutschen Freien Studentenschaft"* (Munich: Vergriffen, 1901); and *Die Freistudententische oder Finkenschaftsbewegung an den deutschen Hochschulen* (Jena: Verlag von Eugen Diederichs,1905).

31. Joseph Gutmann, *Geschichte des Akademischen Vereins für Jüdische Geschichte und Literatur: Zum 50. Stiftungsfest* (Berlin, 1933), 1.

32. Ibid., 6.

33. The *Semester Bericht* of 1884 is quoted in ibid., 6.

34. Jarausch's, *Students, Society and Politics, passim;* Kampe, *Studenten und Judenfrage, passim;* and Fritz Stern, *The Failure of Illiberalism. Essays on the Political Culture of Modern Germany* (New York: Knopf,1972).

35. Gutmann, *Geschichte des Akademischen Vereins,* 9.

36. An Association of Alte Herren of the AJGV was founded in July 1891 and, in the tradition of student corporatism, the members of this "Old Boys" group remained in close contact with the active members of the student association. On the Alte Herren Association see Ibid., 3.

37. Emphasis mine. Ibid., 7.

38. Ibid., 7.

39. The memoir entitled "Erinnerungen eines alten A.J.G.Vers." is found in Gutmann's *Geschichte des Akademischen Vereins,* 9–14.

40. Ibid., 8.

41. A copy of the unpublished biography of Marvin Warschauer written by his son, James Julius Walters (1988), is found in the Leo Baeck Institute in New York, #AR 794.

42. Ibid., 11–13.

43. When considering Warschauer's criticisms about the organization, one has to keep in mind that our knowledge of his feelings is filtered through the prism of his adult life as a rabbi and an active Judaica scholar, and it is relayed to us through the writings of his son.

44. Ibid., 2. These lectures were given during the summer and winter semesters, 1895–96. The titles themselves are found in *Semester-Bericht des Akedemischen Vereins für jüdische Geschichte und Literatur* (winter semester, 1895–96), 17. This document is located in the Wiener Library in Tel Aviv.

45. A *Verein für jüdische Geschichte und Literatur* was founded in Berlin in 1892. A copy of the organizational statutes and miscellaneous information on the association is found in file numbers TD 69 and TD 503 of the Central Archive for the History of the Jewish People (hereafter referred to as the CAHJP). An essay written by Alexander Margolius entitled *Der Verein für Jüdische Geschichte und Literatur in Berlin, 1892–1927*, is located in the Wiener Library at Tel Aviv University.

46. Julius Schoeps, "Modern Heirs of the Maccabees. The Beginning of the Vienna Kadimah, 1882–1897," *Leo Baeck Institute Yearbook* 27 (1982): 155–58.

47. Ibid., 161–68. See also Robert S. Wistrich, *The Jews of Vienna in the Age of Franz Joseph* (New York: Oxford University Press, 1989), 363–69.

48. The document entitled "Ein Wort an Unsere Glaubensgenossen" is found in the Central Zionist Archives (CZA) file A 142–90-11F. A complete translation of this manifesto is contained in Adolph Asch and Johanna Philipson, "Self-Defence at the Turn of the Century: The Emergence of the K.C. (Kartell-Convent)," *Leo Baeck Institute Yearbook* 3 (1958): 122–25. The quotations used in the following discussion are taken from this translation.

49. Ernst I. Jacob, "Life and Work of B. Jacob," in *Paul Lazarus Gedenkbuch. Beiträge zur Wurdigung der Letzten Rabbinergeneration in Deutschland* (Jerusalem: Jerusalem Post Press, 1961), 93–100.

50. Asch and Philipson,"Self-Defence at the Turn of the Century," 124.

51. Ibid., 124.

52. Ibid., 124.

53. Founded in 1893, the *Centralverein* became the major organization of German Jewry. There is a considerable amount of literature on the *Centralverein*, but two important accounts of its establishment are Schorsch, *Jewish Reactions*, 103–48; and Arnold Paucker, "The Jewish Defense Against Antisemitism in Germany, 1893–1933," in *Living With Antisemitism. Modern Jewish Responses*, Jehuda Reinharz, ed. (Hanover: Brandeis University Press, 1987), 104–32.

54. *Ein Wort*, 124.

55. Ibid., 124–25.

56. Ute Frevert, *Ehrenmänner: Das Duell in der Bürgerlichen Gesellschaft* (Munich: C. H. Beck, 1991), 133–66.

57. Kampe, *Studenten und "Judenfrage,"* 185–204; and Schindler, *Studentischer Antisemitismus*, 37–88.

58. Sylvius Pick, "Vor 60 Jahren," 3.

59. Pick, "Vor 60 Jahren," 3.

60. A copy of Posener's unpublished manuscript is located in the National Library of Israel in Jerusalem. This essay functions more as a memoir than as a historical narrative.

61. Ibid., 42–43.

62. Ibid., 57–59.

63. On the founding of the K.C. see Kurt Jakubowski, "Die Gründung des K.C. Eine persönliche Errinerung," in *K.C. Blätter Festschrift: 50 Jahre K.C.* (New York, 1946), 5; Max Mainzer, "50 Jahre K.C.- Ein Beitrag zur Geschichte seiner Gründung und Entwicklung," in *K.C. Blätter Festschrift: 50 Jahre K.C.* (New York, 1946),5–9; Hans Reichmann, "Gedanken Zur KC-Geschichte," in *K.C. Blätter Festschrift: 50 Jahre K.C.* (New York, 1946), 9–11; Asch, *Geschichte des K.C.*, *passim;* Reinharz, *Fatherland or Promised Land*, 32–35; and Schindler, *Studentischer Antisemitismus*, 117–25. The selection of the name *Kartell Convent* was a conscious decision on the part of the students to align themselves with the positions of the *Central Verein deutscher Staatsbürger jüdischen Glaubens*. On the similarities between the K.C. and the C.V. see Reinharz, *Fatherland or Promised Land*, 50–51.

64. Reichmann, "Gedanken Zur KC-Geschichte," 10. The concept of giving and receiving "satisfaction" means that one is perceived to be an honorable student and capable of defending oneself in a duel. The latter part of the quotation is also found in Reinharz, *Fatherland or Promised Land*, 32.

65. Reichmann, "Gedanken Zur KC-Geschichte," 11.

66. *Bericht der freien Verbindung Badenia über das Wintersemester 1894/95* (hereafter referred to as *Semester Bericht*). CZA A 142 90 11B, 2.

67. *Badenia Semester Bericht* (winter 1894/95), 3. The terms "light weapons" and "heavy weapons" refer to different classifications of swords and types of duels. The *Schläger* is classified as a light weapon with the *"Schlägermensur* [being] the most traditional means for settling . . . student disputes." The *Säbel* was considered a heavy weapon and reserved for more serious offenses. The best source for definitions of student terms is *Studentenwörterbuch. 4. überarbeitete und erweiterte Aufluge,* Friedhelm Golücke, ed. (Würzburg, 1987). Jarausch's *Students, Society and Politics* also is useful for sorting out the complex lexicon peculiar to German university students.

68. On the matches between *Badenia* and *Salia,* see *Badenia Semester Berichten* (winter 1894/95 through 1898/99).

69. The *Semester Berichte* of *Sprevia* and *Licaria* are found in CZA A 142 90 11F. This file contains two reports from *Sprevia,* summer 1895 and winter 1899/1900, and a complete set of *Licaria* reports from 1895 through 1902.

70. On March 11, 1896, twenty-two German national and Austrian student organizations of the *Waidhofner Verband* passed a resolution that defined Jews as morally and physically different than Aryans and, consequently, unworthy of duelling with Germans. For a discussion of the *Waidhofner Prinzip,* see Kampe, *Studenten und Judenfrage,* 200–204.

71. On the exclusion of Jewish duelling organizations see Schindler, *Studentischer Antisemitismus,* 147–59; and Kampe, *Studenten und "Judenfrage,"* 185–204. Ze'ev Rosenkranz argues that Jewish student associations ended up, for the most part, arranging duelling matches with one another and, in so doing, perpetuated the social segregation of German Jewry. See his "The Corporate Activities of

Jewish National and Zionist Student Groups in Germany 1895–1914" (in Hebrew) (master's thesis, Hebrew University, 1988).

72. Schindler, *Studentischer Antisemitismus*, 154–55.

73. *Badenia Semester Berichten* (summer 1898–summer 1900).

74. *Licaria Semester Bericht* (winter 1896/97), 3.

75. *Licaria Semester Berichten* (summer 1898; winter 1899/1900).

76. *Badenia Semester Bericht* (summer 1899), 3. A second lecture presented on the same evening was entitled, "A Short Overview of the Jews in the Middle Ages."

77. *Sprevia Semester Bericht* (summer 1895).

78. The titles of the two lectures were "The Origins and History of Modern Antisemitism," and "Jewish Antisemitism." *Licaria Semester Bericht* (winter 1896–97), 7.

79. Ibid., (winter 1898 and winter 1899).

80. Pick, "Vor 60 Jahren," 3.

81. Heinrich Loewe, "Jung-Israel. Ein fünfzigjähriger Gedenktag," in *Meilensteine: Vom Wege des Kartells Jüdischer Verbindungen (KJV) in der zionistischen Bewegung*, Eli Rothschild, ed. (Tel Aviv: Prasidium K.J.V., 1972), 2.

82. Schoeps, "Modern Heirs," 155–64; Wistrich, *The Jews of Vienna*, 363–69; and Marsha L. Rozenblit, "The Assertion of Identity. Jewish Student Nationalism at the University of Vienna before the First World War," *Leo Baeck Institute Yearbook* 27 (1982): 171–86.

83. Under the still valid "Socialist Laws," all organizations holding public meetings had to register with the police. On March 30, 1892, the following document was presented to the *Königliches Polizei-Präsidiums* (the Royal Police Headquarters): "On March 31, 1892, at 8:30 in the evening, a meeting will be held at *Königstraße* 29 for the purpose of establishing a Jewish national association." This document is quoted in Loewe, "Jung-Israel," 2–3. On the founding of *Jung-Israel* see Gross, "The Zionist Students' Movement," 143; Zimmermann, "Jewish Nationalism and Zionism," 134–35; Schindler, *Studentischer Antisemitismus*, 126, ff. #7; and Reinharz, *Fatherland or Promised Land*, 91–96. A typed manuscript entitled "Fuxenunterricht. Kartellgeschichte," written by Benno Cohn in 1914, provides a historical outline of the *Verein Jüdischer Studenten* and the *Bund Jüdischer Corporationen*, the successor organizations to *Jung-Israel*. This document is located in CZA A231 1/1. A discussion of *Jung-Israel* is found on p. 3 of this document.

84. Jehuda Louis Weinberg. *Aus der Frühzeit des Zionismus Heinrich Loewe* (Jerusalem: R. Mass, 1946), 20–25.

85. Ibid., 41–50.

86. Brief references to this organization are found in Cohn, "Fuxenunterricht," 3; Reinharz, *Fatherland or Promised Land*, 95; and Zimmermann, "Jewish Nationalism and Zionism," 135.

87. Loewe's *Bundeslied des jüdisch-nationalen Vereins Jung-Israel* is found in CZA A 146–16, Heinrich Loewe. I am indebted to Paul Fairbrook for rendering these verses into English in a style commensurate with that of the original.

88. This group later became known as the *Verein Jüdischer Studenten and der Universität Berlin* (the Association of Jewish Students at the University of Berlin). On the founding of the V.J.St., see Cohn, "Fuxenunterricht," 3–4; Gross, "The Zionist Students' Movement," 144; Zimmermann, "Jewish Nationalism and Zionism," 135; Schindler, *Studentischer Antisemitismus*, 126–27; and Reinharz, *Fatherland or Promised Land*, 35.

89. Zimmermann, "Jewish Nationalism and Zionism," 135.

90. Untitled poster found in CZA A 231 4/2. (c. 1895).

91. A chapter of the V.J.St. was founded in Leipzig in 1899. A handwritten letter entitled "An unsere jüdischen Commilitonen" was written by the V.J.St. in Leipzig sometime around 1900. No date is given. This document is found in CZA A 231 4/11.

92. Ibid., 1–4.

93. Ibid., 4.

94. Members of the V.J.St.in Leipzig argued that "only if we are complete Jews can we become complete men." Ibid., 2

95. The article appeared in the *Jüdische Turnzeitung* in June 1900 and it is contained in Max Nordau, *Zionistische Schriften* (Berlin: Jüdischer Verlag, 1923), 424–26.

96. George Mosse writes that "the ideal of manliness was basic both to the self-definition of bourgeois society and to the national ideology." *Nationalism and Sexuality: Middle-class Morality and Sexual Norms in Modern Europe* (Madison: University of Wisconsin Press, 1988), 23. Ute Frevert explains that duels fought to defend one's honor and masculinity were a symbolic representation of "courage, bravery, self-discipline and coolness." See Frevert, "Bourgeois honour: middle-class duellists from the late eighteenth to the early twentieth century in Germany," in *The German Bourgeoisie. Essays on the social history of the German middle class from the late eighteenth to the early twentieth century,* David Blackbourn and Richard J. Evans, eds. (London: Routledge, 1991), especially pages 269–71; see also Frevert, *Ehrenmänner, passim;* and Kevin McAleer, *Duelling: The Cult of Honor in Fin-de-Siecle Germany* (Princeton, N.J.: Princeton University Press, 1994).

97. Richarz, *Jewish Life in Germany,* 1–30.

98. The early membership roster of the V.J.St. reads like a veritable "Who's Who" of German Zionism. Heinrich Loewe, Theodor Zlocisti, Arthur Hantke, Erich Rosenkranz, and Martin Buber were active in the V.J.St. and played important roles in the development of a Zionist movement in Germany. Reinharz discusses this phenomenon in *Fatherland or Promised Land,* 35 and 93–98. See also Cohn, "Fuxenunterricht," 3–5.

99. Walter Gross writes that the "V.J.St. took sides against the assimilationist tendency as defended by the *paritätisch* fraternities and the K.C." "The Zionist Students' Movement," 144.

100. Italics mine. *Vereinigung Jüdischer Studenten,* Berlin, *Semester Bericht* (summer 1897), 5. CZA A 231 4/2.

CHAPTER 5

1. Konrad Jarausch estimates that student participation in formal student societies never exceeded 40 percent of the student population. *Students, Society and Politics in Imperial Germany: The Rise of Academic Illiberalism* (Princeton, N.J.: Princeton University Press, 1982), 295–99. No statistical analysis of Jewish participation in formal student associations has been completed.

2. Marion A. Kaplan, *The Making of the Jewish Middle Class: Women, Family and Identity in Imperial Germany* (New York: Oxford University Press, 1991), x.

3. Monika Richarz, *Jewish Life in Germany: Memoirs from Three Centuries,* Stella P. and Sidney Rosenfeld, trans. (Bloomington: Indiana University Press, 1991), ix.

4. Todd Endelman, *Radical Assimilation in English Jewish History, 1656–1945* (Bloomington: Indiana University Press, 1990), 8.

5. On the critical importance of "place" for the creation of cultural knowledge see Hillel J. Kieval, "The Importance of Place: Comparative Aspects of the Ritual Murder Trial in Modern Central Europe," in *Comparing Jewish Societies*, Todd M. Endelman, ed. (Ann Arbor: University of Michigan Press, 1997), 135 66.

6. Endelman makes the comment that "however odd or amusing [the family histories of English Jews] might be in some of their particulars, [they] are intended to represent larger social trends within the English Jewish community." *Radical Assimilation*, 8.

7. Memoir of Eduard Silbermann, ME 601. Portions of Silbermann's memoir are contained in Richarz, *Jewish Life in Germany*, 80–93.

8. Richarz, *Jewish Life in Germany*, 83.

9. Ibid., 85.

10. Ibid., 86.

11. Memoir of Eduard Silbermann, ME 601, 100.

12. Ibid., 101.

13. Ibid., 102.

14. Ibid., 102.

15. Ibid., 102.

16. Richarz, *Jewish Life in Germany*, 86.

17. Memoir of Joseph Gallinger, ME 167, 5.

18. Marjorie Lamberti, *Jewish Activism in Imperial Germany: The Struggle for Civil Equality* (New Haven, Conn.: Yale University Press, 1978), 23–54; Peter Pulzer, *Jews and the German State. The Political History of a Minority, 1848–1933* (Oxford: Blackwell Publishers, 1992); and Jacob Toury, *Die politischen Orientierung der Juden in Deutschland von Jena bis Weimar* (Tübingen: J.C.B. Mohr, 1966).

19. A social history of religious practice among German Jews has yet to be written. For a good overview of the religiosity of German Jews during the Kaiserreich see Mordechai Breuer, *Modernity Within Tradition: The Social History of Orthodox Jewry in Imperial Germany*, Elizabeth Petuchowski, trans. (New York: Columbia University Press, 1992); and Monika Richarz, *Jüdische Leben in Deutschland: Selbstzeugnisse zur Sozialgeschichte im Kaiserreich*, vol. 2 (Stuttgart: Deutsche Verlags-Anstalt, 1976), 46–64.

20. Memoir of Joseph Gallinger, 8.

21. Memoir of Curt Rosenberg, ME 524. A portion of this memoir also appears in *Jüdisches Leben in Deutschland. Selbstzeugnisse zur Sozialgeschichte im Kaiserreich*. Monika Richarz, ed. (Stuttgart, 1979), 298–309.

22. Memoir of Curt Rosenberg, ME 524, 92–93.

23. Ibid., 92–93.

24. Ibid, 105.

25. Ibid., 105–6.

26. Ibid., 107.

27. Ibid., 109.

28. Ibid.

29. Memoir of Ludwig Edinger, ME 718, part 1, 15–16.

30. Ibid., part 2, 66–67.

31. Ibid., part 2, 72–73.

32. Weill's poem is found in Vicki Caron, *Between France and Germany. The Jews of Alsace-Lorraine, 1871–1918* (Stanford, Calif.: Stanford University Press, 1988), footnote #36, p. 208.

33. Memoir of Ludwig Edinger, ME 718, part 1, 73–74.

34. Italics mine. Ibid., 75–76.

35. Ibid., 77–78.

36. Memoir of Arthur Czellitzer, ME 97.

37. Ibid., 35–36.

38. Ibid., 39.

39. Ibid., 42.

40. Memoir of Georg Witkowski entitled "Erzähltes aus Sieben Jahrzehnten," ME 692.

41. Ibid., 84.

42. Ibid., 84–85.

43. Ibid., 86.

44. Ibid., 93.

45. Ibid., 97.

46. Ibid. 98.

47. On female university students see Kaplan, *Making of the Jewish Middle Class*, 137–52.

48. Richarz, *Jüdische Leben in Deutschland*, 41.

49. Jarausch, *Students, Society and Politics*, 259.

50. Memoir of Adolf Heilberg, ME 257, 62.

51. Ibid., 65–66.

52. Ibid., 66.

53. Memoir of Curt Rosenberg, 113.

54. Ibid., 114.

55. On the *Finkenschaft*, or *Freistudentenschaft*, see Gerhard Plaumann, "Die freistudentische Idee," and Adalbert Zoellner, "Mitarbeit in der Freistudenten-schaft," in *Neudeutsches Studentenbrevier: Aufsätze zur Einführung ins akademische Leben in der Gegenwart*, Paul Ssymank, ed. (Munich: Breyslag, 1912), 180–89; Friedrich Schulze and Paul Ssymank, *Das Deutsche Studententum von den ältesten Zeiten bis zur Gegenwart* (Leipzig: R. Voigtländers Verlag, 1910), 361–68; and Jarausch, *Students, Society and Politics*, 277–88.

56. Jarausch, *Students, Society and Politics*, 278–80.

57. Quoted in Ibid., 286.

58. John M. Efron. *Defenders of the Race. Jewish Doctors and Race Science in Fin-de-Siecle Europe* (New Haven, Conn.: Yale University Press, 1994).

59. Memoir of Moritz Goldstein, ME 195, 61–62.

60. Ibid., 63.

61. Ibid., 66–67.

62. Ibid., 67–68.

63. Ibid., 64–65 and 70.

64. Memoir of Ernst Jolowicz, ME 308, 11–12.

65. Ibid., 12–13.

66. Ibid., 15.

67. Ibid., 16–19.

68. Ibid., 19.

69. Memoir of Ernst Herzfeld, ME 287.
70. Ibid., 27.
71. Ibid., 27–28.
72. Ibid., 28.
73. Ibid., 30 and 32.
74. Ibid., 30.
75. Memoir of Arthur Czellitzer, 42–48.
76. Ibid., 45.
77. Ibid., 45–46.
78. Ibid., 47.

CHAPTER 6

1. Helmut Walser Smith, *German Nationalism and Religious Conflict: Culture, Ideology, Politics, 1870–1914* (Princeton, N.J.: Princeton University Press, 1995), 117.

2. Konrad Jarausch, "Students, Sex and Politics in Imperial Germany," *Journal of Contemporary History* 17 (1982): 289–90; and Marion A. Kaplan, *The Making of the Jewish Middle Class: Women, Family and Identity in Imperial Germany* (New York: Oxford University Press, 1991), 137–38 and 277, note 1.

3. According to Stein, Professor Mendel was forced (*gezwungen*) to allow women in as auditors. Memoir of Nathan Stein, ME 618, 63.

4. Memoir of Walter Heinemann, ME 284, 30. Kaplan's comments on the obstacles faced by the first generation of female Jewish university students parallel my own observations. *Making of the Jewish Middle Class*, 138–43.

5. The details of Rahel Straus's life can be found in her unpublished memoirs, ME 636, and her published autobiography, *Wir lebten in Deutschland: Erinnerungen einer deutschen Jüdin, 1880–1933* (Stuttgart: Deutsche Verlag-Anstalt, 1962). Harriet Freidenreich's depiction of Straus as an "example of a new Jewish superwoman of the early twentieth century" is certainly apropos, for Straus raised five children in a fairly traditional, kosher Jewish household, was active in feminist and Zionist organizations, maintained a private medical practice, and gave lectures on birth control and nutrition to women. "Jewish Identity and the'New Woman': Central European Jewish University Women in the Early Twentieth Century," in *Gender and Judaism. The Transformation of Tradition*, Tamar Rudavsky, ed. (New York: New York University Press, 1995), 113–22.

6. Memoir of Rahel Straus, ME 636, 123–24.

7. Ibid., 125.

8. Kaplan, *Making of the Jewish Middle Class*, 138.

9. Ibid., 143.

10. The cost of studying medicine was considerably higher than that of studying the humanities. Upon hearing that Rahel had registered as a literature student rather than pursue her long-held goal of studying medicine, Rahel's uncle, Raphael Lowenfeld, offered to support her studies, provided that she follow her dream of becoming a doctor. Memoir of Rahel Straus, 125–27.

11. Ibid., 127.

12. Ibid., 128. Kaplan also discusses this exchange between Straus and the professor, but does not include Straus's comment about her and the professor becoming "good friends." Instead, Kaplan writes that "These insults only heightened Straus's resolve to attain her degree: 'I wanted to show him, to show all men, that one could

achieve one's chosen profession.'" See Kaplan, *Making of the Jewish Middle Class*, 139. Our different emphases may result from the fact that my source on Straus is her unpublished memoir, whereas Kaplan utilizes the published version. See Straus, *Wir lebten in Deutschland*.

13. Kaplan, *Making of the Jewish Middle Class*, 146–47.

14. Else Croner. *Das Tagebuch eines Fräulein Doktors* (Stuttgart, 1908). Quoted in Kaplan, *Making of the Jewish Middle Class*, 147.

15. Memoir of Rahel Straus, 136.

16. Ibid., 137.

17. Emphasis mine. Ibid., 137.

18. Ibid., 140.

19. Memoir of Frieda Hirsch, ME 303, 6–19.

20. Ibid., 45–48

21. Ibid., 54.

22. Ibid., 55.

23. Ibid., 57.

24. Ibid., 60.

25. Ibid., 68.

26. Ibid., 68–69.

27. Käte Frankenthal, *Der dreifache Fluch: Jüdin, Intellektuelle, Sozialistin. Lebens-errinnerungen einer Ärztin in Deutschland und im Exil* (Frankfurt: Campus, 1981), 1–7.

28. Ibid., 22.

29. Ibid., 23.

30. Ibid., 27–28.

31. Ibid., 29.

32. Ibid., 30.

33. Ibid., 31–32.

34. Moses Auerbach, "Die Gründung der Berliner V.J.A.," *Unser Weg. Jüdisch Akademische Blätter.* 2 (December 1928): 22–23; Isaac Breuer, *Mein Weg* (Jerusalem: Morascha Verlag, 1988), 93–103; and Mordechai Breuer, *Modernity Within Tradition. The Social History of Orthodox Jewry in Imperial Germany*, Elizabeth Petuchowski, trans. (New York: Columbia University Press, 1992), 372–82.

35. On the B.J.A. see Leo Teitz, "Zur Entwicklung des B.J.A.," *Unser Weg,* 28–31; Jacob Levy, "Tradition und Fortschritt im B.J.A.," *Unser Weg,* 24–28; Breuer, *Modernity Within Tradition,* 373; and Thomas Schindler, *Studentischer Antisemitismus und jüdische Studenverbindungen 1880–1933* (Gießen: Schriftenreihe der Studentengeschichtlichen Vereinigung des CC, 1988), 133–37.

36. Paragraph two stated that "the association [was] grounded in halakhic Judaism (*gesetztreuen Judentums*). "*Satzungen der Vereinigung jüdischer Akademiker zu Berlin im Bund jüdischer Akademiker*, p. 1.

37. Isaac Breuer, *Mein Weg,* 71.

38. Levy, "Tradition," 25. For an overview of Hirsch's reform program see Michael Meyer, *Response to Modernity. A History of the Reform Movement in Judaism* (New York: Oxford University Press, 1988), 77–80.

39. Isidor Grunfeld, *Three Generations. The Influence of Samson Raphael Hirsch on Jewish Life and Thought* (London: Jerusalem Post Publications, 1958), 71.

40. *Satzungen der Vereinigung jüdischer Akademiker zu Berlin im Bund jüdischer*

Akademiker, p. 1; *Was Will der Bund Jüdischer Akademiker* (Berlin, n.d.), 23–24; and Grunfeld, *Three Generations,* 71.

41. Mordechai Breuer, *Modernity Within Tradition,* 374.

42. This five-point program is quoted from *Der Jüdische Student. Vierteljahres-schrift der Vereine Jüdischer Studenten (im Bund Jüdischer Corporationen).* Erster Jahr-gang, (Berlin, 1904), 1. This publication appeared from 1902 until March 1903 as a monthly journal, was reconstituted as a quarterly publication in 1904, and reverted to a monthly format in 1907. On the establishment of the B.J.C. see Beno Cohn, "Fuxenunterricht," 6–7; Leopold Ambrunn, *Der V.J.St. München. Ein Rückblick zum 9. Mai 1910.* CZA A 231 4/14, 2; Walter Gross, "The Zionist Students' Movement," *Leo Baeck Institute Yearbook* 4 (1959): 145; Moshe Zimmermann, "Jewish Nationalism and Zionism in German-Jewish Student Organizations," *Leo Baeck Institute Yearbook* 27 (1982): 135; and Schindler, *Studentischer Antisemitismus,* 126–27.

43. Ambrunn, *Der V.J.St. München,* 2–3.

44. Cohn, "Fuxenunterricht," 6–7.

45. This poll was reprinted in an article in *Der Jüdische Student* entitled "Eine Tendenz-Rundfrage vor zehn Jahren," 1 (April 1911): 5. Zimmermann's article on Jewish nationalist student organizations refers at length to this poll; see Zimmermann, "Jewish Nationalism and Zionism," 135–36.

46. Zimmermann, "Jewish Nationalism and Zionism," 135.

47. Max Eschelbacher, "Unser Verhältnis zum Judentum," *Der Jüdische Student* 3 (1902/03): 35.

48. Heinrich Loewe, "Sind die Juden eine Religionsgemeinschaft?," *Der Jüdische Student* 5 (1902/03): 71. Moritz Lazarus (1824–1903) was a philosopher and psychologist who applied a philosophic formalism to the study of Jewish sources and utilized philosophy as "a methodological aid for discovering the objective unity of the "ethical cosmos." Hermann Cohen (1842–1918) was also a philosopher and became one of the few Jews to become a full professor before the First World War. Although a respected expert on Kant, Cohen remained convinced that German Jews could be both loyal Jews and Germans, provided that they take their Judaism seriously.

49. Ibid., 72.

50. Emil Cohn, "Das nationale Bewusstein," *Der Jüdische Student* 1 (April 1904): 5.

51. Ibid., 9.

52. At the B.J.C.'s annual gathering in 1910 the organization passed a reso-lution that declared the organization's official support for Zionism. The B.J.C.'s move toward Zionism is discussed in Cohn, "Fuxenunterricht," 13–15; Zimmer-mann, "Jewish Nationalism and Zionism," 137–42; and Schindler, *Studentischer Antisemitismus,* 127–29.

53. The activities of the various chapters of the V.J.St. and listings of the lectures presented are documented in the organizations' "Semester Reports" and "Monthly Reports." These documents are found in CZA A 231 1/4 and CZA A 231 1/5.

54. On the founding of *Hasmonaea* and the K.Z.V., see Cohn, "Fuxenunter-richt," 25–28; Gross, "Zionist Students' Movement," 146–47; Egon Rosenberg, "Vom Burschenschafter zum K.Z.Ver.," *Jahrgang 1902* (Berlin, 1932), 6, CZA A 231 1/A; and Zimmermann, "Jewish Nationalism and Zionism," 137;

55. Walter Fischer, "Errinerungen Eines Hasmonäers," in *Meilensteine: Vom*

Wege des Kartells Jüdischer Verbindungen (KJV) in der zionistischen Bewegung, Eli Rothschild, ed. (Tel Aviv: Prasidium K.J.V., 1972), 24–29.

56. Ibid., 26. On the study sessions themselves see, Eugen Täubler, "Gedanken aus der Geschichts-Fuxenstunde," in *Meilensteine: Vom Wege des Kartells Jüdischer Verbindungen (KJV) in der zionistischen Bewegung,* Eli Rothschild, ed. (Tel Aviv, 1972), 46–48.

57. "Unser Programm," *Mitteilungen des K.Z.V.* 1 (January 1908): 2–4.

58. Richard Lichtheim,"Erziehung," *Mitteilungen des K.Z.V.* 3 (March 1908): 5.

59. Rosenberg, "Vom Burschenschafter zum K.Z.Ver.," 5.

60. Kurt Blumenfeld, *Erlebte Judenfrage. Ein Vierteljahrhundert deutscher Zionismus* (Stuttgart: Deutsche Verlags-Anstalt, 1962), 27–28.

61. Ibid., 27 and 36; Gross, "Zionist Students' Movement," 147–48; and Zimmermann, "Jewish Nationalism and Zionism," 137.

62. Gross, "Zionist Students' Movement," 147–48.

63. Blumenfeld remarks that the six new members all heralded from Lithuania and most of them were naturalized German citizens. *Erlebte Judenfrage,* 43–44.

64. Gross, "Zionist Students' Movement," 148. On the founding of *Maccabaea* see the collection of essays written in honor of its twenty-fifth anniversary, in which are included: Blumenfeld, "Zur Jubiläum Maccabaea," 1–4; Felix Rosenblüth, "Fünf Generationen Maccabaea: Die Gründung," 4–5; and Gerhard Holdheim, "Die Alte Generation," 5–7. These essays are found in CZA A 231 4/12.

65. Quoted in Marjorie Lamberti, "From Coexistence to Conflict: Zionism and the Jewish Community in Germany, 1897–1914," *Leo Baeck Institute Yearbook* 27 (1982): 63. On the tenth *Kartelltag* and the passage of the new party platform see also, Cohn, "Fuxenunterricht,"13–16; Gross, "Zionist Students' Movement," 148–49; and Zimmermann, "Jewish Nationalism and Zionism," 137–42.

66. A list of the numerous articles in *Der Jüdische Student* that focus on this development is found in Lamberti, "From Coexistence," 63, note 56.

67. Isaak Zwirn, "Erklärung zur Tendenzinterpretation," *Der Jüdische Student* 6, no.11/12 (Feb./March 1910): 255; Erich Cohn, "Der Zionismus im B.J.C.," *Der Jüdische Student* 7, no.7 (October 1910): 179–85; and Felix Rosenblüth, "Auch etwas über den Zionismus im B.J.C.," *Der Jüdische Student* 7, no.8 (Nov. 1911): 206–8.

68. Zimmermann, "Jewish Nationalism and Zionism," 137.

69. On the differences between the K.Z.V. and the B.J.C., see Richard Lichtheim, "K.Z.V. and B.J.C.," *Mitteilungen des K.Z.V.* 10 (December 1910): 3–5; and Egon Rosenberg, "Der Kampf zwischen K.Z.V. und B.J.C.," *Mitteilungen des K.Z.V.* 3 (March 1914): 42–50.

70. "Die Fusionsverhandlungen mit dem B.J.C.," *Mitteilungen des K.Z.V.* 6 (June 1914): 1.

71. Erwin Goldemann, "Die jüdische Korporation," *Der Jüdische Student* 5 (1912/1913): 141–45; "Unser Verhältnis zum K.Z.V.," *Der Jüdische Student* 12 (1912/1913): 443; Cohn, "Fuxenunterricht," 24–28; Gross, "Zionist Students' Movement," 149; and Zimmermann, "Jewish Nationalism and Zionism," 141–42.

72. "Die Fusionsverhandlungen," 3–8.

73. Details of the fusion and the program of the K.J.V. are contained in the last edition of *Mitteilungen des Kartell Zionistischer Verbindungen* 8 (August 1914). I have utilized the translation contained in Gross, "Zionist Students' Movement," 149.

74. "Zwei Programme," *Der Jüdische Student* 8, no. 11 (February 1912): 335–37.

The slanderous comments about the K.C. that appeared in *Der Jüdische Student* are also quoted in numerous articles within the *K.C. Blätter. Monatsschrift der im Kartel-Convent vereinigten Korporationen* (the monthly journal of the K.C.) For example, see Max Mainzer, "K.C. und B.J.C.," 2, no. 9 (June 1912): 165–69; and Karl Löwenstein, "Eine'Berichtigung' des B.J.C.," 3, no.7 (April 1913): 153–54.

75. Lichtheim, "K.Z.V. and B.J.C.," 5.

76. Friederich Loewenthal, "Der K.C. und der Zionismus," *Mitteilungen des K.Z.V.* 10 (December 1910): 7.

77. Ibid., 6–8.

78. Mainzer, "K.C. und B.J.C.," 165.

79. Ludwig Holländer, "K.C. und B.J.C.," *K.C. Blätter* 3, no. 2 (November 1912): 37.

80. Löwenstein,"Eine'Berichtigung' des B.J.C.," 153–54.

81. Lamberti's interpretation of the conflict between the Zionists and the C.V. is presented in "From Coexistence to Conflict." On the interpretive debate that emerged in the wake of Lamberti's article see, Jehuda Reinharz, "Advocacy and History: The Case of the Centralverein and the Zionists," *Leo Baeck Institute Yearbook* 33 (1988): 113–22; and Marjorie Lamberti, "The Centralverein and the Anti-Zionists. Setting the Historical Record Straight," *Leo Baeck Institute Yearbook* 33 (1988): 123–29.

82. "Das F.W.V.er Taschenbuch," *Der Jüdische Student* 11 (February 1909): 243–45.

83. Ibid., 245.

84. V.J.St. election poster, CZA A 231 4/2.

85. Isaac Breuer, *Mein Weg,* 98 and Mordechai Breuer, *Modernity Within Tradition,* 374–75.

86. "Vom Verhältnis zwischen B.J.C. und B.J.A.," *Der Jüdische Student* 6, no. 3 (June 1909): 61–62.

87. Ibid., 62.

88. "Jüdischer Studentverbindungen," *Was Will der Bund Jüdischer Akademiker,* 18.

89. This speech is entitled "An die jüdischen Abiturienten," and it is found in ibid., 5–10.

90. The article is contained in ibid., 11–30.

91. Ibid., 17–19.

92. Ibid., 19–20.

93. Ibid., 20–21.

CONCLUSION

1. See Monika Richarz, *Der Eintritt der Juden in die Akademischen Berufe* (Tübingen: J.C.B. Mohr, 1974), 157–63.

Bibliography

PRIMARY SOURCES

Central Archives for the History of the Jewish People, Jerusalem:

TD-69 Verein für Jüdische Geschichte und Literatur
TD-503 Deutschland-Verband der Vereine für Jüdische Geschichte

Central Zionist Archives, Jerusalem:

A 142-90-11A
A 142-90-11B
A 142-90-11C
A 142-90-11E
A 142-90-11F
A 231 1/A
A 231 1/1
A 231 1/2
A 231 1/3
A 231 1/4
A 231 1/5
A 231 1/6
A 231 1/7
A 231 1/8
A 231 1/9
A 231 1/11
A 231 1/12
A 231 2/15
A 231 4/2

A 231 4/11
A 231 4/12
A 231 4/14
A 231 4/15
A 231-75

The Leo Baeck Institute, New York: Memoir Collection

Elisabeth Bab, ME 21
Friederich Bilski, ME 261
Rudolf Bing, ME 267
Moses Cavalry, ME 80
Ludwig Adolf Cohn, ME 91
Arthur Czellitzer, ME 97
Ludwig Edinger, ME 718
Joseph Gallinger, ME 167
Else Gerstel, ME 184
Hermann Gessner, ME 378
Moritz Goldstein, ME 195
Sammy Gronemann, ME 203
Frieda Hirsch, ME 303
Judith Schrag-Haas, ME 581
Berthold Haase, ME 249
Simon Hayum, ME 560
Adolf Heilberg, ME 257
Walter Heinemann, ME 284
Ernst Herzfeld, ME 287
Robert Hirsch, ME 312
Bernhard Hirschel, ME 316
Eduard Isaac, ME 326
Monty Jacobs, ME 334
Ernst Jolowicz, ME 308
Richard Koch, ME 735
Max Kollenscher, ME 368
Phillip Loewenfeld, ME 404
Adolf Magnus-Levy, ME 410
Ernst Marcus, ME 423
Hermann Makower, ME 417
Paul Muehsam, ME 451
Hertha Nathorff, ME 460
Alfred Neumayer, ME 471
Richard Offenbacher, ME 480
Alfred Philippson, ME 803
Paul Posener, MS 122
Curt Rosenberg, ME 524
Louis Rosendahl, ME 525
Recha Rothschild, ME 243
Margarete Sallis, ME 550
Albert Salomon, ME 580.
Alice Salomon, ME 810

Bibliography

Georg-Anton Salomon, ME 551
Aron Sandler, ME 556
Hans Schaefer, ME 563
Alfred Schweizer, ME 592
Caesar Seligmann, ME 595
Eduard Silbermann, ME 601
Friederich Solon, ME 607
Meier Spanier, ME 609
Selmar Speier, ME 611
S. Spiro, ME 614
Nathan Stein, ME 618
Margarethe Steinberg, ME 620
Alfred Stern, ME 621
Arthur Stern, ME 622
Alfred Sternthal, ME 630
Rahel Straus, ME 636
Eugen Strauss, ME 633
Paul Tachau, ME 639
Marvin Warschauer, AR 794
Georg Witkowski, ME 692

Student Publications

Biographisches Corpsalbum der Borussia zu Bonn 1827–1902. Düsseldorf: 1902.
Die Burschenschaft Allemania zu Heidelberg. Ein Album herausgegeben zum dreißig-
    jährigen Stiftungsfeste und fünfhundertjährigen Universitätsjubiläum. Heidelberg:
    1886.
Die Burschenschaft Franconia zu Heidelberg, 1856–1886. Eine Festgabe zum dreissigjähr-
    igen Stiftungsfest. Heidelberg: 1886.
Die Burschenschaft Franconia zu Heidelberg. 1856–1886. Heidelberg: 1886.
Chelius, Richard V., ed. Ein Rückblick auf die Geschichte des Korps Suevia zu Heidelberg
    von 1810–1910 zur Feier des hundertjährigen Stiftungsfest. Heidelberg: 1910.
Die Corps der deutschen Hochschulen. Nebst einer eingehenden Darstellung studentischer
    Verhältnisse. Anhang: Die modernen Burschenschaft. Leipzig: 1870.
Corps Rhenania zu Heidelberg. Mitglieder-Verzeichniss der Jahre 1849 bis 1879. Heidel-
    berg: 1879.
Corps Suevia zu Heidelberg, 1810–1935 Zum 125. Stiftungsfeste Juni 1935. Heidelberg:
    1935.
Die deutsche Studentenschaft. Eine akademische Zeitstudie. Zugleich Entgegnung auf die
    neuesten Flugschriften der Corpsstudent und Burschenschafter. Würzburg: 1869.
100 Jahre Allemania zu Heidelberg. 1856–1956. Heidelberg: 1856.
Fraenkel, Ernst. Viadrina Suspensa! Vivat Thuringia! 40 Jahre in Kampf für Recht und
    Ehre. Breslau: 1926.
Freie Wissenschaftlicher Taschenbüche in zwei Bearbeitung. hrsg. vom Bund der Alten
    Herren der Freien Wissenschaftliche Vereinigung an der Universität Berlin.
    Berlin: 1931.
Das gegenwärtige deutsche Studententhum, Seine Parteien und die Grundzüge Seiner
    Entwickelung. Dargelegt in der Form einer Erwiderung auf die Schrift: Was sind
    und wollen die Corps? Göttingen: 1869.
Geschichte der Burschenschaft Allemania zu Heidelberg, 1856–1906. Heidelberg: 1906.

Bibliography

Geschichte des Corps Rhenania zu Würzburg von 1842 bis 1892. Ludwigshafen: 1893.

Geschichte des Corps Saxonia zu Leipzig 1812 bis 1912. Leipzig: 1912.

Geschichte der Freien schlagenden Verbindungen Salia. Würzburg: 1914.

Handbuch der deutschen Burschenschaft. Herausgegeben vom Hauptausschuß der deutschen Burschenschaft im Geschäftsjahr 1981/82. Bad Neuheim: 1982.

Howitt, William, ed. *The Student-Life of Germany. From the unpublished manuscripts of Dr. Cornelius.* London: Longman, Brown, Green and Longmans, 1841.

Juden, Studenten, Professor. Frage und Antwortspiel. Leipzig: 1881.

K.C. Blätter Festschrift. 50 Jahre K.C. New York: 1946.

K.C. Jahrbuch. Berlin: 1906 and 1908.

Mitglieder der Guestphalia zu Heidelberg, 1818–1928. Heidelberg: 1928.

Die Mitglieder der Vandalia zu Heidelberg, Juni 1907. Heidelberg: 1907.

Müller, Kurt. *Das Judentum in der deutschen Studenschaft.* Leipzig: 1891.

Pfister, Otto von. *Das Wesen und Ideal der Burschenschaft.* Darmstadt: n.d.

Quidde, L. *Die Antisemitenagitation und die deutsche Studentenschaft.* Göttingen: Verlag von Robert Peppmüller, 1881.

Rhenania, 1862–1869. Von der Wiedererrichtung 1862 bis zur Feier des zwanzigjährigen Stiftungsfestes 1869. Heidelberg: 1869.

Semester-Bericht des Akedemischen Vereins für jüdische Geschichte und Literatur, winter semester, 1895–96.

Spangenberg, Max. *Der Standpunkt der "Freien Wissenschaftliche Vereinigung" an der Universität Berlin: Zur Judenfrage und zur Wissenschaft; Zwei Reden an seine Vereingenossen gehalten am 4. Juli 1881 und 30. Oktober 1882.* Berlin: 1882.

Die studentische Petition als Annex der allgemeinen Petition betreffend die Einschränkung der jüdischen Machstellung. Reden gehalten in dem am 22. Nov. u. 10. Dec. zur Besprechung der Frage in Tritschlers Saal u. der Central-Halle privat abgehaltenen Versammlungen. Leipzig: 1881.

Ssymank, Paul. *Die Finkenschaftsbewegung. Ihr Entstehen und ihre Entwicklung bis zur Gründung der "Deutschen Freien Studentenschaft."* Munich: Vergriffen, 1901.

———. *Die Freistudententische oder Finkenschaftsbewegung an den deutschen Hochschulen.* Jena: Verlag von Eugen Diederichs, 1905.

———. *Neudeutsches Studentbrevier; Aufsätze zur Einführung ins akademische Leben in der Gegenwart.* Munich: Breyslag, 1912.

Statuten der Freien schlagenden Verbindung Salia. Würzburg: 1914.

Ullmer, Fritz. *Geschichtstafel der Burschneschaft der Frankonia zu Heidelberg: 1856–1920.* Heidelberg: 1920

———. *Die Heidelberger Burschenschaft: 1814–1920.* Heidelberg: 1920.

Was sind und wollen die Corps? Entwurf einer Zusammenstellung der allgemeinen deutschen Corps Principien. Göttingen: 1869.

Was will der Bund Jüdischer Akademiker? Berlin: n.d.

Was will und soll die Burschenschaften? Ein Wort zur Aufklärung. Breslau: 1864.

Weil, Bruno. *Juden in der deutschen Burschenschaften. Ein Beitrag zum Streit und die Konfessionelle Studentenverbindung.* Strassburg: 1905.

Student Journals and Newspapers

Akademische Monatsschrift. Centralorgan die gesamminteressen deutscher Universitäten.

Akademische Zeitschrift. Organ für die gesammten Interessen der deutschen Hochschulen.

Deutsche Universitäts Zeitung. Centralorgan für die Gesammtinteressen deutscher Universitäten.

Bibliography

Der Jüdische Student. Organ des Bundes Jüdischer Corporationen.
K.C. Blätter. Monatsschrift der im Kartell-Convent Vereinigten Korporationen
Unser Weg. Jüdisch Akademische Blätter. Bund Jüdischer Akademiker
Der Zionistische Student. Flugschrift des Kartell Zionistischer Verbindungen.

Published Primary Sources

Boehlich, Walter, ed. *Der Berliner Antisemitismusstreit.* Frankfurt am Main: Insel Verlag, 1965.

Jewish Emancipation, A Selection of Documents by R. Mahler. Pamphlet Series, Jews and the Post-War World, no. 1. New York: 1941.

Mendes-Flohr, Paul and Jehuda Reinharz, eds. *The Jew in the Modern World. A Documentary History.* New York: Oxford University Press, 1980.

Rivkin, Ellis, ed., and Helen Lederer, trans. *Readings in Modern Jewish History.* Cincinnati: Hebrew Union College, 1957.

Toepke, Gustav, ed. *Die Matrikel der Universität Heidelberg.* vols 5 and 6. Heidelberg: Carl Winter's Universitätbuchhandlung, 1904.

Published Memoirs

Blumenfeld, Kurt. *Erlebte Judenfrage: Ein Vierteljahrhundert Deutscher Zionismus.* Stuttgart: Deutsche Verlags-Anstalt, 1962.

Braun-Vogelstein, Julie. *Was Niemals Stirbt. Gestalten und Erinnerungen.* Stuttgart: Deutsche Verlags-Anstalt, 1966.

Breuer, Isaac. *Mein Weg.* Jerusalem: Morascha Verlag, 1988.

Croner, Else. *Das Tagebuch eines Fräulein Doktors.* Stuttgart, 1908.

Frankenthal, Käte. *Der dreifache Fluch: Jüdin, Intellektuelle, Sozialistin. Lebenserinnerungen einer Ärztin in Deutschland und im Exil.* Frankfurt, 1981.

Lichtheim, Richard. *Rückkehr. Lebenserinnerungen aus der Frühzeit des deutsche Zionismus.* Stuttgart: Deutsche Verlags-Anstalt, 1970.

Richarz, Monika. *Jewish Life in Germany. Memoirs From Three Centuries.* Stella P. and Sidney Rosenfeld, trans. Bloomington: Indiana University Press, 1991.

———. *Jüdisches Leben in Deutschland. Selbstzeugnisse zur Sozialgeschichte im Kaiserreich.* 3 vols. Stuttgart: Deutsche Verlags-Anstalt, 1976.

Straus Rahel. *Wir lebten in Deutschland: Erinnerungen einer deutschen Jüdin.* Stuttgart, 1962.

SECONDARY SOURCES

Allenhofer, Norbert, and Renate Heuer, eds. *Probleme deutsch-jüdischer Identität.* Frankfurt am Main: Archiv Bibliographia Judaica, 1985.

Angerer, Albin. "Die Entwicklung des Toleranzgedankens in Studentischen Zusammenschlüssen. Eine Studie aus dem Institut für Hochschulkunde in Würzburg." *Einst und Jetzt. Jahrbuch des Vereins für corpsstudentische Gesichtsforschung* 3 (1958): 92–101.

Angress, Werner T. "Prussia's Army and the Jewish Reserve Officer Controversy Before World War I." *Leo Baeck Institute Yearbook* 17 (1972): 19–42.

Asch, Adolph. *Geschichte des K.C. (Kartell jüdischer Studenten) im Lichte der deutschen Kulturellen und politische Entwicklung.* London, 1964.

Asch, Adolph, and Johanna Philippson. "Self Defence at the Turn of the Century. The Emergence of the K.C. (Kartell-Convent)." *Leo Baeck Institute Yearbook* 3 (1958): 122–39.

Bibliography

Ascheim, Steven. "Between East and West: Reflections on Migrations and the Making of German-Jewish Identity, 1800–1880." Proceedings of the 5th Symposium on the History of the Jews in the Netherlands. *Studia Rosenthaliana,* special issue published in 23, no. 2 (fall 1989): 77–87.

———. *Brothers and Strangers: The Eastern European Jew in German and Jewish Consciousness, 1800–1923.* Madison: University of Wisconsin Press, 1982.

Barkai, Avraham. "German Jewish Migrations in the 19th Century, 1830–1910." *Leo Baeck Institute Yearbook* 30 (1985): 301–18.

———. "The German Jews at the Start of Industrialization: Structural Change and Mobility 1835–1860." In *Revolution and Evolution: 1848 in Jewish History,* Werner E. Mosse, et al., eds., 123–49. Tübingen: J.C.B. Mohr, 1981.

———. *Die Jüdische Minderheit und Industrialisierung. Demographie, Berufe und Einkommen der Juden in Westdeutschland, 1850–1914.* Tübingen: J.C.B. Mohr, 1988.

Bausinger, Hermann. "Bürgerlichkeit und Kultur." In *Bürgertum und Bürgerlichkeit in 19. Jahrhundert,* J. Kocka, ed., 121–42. Göttingen: Vandenhoeck and Ruprecht, 1987.

Berger, Gerhart, and Detlev Aurand, eds. *Weiland Bursch zu Heidelberg. Eine Festschrift der Heidelberger Korporationen zur 600-Jahr-Feier der Ruperto Carola.* Heidelberg: Heidelberger Verlagsanstalt u. Druckerei, 1986.

Berghahn, Marion. *Continental Britons: German Jewish Refugees from Nazi Germany.* Oxford: Berg Publishers, 1988.

Blackbourn, David. *Class, Religion and Local Politics in Wilhelmine Germany. The Centre Party in Württemberg Before 1914.* New Haven: Yale University Press, 1980.

———. *Populists and Patricians. Essays in Modern German History.* London: Allen and Unwin, 1987.

Blackbourn, David, and Geoff Ely. *The Peculiarities of German History. Bourgeois Society and Politics in 19th Century Germany.* Oxford: Oxford University Press, 1984.

Bohrmann, Hans. *Strukturwandal der deutsche Studentpresse: Studentpolitik und Studentzeitschriften, 1848–1974.* Munich: Verlag Dokumentation, 1975.

Brenner, Michael. *The Renaissance of Jewish Culture in Weimar Germany.* New Haven, Conn.: Yale University Press, 1996.

Breuer, Mordechai. *Modernity Within Tradition. The Social History of Orthodox Jewry in Imperial Germany,* Elizabeth Petuchowski Trans. New York: Columbia University Press, 1992.

Bruchmueller, Wilhelm. *Das deutsche Studententum von seinem Anfängen bis zur Gegenwart.* Leipzig: 1922.

Buford, W. H. *The German Tradition of Self-Cultivation. Bildung from Humboldt to Thomas Mann.* Cambridge: Cambridge University Press, 1975.

Caron, Vicki. *Between France and Germany. The Jews of Alsace Lorraine, 1871–1918.* Stanford, Calif.: Stanford University Press, 1988.

Comaroff, John L. "Of Totemism and Ethnicity: Consciousness, Practice and the Signs of Inequality" *Ethnos* 3–4 (1987): 301–23.

Cohen, Anthony P. "Culture As Identity: An Anthropologist's View." *New Literary History: A Journal of Theory and Interpretation* 24, no. 1, (winter 1993): 195–209.

Cohen, Gershon D. "German Jewry as a Mirror of Modernity." *Leo Baeck Institute Yearbook* 20 (1975): 9–31.

Craig, John E. "Education and Social Mobility in Germany." In *The Transformation of Higher Learning: Expansion, Diversification, Social Opening and Professionalization in England, Germany, Russia and the United States,* Konrad Jarausch, ed. Chicago: University of Chicago Press, 1983.

Dashevsky, Arnold. "Being Jewish: An Approach to Conceptualization and Operationalization." In *Gratz College Anniversary Volume, 1895–1970,* Isidore D. Passow and Samuel T. Lachs, eds. Philadelphia: Jewish Publication Society, 1971.

Efron, John Maurice. *Defenders of the Race. Jewish Doctors and Race Science in Fin-de-Siècle Europe.* New Haven, Conn.: Yale University Press, 1994

Eisen, George. "Zionism, Nationalism and the Emergence of the Jüdische Turnerschaft." *Leo Baeck Institute Yearbook* 28 (1983): 247–62.

Elbogen, Ismar. *Geschichte der Juden in Deutschland.* Berlin: Juedische Buch-Vereinigung, 1935.

Eley, Geoff. *From Unification to Nazism. Reinterpreting the German Past.* Boston: Allen and Unwin, 1986.

Eliav, Mordechai. *Jewish Education in Germany in the Period of Enlightenment and Emancipation* (in Hebrew). Jerusalem: 1960.

———. "Jüdische Erziehung in Deutschland im Zeitalter der Aufklärung und der Emanzipation." *Bulletin des Leo Baeck Instituts* 3 (1960): 207–15.

Endelman, Todd, ed. *Jewish Apostasy in the Modern World.* New York: Holmes and Meier, 1987.

———. *Radical Assimilation in English Jewish History, 1656–1945.* Bloomington: Indiana University Press, 1990.

Epstein, A. L. *Ethos and Identity.* London: Tavistock Publications, 1978.

Erb, Rainer. "Warum ist der Jude zum Ackerbürger nicht Tauglich? Zur Geschichte eines antisemitischen Steterotyps." In *Antisemitismus und Jüdische Geschichte: Studien zu Ehren Herbert A. Strauss,* Rainer Erb and Michael Schmidt, eds., 99–120. Berlin: Wissenschaftlicher Autorenverlag, 1987.

Erikson, Erik. *Childhood and Society.* New York: W.W. Norton and Co., 1950.

Evans, Richard. *Rethinking German History. Nineteenth Century Germany and the Origins of the Third Reich.* Boston: Allen and Unwin, 1987.

———, ed. *Society and Politics in Wilhelmine Germany.* London: Croom Helm, 1978.

Faber, Karl-Georg. "Student und Politik in der ersten deutschen Burschenschaft." *Geschichte in Wissenschaft und Unterricht,* 21, no. 2 (1970): 68–80.

Fabricius, Wilhelm. *Die Deutschen Corps. Eine historische Darstellung der Entwicklung des Studentischen Verbindungswesens in Deutschland bis 1815, der Corps bis zur Gegenwart.* Frankfurt am Main: Im Verlag der Deutschen Corpszeitung, 1926.

Faierstein, Morris M. "The Liebes Brief. A Critique of Jewish Society in Germany (1749)." *Leo Baeck Institute Yearbook* 27 (1982): 219–41.

Frankel, Jonathon, and Steven Zipperstein, eds. *Assimilation and Community. The Jews in Nineteenth-Century Europe.* Cambridge: Cambridge University Press, 1992.

Fischer, Walter. "Errinerungen Eines Hasmonäers." In *Meilensteine: Vom Wege des Kartells Jüdischer Verbindungen (KJV) in der zionistischen Bewegung,* Eli Rothschild, ed., 24–29. Tel Aviv: Prasidium K.J.V., 1972.

Freidenreich, Harriet. "Jewish Identity and the 'New Woman': Central European Jewish University Women in the Early Twentieth Century." In *Gender and Judaism. The Transformation of Tradition,* Tamar Rudavsky, ed., 113–22. New York: New York University Press, 1995.

Frevert, Ute. "Bourgeois Honour: Middle-Class Duellists in Germany from the Late

Eighteenth to the Early Twentieth Century." In *The German Bourgeoisie. Essays on the Social History of the German Middle Class from the Late Eighteenth to the Early Twentieth Century,* David Blackbourn and Richard J. Evans, eds. London: Routledge, 1991.

———. *Ehrenmänner. Das Duell in der Bürgerlichen Gesellschaft.* Munich: C.H. Beck, 1991.

Friedlander, Albert Hoschander. "The Wohlwill-Moser Correspondence." *Leo Baeck Institute Yearbook* 11 (1966): 262–99.

Friesel, Evyatar. "The Political and Ideological Development of the Centralverein Before 1914." *Leo Baeck Institute Yearbook* 31 (1986): 121–46.

Geschichte der deutschen Burschenschaft. Vor und Frühzeit bis zu den Karlsbader Beschlüssen. Vol. 1. Paul Wentzcke, ed. Published as *Quellen und Darstellungen zur Geschichte der Burschenschaft und der deutschen Einheitsbewegung.* Vol 6. Heidelberg: 1919.

Gilbert, Felix. "Bismarckian Society's Image of a Jew." *Leo Baeck Memorial Lecture,* no. 22. New York: 1978.

Gilman, Sander. *Jewish Self-Hatred. Anti-Semitism and the Hidden Language of the Jews.* Baltimore: Johns Hopkins University Press, 1986.

Goldscheider, Calvin. *Jewish Continuity and Change: Emerging Patterns in America.* Bloomington: Indiana University Press, 1986.

Gordon, Milton M. *Assimilation in American Life: The Role of Race, Religion, and National Origins.* New York: Oxford University Press, 1964.

Gordis, David M., and Yoav ben Horin. *Jewish Identity in America.* Los Angeles: University of Judaism Press, 1991.

Graebke, Hans Dietrich. "Der Heidelberger Seniorenconvent (SC) vom beginn des 19. Jahrhunderts bis Heute." In *Weiland Bursch zu Heidelberg. Eine Festschrift der Heidelberger Korporationen zur 600-Jahr-Feier der Ruperto Carola,* Gerhart Berger and Detlev Aurand, eds., 17–36. Heidelberg: Heidelberger Verlagsanstalt u. Druckerei, 1986.

Greenbaum, Alfred Abraham. "The Verein für Cultur und Wissenschaft der Juden in Jewish Historiography: An Analysis and Some Observations." In *Text and Responses. Studies Presented to Nahum N. Glatzer on the Occasion of His Seventieth Birthday by His Students,* Michael A. Fishbane and Paul R. Flohr, eds., 173–85. Leiden: E.J. Brill, 1975.

Grieve, Hermann. "On Jewish Self-Identification: Religion and Political Orientation." *Leo Baeck Institute Yearbook* 20 (1975): 35–46.

Gross, Walter. "The Zionist Students' Movement." *Leo Baeck Institute Yearbook* 4 (1959): 143–65.

Grunfeld, Isidor. *Three Generations. The Influence of Samson Raphael Hirsch on Jewish Life and Thought.* London: Jerusalem Post Publications, 1958.

Gutmann, Joseph. *Geschichte des Akademischen Vereins für Jüdische Geschichte und Literatur. Zum 50. Stiftungsfest.* Berlin: 1933.

Hall, Stuart. "Cultural Identity and Diaspora." In *Identity: Community, Culture, Difference,* Jonathon Rutherford, ed., 222–37. London: Lawrence and Wishart, 1990.

———. "Ethnicity: Identity and Difference," *Radical America* 23, no. 4 (June 1991): 9–20.

Hamburger, Ernst. *Juden im öffentlichen Leben Deutschlands. Regierungsmitglieder,*

Bibliography

Beamte und Parlamentarier in der Monarchischen Zeit, 1848–1914. Tübingen: J.C.B. Mohr, 1968.

Hardtwig, Wolfgang. "Strukturmerkmale und Entwicklungstendenzen des Vereinswesens in Deutschland, 1789–1848" In *Historische Zeitschrift Beiheft #9: Vereinswesen und bürgerliche Gesellschaft in Deutschland,* Otto Dann, ed., 11–50. Munich, 1984.

———. "Studentenschaft und Aufklärung. Landsmannschaften und Studentenorden in Deutschland im 18. Jahrhundert." In *Geselligkeit, Vereinswesen und bürgerliche Gesellschaft in Frankreich, Deutschland und in der Schweiz,* Etienne Francios, ed., 239–60. Paris: 1986.

———. "Studentische Mentalität Politische Jugendbewegung: Nationalismus, Die Anfänge der deutschen Burschenschaften." *Historische Zeitschrift* 242 (1986): 581–628.

Herman, Simon N. *Jewish Identity: A Social Psychological Perspective.* Beverly Hills: Sage Publications, 1977.

Hertz, Debra. *Jewish High Society in Old Regime Berlin.* New Haven, Conn.: Yale University Press, 1988.

Herzig, Arno. "Das Problem der Jüdischen Identität in der Deutschen Bürgerlichen Gesellschaft." In *Deutsche Aufklärung und Judenemanzipation. Jahrbuch des Instituts für Deutsche Geschichte.* Beiheft 3, Walter Grab, ed., 243–62. Tel Aviv: Institut für Deutsche Geschichte, 1980.

Holeczek, Heinz. "The Jews and the German Liberals." *Leo Baeck Institute Yearbook* 28 (1983): 77–91.

———. "Judenemanzipation in Preußen." In *Die Juden als Minderheit in der Geschichte,* Bernd Martin and Ernst Schulin, eds., 131–60. Munich: Deutscher Taschenbuch Verlag, 1981.

Hughes, Michael. *Nationalism and Society. Germany 1800–1945.* London: Edward Arnold, 1988.

Humboldt, Wilhelm von. *The Limits of State Action.* J. W. Burrow, ed. Cambridge: Cambridge University Press, 1969.

Hyman, Paula. *The Emancipation of the Jews of Alsace: Acculturation and Tradition in the Nineteenth Century.* New Haven, Conn.: Yale University Press, 1991.

Israel, Jonathon. *European Jewry in the Age of Mercantilism: 1550–1750.* Oxford: Clarendon Press, 1985.

Jacob, Ernst I. "Life and Work of B. Jacob" In *Paul Lazarus Gedenkbuch. Beiträge zur Wurdigung der Letzten Rabbinergeneration in Deutschland,* 93–100. Jerusalem: Jerusalem Post Press, 1961.

Jarausch, Konrad. *Deutsche Studententum 1800–1970.* Frankfurt am Main: Suhrkamp Verlag, 1984.

———. "Higher Education and Social Change, 1860–1930." In *The Transformation of Higher Learning, 1860–1930: Expansion, Diversification, Social Opening and Professionalization in England, Germany, Russia and the United States.* Konrad Jarausch, ed. Chicago: University of Chicago Press, 1983.

———. "Die Neuhumanistische Universität und die Bürgerliche Gesellschaft 1800–1870. Eine quantitative Untersuchung zur Sozialstruktur der Studentenschaften deutscher Universitäten." *Darstellung und Quellen. zur Geschichte der deutschen Einheitsbewegung in neunzehnten und zwanzigsten Jahrhundert. Im Auflrage der Gesellschaft für Burschenschaftliche Geschichtsforschung* 11 (1981): 11–58.

————. "The Social Transformation of the University: The Case of Prussia 1865–1914." *Journal of Social History* 12 (1979): 609–36.

————. "The Sources of German Student Unrest: 1815–1848." In *The University in Society, Vol. 2: Europe, Scotland, and the United States from the 16th–20th Century,* Lawrence Stone, ed. Princeton, N.J.: Princeton University Press, 1974.

————. "Students, Sex and Politics in Imperial Germany." *Journal of Contemporary History,* 17 (1982): 285–304.

————. *Students, Society and Politics in Imperial Germany. The Rise of Academic Illiberalism.* Princeton, N.J.: Princeton University Press, 1982.

Jochmann, Werner. "Struktur und Funktion des deutschen Antisemitismus," In *Juden im Wilhelminischen Deutschland 1890–1914,* Werner E. Mosse, ed., 411–29. Tübingen: J.C.B. Mohr, 1976.

Kaiser, Nancy A. *Social Integration and Narrative Structure: Patterns of Realism in Auerbach, Freytag, Fontane and Raabe.* New York: Lang, 1986.

Kampe, Norbert. "Jews and Antisemites at Universities in Imperial Germany (I): Jewish Students: Social History and Social Conflict." *Leo Baeck Institute Yearbook* 30 (1985): 357–94.

————. "Jews and Antisemites at Universities in Imperial Germany (II): The Friedrich-Wilhelms-Universität of Berlin: A Case Study of the Students' Jewish Question." *Leo Baeck Institute Yearbook* 30 (1987): 43–101.

————. "Jüdische Professoren im Deutschen Kaiserreich." In *Antisemitismus und Judische Geschichte,* Rainer Erb and Michael Schmidt eds. Berlin: Wissenschaftlicher Autorenverlag, 1987.

————. *Studenten und "Judenfrage" im Deutschen Kaiserreich : Die Entstehung einer akademischen Trägerschicht des Antisemitismus.* Göttingen: Vandenhoeck and Ruprecht, 1988.

Kaplan, Marion A. *The Making of the Jewish Middle Class: Women, Family and Identity in Imperial Germany.* New York: Oxford University Press, 1991.

————. "Gender and Jewish History in Imperial Germany." In *Assimilation and Community. The Jews in Nineteenth Century Europe,* Jonathon Frankel and Steven J. Zipperstein, eds., 198–224. Cambridge: Cambridge University Press, 1992.

————. "Tradition and Transition. The Acculturation, Assimilation and Integration of Jews in Imperial Germany—A Gender Analysis." *Leo Baeck Institute Yearbook* 27 (1982): 3–36.

Katz, Jacob. *Exclusiveness and Tolerance: Studies in Jewish-Gentile Relations in Medieval and Modern Times.* West Orange, N.J.: Behrman House, 1961.

————. *Out of the Ghetto: The Social Background of Jewish Emancipation, 1770–1870.* New York: Schocken Books, 1973.

————.*Tradition and Crisis. Jewish Society at the End of the Middle Ages.* New York: Schocken Books, 1961.

Kieval, Hillel J. "Caution's Progress: The Modernization of Jewish Life in Prague, 1780–1830." In *Toward Modernity. The European Jewish Model,* Jacob Katz, ed., 71–105. New Brunswick: Transaction Books, 1988.

————. "The Importance of Place: Comparative Aspects of the Ritual Murder Trial in Modern Central Europe." In *Comparing Jewish Societies,* Todd M. Endelman, ed. Ann Arbor: University of Michigan Press, 1997.

————. *The Making of Czech Jewry. National Conflict and Jewish Society in Bohemia, 1870–1918.* New York: Oxford University Press, 1988.

Bibliography

Kisch, Guido. *Die Universitäten und die Juden: Eine Historische Betrachtung zur Fünfhundertjahrfeier der Universität Basel.* Tübingen: J.C.B. Mohr, 1961.

Knowles, Lee. *A Day With Korps-Students in Germany. Being an Account of Some Heidelberg Duels.* Heidelberg, 1908.

Kocka, Jürgen, ed. *Bürger und Bürgerlichkeit im 19 Jahrhundert.* Göttingen: Vandenhoeck and Ruprecht, 1987.

———. "Theorien in der Sozial-und Gesellschaftsgeschichte. Vorschläge zur historischen Sichtungsanalyse." *Geschichte und Gesellschaft* 1 (1975): 9–42.

Lamberti, Marjorie. "The Centralverein and the Anti-Zionists: Setting the Historical Record Straight." *Leo Baeck Institute Yearbook* 33 (1988): 123–29.

———. "From Coexistence to Conflict: Zionism and the Jewish Community in Germany, 1897–1914." *Leo Baeck Institute Yearbook* 27 (1982).

———. *Jewish Activism in Imperial Germany. The Struggle for Civil Equality.* New Haven, Conn.: Yale University Press, 1978.

———. "Liberals, Socialists and the Defence Against Antisemitism in the Wilhelmine Period." *Leo Baeck Institute Yearbook* 25 (1980): 147–62.

Levenson, Alan. "German Zionism and Radical Assimilation Before 1914." *Studies in Zionism* 13, no. 1 (spring 1992): 21–41.

———. "Jewish Reactions to Intermarriage in Nineteenth Century Germany." Ph.D. diss., Ohio State University, 1990.

Levy, Richard S. *The Downfall of the Antisemitic Political Parties in Imperial Germany.* New Haven, Conn.: Yale University Press, 1975.

Lewin, Erich. *Vergangenheit und Zukunft des K.C. Eine Sozialkritische Studie. Positiver aus derselben Zeitspanne, Hans Reichmann, Gedanken zur K.C. Geschichte.* Unpublished Manuscript of the Leo Baeck Institute London, n.d.

Lewin, Louis. "Aus dem jüdischen Kulturkampfe." *Jahrbuch der jüdisch-Literarischen Gesellschaft* 12 (1918): 182–94.

Liberles, Robert. "Dohm's Treatise on the Jews. A Defence of the Enlightenment." *Leo Baeck Institute Yearbook* 33 (1988): 29–42.

———. "Was There a Jewish Movement for Emancipation in Germany?" *Leo Baeck Institute Yearbook* 31 (1986): 35–49.

Lichtheim, Richard. *Die Geschichte des deutschen Zionismus.* Jerusalem: 1954.

———. *Das Programm des Zionismus.* Berlin: 1913.

Lidtke, Vernon L. *The Alternative Culture: Socialist Labor in Imperial Germany.* New York: Oxford University Press, 1985.

Liebeschütz, Hans. "Treitschke and Mommsen on Jewry and Judaism." *Leo Baeck Institute Yearbook* 7 (1962): 153–82.

Locher, Torsten "Burschenschaft Frankonia in der DB." In *Weiland Bursch zu Heidelberg. Eine Festschrift der Heidelberger Korporationen zur 600-Jahr-Feier der Ruperto Carola,* Gerhart Berger and Detlev Aurand, eds. Heidelberg: Heidelberger Verlagsanstalt u. Druckerei, 1986.

Loewe, Heinrich. "Jung-Israel. Ein fünfzigjähriger Gedenktag." In *Meilensteine: Vom Wege des Kartells Jüdischer Verbindungen (KJV) in der zionistischen Bewegung,* Eli Rothschild, ed. Tel Aviv: Prasidium K.J.V., 1972.

London, Perry, and Alissa Hirshfeld. "The Psychology of Identity Formation." In *Jewish Identity in America,* David M. Gordis and Yoav ben Horin, eds., 32–41. Los Angeles: Univeristy of Judaism Press, 1991.

Low, Alfred D. *Jews in the Eyes of the Germans; From the Enlightenment to Imperial Germany.* Philadelphia: Institute for the Study of Human Issues, 1979.

Bibliography

Lowenstein, Steven. "The Pace of Modernization of German Jewry in the Nineteenth Century." *Leo Baeck Institute Yearbook* 21 (1976): 41–56.

———. "The Rural Community and the Urbanization of German Jewry," in *Central European History* 13, no. 3 (1980): 218–36.

Macdonald, Sharon. "Identity Complexes in Western Europe: Social Anthropological Perspectives." In *Inside European Identities. Ethnography in Western Europe*, Sharon Macdonald, ed. Providence: Berg Publishers, 1993.

Massing, Paul W. *Rehearsal for Destruction: A Study of Political Anti-Semitism in Imperial Germany*. New York: Harper, 1949.

McAleer, Kevin. *Duelling: The Cult of Honor in Fin-de-Siècle Germany*. Princeton, N.J.: Princeton University Press, 1994.

McClelland, Charles E. *State, Society and University in Germany, 1700–1914*. Cambridge: Cambridge University Press, 1980.

Mechow, G. *Berliner Studenten 1810–1914*. Berlin: Haude and Spenersche Verlagsbuchhandlung, 1976.

Mendes-Flohr, Paul. "The Study of the Jewish Intellectual: Some Methodological Proposals." In *Essays in Modern Jewish History*. East Brunswick, N.J.: 1982.

Meyer, Michael, A. "Great Debate on Antisemitism. Jewish Reaction to New Hostility in Germany 1879–1881." *Leo Baeck Institute Yearbook* 11 (1966): 137–70.

———. *Jewish Identity in the Modern World*. Seattle: University of Washington Press, 1990.

———. *The Origins of the Modern Jew: Jewish Identity and European Culture in Germany, 1749–1824*. Detroit: Wayne State University Press, 1979.

———. *Response to Modernity. A History of the Reform Movement in Judaism*. New York: Oxford University Press, 1988.

Michael, Reuven. "Die Antijudaistische Tendenz in Christian Wilhelm Dohm's Buch über die Bürgerliche Verbesserung der Juden." *Bulletin des Leo Baeck Institut* 77 (1987): 12–48.

Miller, George Morey. *Alt Heidelberg and its Student Life*. Heidelberg: Otto Peters, 1911.

Möller, Horst. "Aufklärung, Judenemanzipation und Staat. Ursprung und Wirkung von Dohms Schrift 'Über die bürgerliche Verbesserung der Juden.'" In *Deutsche Aufklärung und Judenemanzipation. Jahrbuch des Instituts für Deutsche Geschichte*. Beiheft 3, Walter Grab, ed., 119–49. Tel Aviv: Institut für Deutsche Geschichte, 1980.

Mosse, George. *The Crisis of German Ideology. Intellectual Origins of the Third Reich* New York: Grosset and Dunlap, 1964.

———. *German Jews Beyond Judaism*. Bloomington: Indiana University Press, 1985.

———. "The Image of the German Jew in Popular Culture." *Leo Baeck Institute Yearbook* 2 (1957): 218–27.

———. "Jewish Emancipation: Between *Bildung* and Respectability." In *The Jewish Response to German Culture. From the Enlightenment to the Second World War*, Jehuda Reinharz and W. Schatzberg, eds., 1–16. Hanover, N.H.: University Press of New England, 1985.

———. *Nationalism and Sexuality: Middle-class Morality and Sexual Norms in Modern Europe*. Madison: University of Wisconsin Press, 1988.

Mosse, Werner E., ed. *Juden im Wilhelminischen Deutschland 1890–1914*. Tübingen: J.C.B. Mohr, 1976.

Bibliography

Mosse, Werner E., Arnold Paucker, and Reinhard Rürup, eds. *Revolution and Evolution: 1848 in Jewish History.* Tübingen: J.C.B. Mohr, 1981.

Nipperdey, Thomas. *Gesellschaft, Kultur, Theorie. Gesammelte Aufsätze zur neueren Geschichte.* Göttingen: Vandenhoeck and Ruprecht, 1976.

Nordau, Max. *Zionistische Schriften.* Berlin: Jüdischer Verlag, 1923.

Oppenheim, Michael. "A 'Fieldguide' to the Study of Modern Jewish Identity." *Jewish Social Studies* 46 (1984): 215–30.

Paucker, Arnold. *Der jüdische Abwehrkampf.* Hamburg: Leibniz Verlag, 1968.

Paulsen, Friedrich. *Die deutschen Universitäten und das Universitätsstudium.* Berlin: 1902. Trans. by Frank Tilly as *The German Universities and University Study.* New York: C. Scribner's Sons, 1906.

———. "Die Entwicklung der Realschule zum Realgymnasium in Preußsen." In *Das Gymnasium in Geschichte und Gegenwart,* Hermann Röhrs, ed., 14–41. Frankfurt a.M.: Akademische Verlagsgesellschaft, 1969.

Philipson, Ilene. "What's the Big I.D.? The Politics of the Authentic Self." *Tikkun* 6, no.6 (Nov/Dec 1991): 51.

Pick, Sylvius. "Vor 60 Jahren"

Pickus, Keith H. "German Jewish Identity in the Kaiserreich: Observations and Methodological Considerations," *Jewish History* 9, no. 2 (1995): 73–91.

———. "Images of God and Country: Jewish National and Religious Identities in Wilhelmine Germany." *Aschkenas* 8 (Fall, 1998): 1–14.

———. "Jewish University Students in Germany and the Construction of a Post-Emancipatory Identity: The Model of the *Freie Wissenschaftliche Vereinigung.*" *Leo Baeck Institute Yearbook* 39 (1994): 65–81.

Poppel, Stephen M. *Zionism in Germany 1897–1933: The Shaping of Jewish Identity.* Philadelphia: Jewish Publication Society, 1977.

Preston, David L. "The German Jews in Secular Education, University Teaching and Science: A Preliminary Inquiry," *Jewish Social Sciences* 2 (spring 1976): 99–116.

Pulzer, Peter. *Jews and the German State. The Political History of a Minority, 1848–1933.* Oxford: Blackwell Publishers, 1992.

———. "Religion and Judicial Appointments in Germany: 1869–1918." *Leo Baeck Institute Yearbook* 28 (1983): 185–204.

———. *The Rise of Political Anti-Semitism in Germany and Austria.* New York: John Wiley and Sons, 1964.

———. "Why Was There a Jewish Question in Imperial Germany?" *Leo Baeck Institute Yearbook* 25 (1980): 133–46.

Ragins, Sanford. *Jewish Responses to Antisemitism in Germany: A Study in the History of Ideas.* Cincinnati: Hebrew Union College Press, 1980.

Reichold, Hartmut. "Dr. jur. David Morgenstern. Juden in der Burschenschaft des Vormärz." *Israelistische Kultusgemeinde Fürth* (September 1983): 15–18.

Reinharz, Jehuda. "Advocacy and History: The Case of the Centralverein and the Zionists." *Leo Baeck Institute Yearbook* 33 (1988): 113–22.

———. *Fatherland or Promised Land: The Dilemma of the German Jew, 1893–1914.* Ann Arbor: University of Michigan Press, 1975.

———. "The Zionist Response to Antisemitism in Germany." *Leo Baeck Institute Yearbook* 30 (1985): 104–40.

———, ed. *Living With Antisemitism: Modern Jewish Responses.* Hanover, N.H.: Brandeis University Press, 1987.

Reinharz, Jehuda, Michael Fishbane, and Paul Flohr, eds. *Consensus and Conflict between Zionists and Liberals in Germany before World War I. Texts and Responses.* Studies presented to Nahum N. Glatzer. Leiden: Brill, 1975.

Reinharz, Jehuda, and Walter Schatzberg, eds. *The Jewish Response to German Culture: From the Enlightenment to the Second World War.* Hanover, N.H.: Clark University Press, 1985.

Reissner, H. G. "Rebellious Dilemma: The Case Histories of Eduard Gans and Some of his Partisans." *Leo Baeck Institute Yearbook* 2 (1956): 179–93.

Richarz, Monika. *Der Eintritt der Juden in die Akademischen Berufe.* Tübingen: J.C.B. Mohr, 1974.

———. "Jewish Social Mobility in Germany during the Time of Emancipation (1790–1871)." *Leo Baeck Institute Yearbook* 20 (1975): 69–77.

Ringer, Fritz K. *The Decline of the German Mandarins.* Cambridge: Wesleyan University Press, 1969.

———. *Education and Society in Modern Europe.* Bloomington: Indiana University Press, 1979.

———. "The German Academic Community 1871–1914." *Internationalisches Archiv für Sozialgeschichte der deutschen Literatur.* 3 (1978).

Röhrs, Hermann, ed. *Das Gymnasium in Geschichte und Gegenwart.* Frankfurt am Main: Akademische Verlagsgesellschaft, 1969.

Roos-Schumacher, Hedwig. *Der Kyffhäuserverband der Vereine Deutscher Studenten 1880–1914/18. Ein Beitrag zum nationalen Vereinwesen und zum politischen Denken im Kaiserreich.* Gifhorn: Deutsche Akademische Schriften, 1986.

Rosenkranz, Ze'ev. "The Corporate Activities of Jewish National and Zionist Student Groups in Germany 1895–1914" (in Hebrew). Master's thesis, Hebrew University, 1988.

Ross, R. J. *The Beleaguered Tower. The Dilemma of Political Catholicism in Wilhelmine Germany.* Notre Dame: University of Notre Dame Press, 1976.

Roth, Guenther, *The Social Democrats in Imperial Germany.* Totowa, N.J.: Bedminster Press, 1963.

Rothschild, Eli, ed. *Meilensteine: Vom Wege des Kartells Jüdischer Verbindungen (KJV) in der zionistischen Bewegung.* Tel Aviv: Prasidium K.J.V., 1972.

Rozenblit, Marsha L. "The Assertion of Identity: Jewish Student Nationalism at the University of Vienna Before the First World War." *Leo Baeck Institute Yearbook* 27 (1982): 171–86.

———. *The Jews of Vienna: Assimilation and Identity.* Albany: State University of New York Press, 1983.

Rubaschoff, S. "Erstlinge der Entjudung." *Der Jüdische Wille* (1918–19): 26–41, 108–21, 193–203.

Ruppin, Arthur. *Soziologie der Juden.* 2 vols. Berlin: Jüdischer Verlag, 1930–31.

Rürup, Reinhard. *Emanzipation und Antisemitisimus. Studien zur Judenfrage der bürgerliche Gesellschaft.* Göttingen: Vandenhoeck and Ruprecht, 1975.

———. "Emanzipation und Krise. Zur Geschichte der Judenfrage in Deutschland vor 1890." In *Juden in Wilhelminischen Deutschland. 1890–1914,* Werner Mosse and Arnold Paucker, eds., 1–56. Tübingen: J.C.B. Mohr, 1976.

———. "German Liberalism and the Emancipation of the Jews." *Leo Baeck Institute Yearbook* 20 (1975): 59–68.

———. "Jewish Emancipation and Bourgeois Society." *Leo Baeck Institute Yearbook* 14 (1969): 67–91.

Bibliography

Schatzker, Chaim. *Jüdische Jugend im zweiten Kaiserreich: Sozializations und Erziehungs-prozesse der Jüdische Jugend in Deutschland: 1870–1917*. Frankfurt am Main: Verlag Peter Lang, 1986.

Scherrer, Hans-Carl. "Die akademisch-wissenschaftlichen Vereine im 19. Jahrhundert. Gründe ihres Enstehens, ihr Leben und ihr Schiksal." *Einst und Jetzt* (1975): 131–47.

Scheuer, Oskar Franz. *Burschenschaft und Judenfrage: Der Rassenantisemitismus in der deutschen Studentenschaft*. Berlin: Verlag Berlin-Wien, 1927.

Schindler, Thomas. *Studentischer Antisemitismus und jüdische Studentverbindungen 1880–1933*. Gießen: Schriftenreihe der Studentengeschichtlichen Vereinigung des CC, 1988.

Schmelz, Usiel O. "Die Demographische Entwicklung der Juden in Deutschland von der Mitte des 19. Jahrhunderts bis 1933." *Bulletin des Leo Baeck Instituts* 83 (1989): 15–62.

Schmidt, Hans. "The Terms of Emancipation 1781–1812: The Public Debate in Germany and its Effect on the Mentality and Ideas of German Jewry." *Leo Baeck Institute Yearbook* 1 (1956): 28–45.

Schoeps, Julius. "Modern Heirs of the Maccabees. The Beginning of the Vienna Kadimah: 1882–1897." *Leo Baeck Institute Yearbook* 27 (1982): 155–70.

Schorsch, Ismar. "Breakthrough into the Past: The *Verein für Cultur und Wissenschaft der Juden,*" *Leo Baeck Institute Yearbook,* 33 (1988), 3–28.

———. *From Text to Context. The Turn to History in Modern Judaism*. Hanover, N.H.: University Press of New England, 1993.

———. "German Antisemitism in Light of Post-War Historiography." *Leo Baeck Institute Yearbook* 19 (1974): 257–71.

———. *Jewish Reactions to German Antisemitism: 1870–1914*. New York: Columbia University Press, 1972.

———. "The Religious Parameters of Wissenschaft. Jewish Academics at Prussian Universities." *Leo Baeck Institute Yearbook* 25 (1980): 3–19.

Schulze, Friedrich, and Paul Ssymank. *Das deutsche Studentum von den ältesten Zeiten bis zur Gegenwart*. Leipzig: R. Voigtländers Verlag, 1910.

Schwarz, Jürgen. "Deutsche Studenten und Politik im 19. Jahrhundert." *Geschichte in Wissenschaft und Unterricht* 20, no. 2 (1969): 72–94.

Scott, Joan Walloch. *Gender and the Politics of History*. New York: Columbia University Press, 1988.

Seiffert, Paul. *Geschichte und Entwicklung der studentischen Verbände*. Breslau, 1913.

Seltzer, Robert. *Jewish People, Jewish Thought. The Jewish Experience in History*. New York: Macmillan Publishing, 1980.

Sheehan, James. *German Liberalism in the 19th Century*. Chicago: University of Chicago Press, 1978.

Smith, Anthony D. *The Ethnic Revival in the Modern World*. London: Cambridge University Press, 1981.

Smith, Helmut Walser. *German Nationalism and Religious Conflict: Culture, Ideology, Politics, 1870–1914*. Princeton, N.J.: Princeton University Press, 1995.

Sommerlad, Bernhard. "Wartburgfest und Corpsstudenten." *Einst und Jetzt* (1979): 16–42.

Sorkin, David. "Emancipation and Assimilation: Two Concepts and their Application to German-Jewish History." *Leo Baeck Institute Yearbook* 35 (1990): 17–33.

———. "The Invisible Community: Emancipation, Secular Culture and Jewish

Identity in the Writings of Berthold Auerbach." In *Jewish Response to German Culture. From the Enlightenment to the Second World War,* Jehuda Reinharz and W. Schatzberg, eds., 100–119. Hanover, N.H.: University Press of New England, 1985.

———. *The Transformation of German Jewry, 1780–1840.* New York: Oxford University Press, 1987.

———. "Wilhelm von Humboldt: The Theory and Practice of Self-Formation (*Bildung*), 1791–1810." *Journal of the History of Ideas* 44 (1983): 55–73.

Spindler, George. *The Life of Karl Follen. A Study in German-American Cultural Relations.* Chicago: University of Chicago Press, 1917.

Stanislawski, Michael. *For Whom do I Toil. Judah Leib Gordon and the Crisis of Russian Jewry.* New York: Oxford University Press, 1988.

Stern, Fritz. *The Failure of Illiberalism. Essays on the Political Culture of Modern Germany.* New York: Knopf,1972.

Strauss, Herbert. "Emancipation and Post-Emancipation Identities: Reflections on On-Going Research." *American Jewish Archives* 40, no. 2: 289–96.

Studier, Manfred. *Der Corpsstudent als Idealbild der Wilhelminischen Ära. Untersuchnungen zum Zeitgeist 1888 bis 1914.* Würzburg: Gemeinschaft für deutsche Studentgeschichte, 1990.

Täubler, Eugen. "Gedanken aus der Geschichts-Fuxenstunde." In *Meilensteine: Vom Wege des Kartells Jüdischer Verbindungen (KJV) in der zionistischen Bewegung,* Eli Rothschild, ed., 46–48. Tel Aviv, 1972.

Tiltze, H. "Enrollment Expansion and Academic Overcrowding in Germany." In *The Transformation of Higher Learning: Expansion, Diversification, Social Opening and Professionalization in England, Germany, Russia and the United States,* Konrad Jarausch, ed. Chicago: University of Chicago Press, 1983.

Toury, Jacob. "Organizational Problems of German Jewry. Steps Towards the Establishment of a Central Organization: 1893–1920." *Leo Baeck Institute Yearbook* 13 (1968): 57–92.

———. *Die politischen Orientierung der Juden in Deutschland von Jena bis Weimar.* Tübingen: J.C.B. Mohr, 1966.

———. *Soziale und politische Geschichte der Juden in Deutschland, 1847–1871. Zwischen Revolution, Reaktion und Emanzipation.* Düsseldorf: Droste Verlag, 1977.

Ucko, Siegfried. "Geistesgeschichtliche Grundlagen der Wissenschaft des Judentums. (Motive des Kulturvereins vom Jahre 1819.)" *Zeitschrift für die Geschichte der Juden in Deutschland* 5 (1935): 1–42.

Vascik, George. "The German Peasant League and the Limits of Rural Liberalism in Wilhelminian Germany." *Central European History* 24, no. 2 (1991): 147–75.

Volkov, Shulamit. "Antisemitism as a Cultural Code. Reflections on the History and Historiography of Antisemitism in Imperial Germany." *Leo Baeck Institute Yearbook* 23 (1978): 25–46.

———. "The Dynamics of Dissimilation: *Ostjuden* and German Jews." In *The Jewish Response to German Culture. From the Enlightenment to the Second World War,* Jehuda Reinharz and W. Schatzberg, eds., 195–211. Hanover, N.J.: University Press of New England, 1985.

———. *Jüdisches Leben und Antisemitismus im 19. und 20. Jahrhundert.* Munich: C.H. Beck, 1990.

Bibliography

———. *The Rise of Popular Anti-Modernism in Germany 1873–1893. The Urban Master Artisans*. Princeton, N.J.: Princeton University Press, 1978.

Wassermann, Henry. "Jews and Judaism in the *Gartenlaube*." *Leo Baeck Institute Yearbook* 23 (1978): 47–60.

———. *Yehudim, Burganut ,ve- "Hevrah Burganit" be-Idan Liberali be-Germaniah*. (Jews, Bürgertum and Bürgerlich Gesellschaft in a liberal era: 1840–1880). Ph.D. diss., Hebrew University, 1980.

Wehler, Hans-Ulrich. *The German Empire, 1871–1918*. Leamington Spa, U.K.: Berg Publishers, 1985.

Weinberg, Jehuda Louis. *Aus der Frühzeit des Zionismus Heinrich Loewe*. Jerusalem: R. Mass, 1946.

Weiß, Egbert. "Burschenschaftliche Ideen im Corps. Ein Beitrag zum 160. Jahrestag des Wartburgfestes." *Einst und Jetzt* (1977): 89–98.

Wertheimer, Jack. "The Ausländerfrage at Institutions of Higher Learning: A Controversy Over Russian-Jewish Students in Imperial Germany." *Leo Baeck Institute Yearbook* 27 (1982): 187–215.

———. "Between Tsar and Kaiser: The Radicalisation of Russian-Jewish University Students in Germany." *Leo Baeck Institute Yearbook* 28 (1983): 329–49.

———. *Unwelcome Strangers: East European Jews in Imperial Germany*. New York: Oxford University Press, 1987.

White, Hayden. *Tropics of Discourse: Essays in Cultural Criticism*. Baltimore, Md.: Johns Hopkins University Press, 1978.

Wistrich, Robert S. *The Jews of Vienna in the Age of Franz Joseph*. New York: Oxford University Press, 1989.

Wolf, Immanuel. "Über den Begriff einer Wissenschaft des Judentums." *Zeitschrift für die Wissenschaft des Judentums* 1 no. 1 (1822), trans. Lionel E. Kochen, *Leo Baeck Institute Yearbook* 2 (1957): 194–204.

Wreden, Ernst Wilhelm. "Die Heidelberger Burschenschaft 1814–1986." In *Weiland Bursch zu Heidelberg. Eine Festschrift der Heidelberger Korporationen zur 600-Jahr-Feier der Ruperto Carola*, Gerhart Berger and Detlev Aurand, eds., 45–67. Heidelberg: Heidelberger Verlagsanstalt u. Druckerei, 1986.

Yerushalmi, Yosef. "Assimilation and Racial Antisemitism: The Iberian and the German Models." *Leo Baeck Memorial Lecture*, no. 26 (1982).

Zimmermann, Moshe. "Das Gesellschaftsbild der deutschen Zionisten vor dem 1 Weltkrieg." *Trumah* (Hochschule für Jüdische Studien, Heidelberg) 1987: 129–53.

———. "Jewish Nationalism and Zionism in German-Jewish Students' Organizations." *Leo Baeck Institute Yearbook* 27 (1982): 129–53.

Index